SUPERCAPITALISM

SUPERCAPITALISM

*The Battle for Democracy
in an Age of Big Business*

ROBERT REICH

ICON BOOKS

This edition published in the UK in 2008 by
Icon Books Ltd, The Old Dairy,
Brook Road, Thriplow,
Cambridge SG8 7RG
email: info@iconbooks.co.uk
www.iconbooks.co.uk

Previously published in the USA in 2007
by Alfred A. Knopf

Sold in the UK, Europe, South Africa and Asia
by Faber & Faber Ltd, 3 Queen Square,
London WC1N 3AU
or their agents

Distributed in the UK, Europe, South Africa and Asia
by TBS Ltd, TBS Distribution Centre, Colchester Road,
Frating Green, Colchester CO7 7DW

This edition published in Australia in 2008
by Allen & Unwin Pty Ltd,
PO Box 8500, 83 Alexander Street,
Crows Nest, NSW 2065

ISBN 978-184831-007-0

Typeset in 11.25pt AGaramond by Marie Doherty

Printed in the UK by CPI Mackays, Chatham, ME5 8TD

To the memory of Mildred Reich

The imperatives of technology and organization, not the images of ideology, are what determine the shape of economic society.

– John Kenneth Galbraith, *The New Industrial State* (1967)

The kind of economic organization that provides economic freedom directly, namely, competitive capitalism, also promotes political freedom because it separates economic power from political power and in this way enables the one to offset the other.

– Milton Friedman, *Capitalism and Freedom* (1962)

CONTENTS

SUPERCAPITALISM

The Paradox

In March 1975, economist Milton Friedman accepted an invitation to Chile to meet with Augusto Pinochet, who some eighteen months before had toppled the democratically elected government of Salvador Allende. Friedman was criticized in the American press for making the trip, but there is no reason to suppose he approved of Pinochet. Friedman went to Chile to urge Pinochet's junta to adopt free-market capitalism – to trim the business regulations and welfare state that had grown under Chile's many years of democratic government and to open itself to trade and investment with the rest of the world. In a series of lectures he delivered in Chile, Friedman reiterated his long-held belief that free markets were a necessary precondition to political freedom and sustainable democracy. Pinochet took Friedman's free-market advice, but Pinochet's brutal dictatorship lasted another fifteen years. The men died within weeks of each other in late 2006.

Of all the nations of the world, America is assumed to best exemplify the idea that capitalism and democracy go hand in hand.[1] But in the years since Friedman visited Chile, the relationship has become strained. Free-market capitalism has triumphed. Yet democracy has weakened.

Since the 1970s, and notwithstanding three recessions, the United States economy has soared. Consumers have been treated to a vast array of new products – personal computers, iPods, antidepressants, hybrid cars, to name just a few – while the prices of standard goods and services have declined, adjusted for inflation. Health care costs more, but Americans live almost fifteen years longer than they did in 1950 on average, largely due to new drugs and new medical equipment.

Companies have also become far more efficient and the stock market has surged. In 1975, the Dow Jones Industrial Average hovered close to 600. It had not advanced very far in years. By late 2006, it hit 12,000. Moreover, since the early 1980s inflation has been well under control.

These successes have been replicated elsewhere. American capitalism won the contest with communism and has now spread almost everywhere in the world. Most nations have become part of a single integrated system of global capitalism. Eastern Europe has been absorbed into a capitalist Europe and Russia is becoming a capitalist power. China, although officially still communist, has become a hotbed of global capitalism.

All this is a triumph, by almost anyone's definition.

Some observers rightly point out that these gains have been accompanied by widening inequalities of income and wealth. The gains have also accompanied other problems such as heightened job insecurity, and environmental hazards such as global warming. Strictly speaking, though, these are not failings of capitalism. Capitalism's role is to enlarge the economic pie. How the slices are divided and whether they are applied to private goods like personal computers or public goods like clean air is up to society to decide. This is the role we assign to democracy.

Democracy means more than a process of free and fair elections. Democracy, in my view, is a system for accomplishing what can only be achieved by citizens joining together with other citizens – to determine the rules of the game whose outcomes express the common good. The rules of course can affect how fast the economy grows: At the extreme, a rule that divided the pie into equal slices would squelch personal incentives to save, invest, and innovate. Another rule might do more to spur economic growth. Democracy is supposed to enable us to make such tradeoffs, or help us achieve both growth and equity or any other goals we share in common.

Yet democracy is struggling to perform these basic functions. As inequality has widened, the means America once used to temper it – progressive income taxes, good public schools, trade unions that bargain for higher wages – have eroded. As the risks of sudden loss of job or income have grown, the social safety net has become less reliable. More of us lack health insurance. As a nation, the United States seems incapable of doing what is required to reduce climate change. Many Americans are also concerned about the crassness and coarseness of much of contemporary culture, and about the loss of Main Streets and their surrounding communities. In all these respects, democracy has been unable to take effective action, or even articulate the tradeoffs and sacrifices doing so would entail.

Capitalism has become more responsive to what we want as individual purchasers of goods, but democracy has grown less responsive to what we want together as citizens. Surveys suggest a growing sense of powerlessness. While in 1964 only 36 percent of Americans felt 'public officials don't care much what people like me think', by 2000 that sentiment was shared by more than 60 percent. In 1964, almost two-thirds of Americans believed government was run for the benefit of all and only 29 percent said it was 'run by a few big interests looking out only for themselves'. But by 2000, the ratio was almost reversed: Only 35 percent believed government was run for the benefit of all, while more than 60 percent thought it was run by a few big interests.[2]

Why has capitalism become so triumphant and democracy so enfeebled? Are these two trends connected? What, if anything, can be done to strengthen democracy?

THE DANGER of summarizing my argument in advance is oversimplification, yet I want to give you a basic sense of it. The last several decades have involved a shift of power away from us in our capacities as citizens and toward us as consumers and investors.

America emerged victorious from World War II, already having survived the Great Depression, with both its economy and its democracy in good working order. Then it experienced unprecedented prosperity, widely shared. It was not quite a golden age – women and minorities were still relegated to second-class citizenship, and communist witch hunts scarred politics – yet every income group and social class gained ground, inequality of income and wealth declined, and a far larger middle class emerged. Larger middle classes also emerged, after some lag time, in Europe and Japan. Most Americans professed high levels of confidence in American democracy, as they filled their newly acquired homes with dishwashers, refrigerators, television sets, and stereo systems, and their driveways with Fords, Chevrolets, or Plymouths. The two systems – capitalism and democracy – seemed to be working in such remarkable tandem that they came to be seen as one system, the American system of democratic capitalism, which was to be a model to the world and history's alternative to Soviet communism.

The system for producing goods and services was far more predictable and stable than it is today, and more concentrated in a relatively few large firms, like the big three automakers (GM, Ford, and Chrysler). In order to reap the vast economies of large scale, the huge companies needed predictability and stability, and minimal competition. They also needed the willing cooperation of blue-collar workers because strikes or work stoppages would interrupt the smooth flows of production on which they depended. So the companies agreed to give their workers, organized by industry, a higher share of the profits. These giant companies played such large and conspicuous roles in the economy that they also needed the support of the public. So they negotiated with government over how the additional benefits of economic growth would be distributed, while also protecting jobs, communities, and, eventually, the environment. Some of these deals were struck within regulatory agencies, some within legislatures, some through the mediation of CEOs who played the roles of 'corporate statesmen'. The result was an expression – however indirect and approximate – of what was then understood as the common good.

The tradeoff for this relatively stable and equitable system was a very limited range of choice for consumers and investors. Better deals could be found only with great difficulty. Major product innovations were rare. Fins grew longer, grilles more ornate, and chrome more expansive in automobiles, but the underlying technology did not undergo major alteration. My father stuck with Plymouths, but he admitted the choice didn't much matter. Investors also tended toward passivity, rarely moving their money. There was little point because almost all investments offered about the same moderate returns. The Dow Jones Industrial Average plodded along.

Since the 1970s, this has all changed radically. Large firms became far more competitive, global, and innovative. Something I call supercapitalism was born. In this transformation, we in our capacities as consumers and investors have done significantly better. In our capacities as citizens seeking the common good, however, we have lost ground. The shift began when technologies developed by government to fight the Cold War were incorporated into new products and services. This created possibilities for new competitors, beginning in transportation, communications, manufacturing, and finance. These cracked open the stable production system and, starting in the late 1970s and escalating thereafter, forced all companies to compete more intensively for customers and investors. Consumer power became aggregated and enlarged by mass retailers like Wal-Mart that used the collective bargaining clout of millions of consumers to get great deals from suppliers. Investor power became aggregated and enlarged by large pension funds and mutual funds, which pushed companies to generate higher returns.

As a result, consumers and investors had access to more choices and better deals. But the institutions that had negotiated to spread the wealth and protect what citizens valued in common began to disappear. Giant firms that dominated entire industries retreated, and labor unions shrank. Regulatory agencies faded. CEOs could no longer be corporate statesmen. And as the intensifying competition among companies spilled over into politics, elected officials became less concerned about the Main Streets and communities in their districts and more concerned with attracting money for their campaigns. Lobbyists swarmed over Washington and other capital cities seeking laws and rules that would give them a competitive advantage (or avoid competitive disadvantage) relative to their rivals, wielding greater and greater influence over decision making. Thus did supercapitalism replace democratic capitalism.

To understand what has happened, and what can be done to make democracy function properly once more, requires a detailed inquiry into the changing structure of the political economy. I offer this in the coming chapters.

Along the way, several puzzles will be unraveled: Why, for example,

CEO pay has soared into the stratosphere and what prevented it from soaring before. Why inflation has become less of a threat than it was three or four decades ago. And why antitrust laws are less important today as a means of restraining economic power than they were previously. I'll also explain why there are so many more corporate lobbyists and lawyers in Washington, D.C., than there were three decades ago, when there would seem to be less reason for them now (after all, discretionary government spending is lower as a portion of the national economy than it was then, there are proportionately fewer regulations, and organized labor's power in Washington is a pale shadow of its former self). Why politicians demand that companies be patriotic and put America before other nations, even though companies are less and less able to play national favorites if they want to compete successfully. And why a bigger and bigger fuss is being made over corporate philanthropy when corporations were never set up to be charitable institutions and are less able to operate in that sphere now.

I'll also account for some hypocrisies: How someone can fret about the decline in hourly wages and simultaneously hunt for the best deal from China or India, which is often at the expense of an American's wages or even job. How someone can lament the decline of independent retailers on Main Street while at the same time do most of their shopping at big-box retailers and online. Why a person who is deeply concerned about global warming might nonetheless buy an SUV. And why politicians like to publicly excoriate CEOs (oil company executives who enjoy ballooning profits, tobacco company CEOs who encourage smoking, high-tech executives who trample on human rights in China) but then enact no laws making what they did illegal.

Finally, I will come to some conclusions you may find surprising – among them, why the move toward improved corporate governance makes companies *less* likely to be socially responsible. Why the promise of corporate democracy is illusory. Why the corporate income tax should be abolished. Why companies should not be held criminally liable. And why shareholders should be protected from having their money used by corporations for political purposes without their consent.

My primary focus in this book is America, although the changes that have occurred here have spawned similar changes elsewhere. People around the globe are more able to pursue their own desires and profit from their investments with increasing fervor. Yet despite the satisfaction they feel as consumers and investors, many are frustrated in their capacities as citizens. Their democracies, too, are finding it more and more difficult to articulate and act upon the common good. Voter surveys in Britain, Italy, Spain, Belgium, the Netherlands, Norway, Sweden, Ireland, and Japan show citizens who have grown to feel almost as disempowered as Americans.[3]

Capitalism is almost certainly a precondition for democracy, as Milton Friedman argued. Democracy requires private centers of economic power independent of a central authority; otherwise, people can't dissent from official orthodoxy and also feed their families. Yet as we've seen over the past several decades, particularly in Southeast Asia, democracy may not be essential to capitalism. China, the world's second largest capitalist nation after the United States, whose economy will surpass America's in some twenty years at current rates of growth, has embraced market freedom but not political freedom. China's market freedom does seem essential to its capitalist success; unless people there can own their property and exchange it without worrying that the central authority will confiscate their goods, they have no incentive to save and invest. And only if they're confident the capitalist game isn't rigged against them are they willing to play it to the best of their abilities. But *political* freedom may not be essential. Some observers believe China will move toward democratic capitalism, eventually. Others think China represents a new kind of system that might be termed authoritarian capitalism.[4]

Many more nations today call themselves 'democracies' than did thirty years ago. Former Soviet Eastern European satellites have become independent democracies. Russia views itself as a democracy. Many former colonial nations in Africa and Asia have emerged as democracies. Latin America has embraced democracy. Three decades ago, about a third of the world's nations held free elections; today that number is closer to two-thirds. In the 1970s, fewer than fifty countries possessed the sort of civil liberties we associate with democracy; by the end of the twentieth century, nearly ninety did.[5]

That's surely cause for optimism, until you look more closely. Many of these places are democracies in name only. They are encumbered by the same problems that have hobbled American democracy in recent years, only to a greater degree – endemic corruption, political dominance by small elites, or one-party rule. None is coping effectively with supercapitalism's negative side effects.

MY ACCOUNT is at odds with several established views. Some observers attribute the triumph of capitalism and the weakening of democracy to the rise of global corporations powerful enough to play nations off against one another and buy off politicians in order to enhance the wealth of their owners. But, in fact, large corporations have less economic power now than they had three decades ago. Then, for example, the United States harbored three giant auto companies that informally coordinated prices and investments. Now at least six major companies produce cars in the United States, and competition among them is fierce. Three decades ago there were only three major television networks, one giant telephone company, and a handful of movie and recording studios. Today, thousands of businesses compete intensely within a large and amorphous space where telecommunications, high-tech, and entertainment overlap. Three decades ago, most people put their savings into banks, and had access to only two or three of them within their own towns or cities. Today, thousands of financial institutions – including mutual funds and pension funds – compete for people's savings. Look almost anywhere in today's economy and you find the typical company has less market power than the typical company of three decades ago.

To be sure, some corporations are very large and many have global reach. But companies of all sizes are competing more vigorously than before. The world economy contains far fewer oligopolies than it did decades ago, and almost no monopolies apart from those created or maintained by government. The power and the impetus that once came from the giant corporation – the planning and execution of large-scale production – are gone.

As for politicians, they have not grown noticeably more corrupt, rapacious, or otherwise irresponsible than they were three decades ago. Politics has no more rotten apples than most occupations, although other occupations are typically spared the rotten headlines. In recent decades, however, politicians have been subjected to a great deal more lobbying than before, and the need for money to finance their campaigns has grown. For this reason, their behavior has changed. The immense increase in lobbying and campaign money, however, is not due to any increase in the market power of any individual corporations; as I will show, it stems, paradoxically, from a decrease in their market power.

Others want to credit or blame Ronald Reagan, Margaret Thatcher, or the predominance of conservative leaders in general over the last several decades. Politicians are important, but they cannot effectuate economic and social change unless the preconditions for change already exist, or unless extraordinary circumstances allow it. By the time Reagan came to power, the economy had already started to shift. Deregulation, for example, unleashed many of America's industries before Reagan took office. Small, profitable airlines, banks, and high-tech companies had already gained a competitive foothold and were intent on bringing down regulatory barriers. The percentage of American workers belonging to labor unions was already declining. And the number of business lobbyists in Washington, D.C., had already begun rising; indeed, the number escalated sharply during the Democratic administration of Bill Clinton.

A final theory is that America, followed by much of the rest of the world, became captivated in recent decades by a certain set of ideas about how societies should be organized. Variously dubbed 'neoliberalism', 'neoclassical economics', 'neoconservatism', or 'the Washington consensus', these precepts included free trade, deregulation, privatization, and, in general, more reliance on markets than on government and more concern for efficiency than equity. That these ideas emerged from academics based in universities may suggest why those who give them most credit for altering the world over the last thirty years are usually themselves academics who harbor a generous view of the impact of academic ideas. It is true that policy makers occasionally pay attention to those in the academy, as did Pinochet when he took Friedman's advice. 'Madmen in authority, who hear voices in the air,' wrote the economist John Maynard Keynes, 'are distilling their frenzy from some academic scribbler of a few years back.'[6] But the particular academic scribblings at issue here had been around in much the same form since Adam Smith divined them in the eighteenth century. Most likely they suddenly gained prominence in the last decades of the twentieth century, in the United States and elsewhere, because they offered a convenient justification for the shift already under way. They did not cause the shift; at most, they legitimized it.

Stories about heroic or villainous CEOs and financiers, brilliant or corrupt politicians, or diabolically powerful merchants of ideas, however gratifying they may be, should be surrendered to reality. Although a few of these figures have been especially insightful or particularly unscrupulous, in terms of the big picture their deeds are almost completely beside the point. The changes at issue here are structural, not personal. Similar assumptions about immoral and economically powerful corporations conspiring against the public also need to be abandoned because they are too simplistic. Companies are neither moral nor immoral. Any such explanation is a convenient diversion, assigns credit or blame incorrectly, and thereby imperils meaningful reform of capitalism and democracy.

The fact is, most of us are consumers and investors, and as such are benefiting enormously from supercapitalism. Wal-Mart, for example, has caused prices on a wide range of items to be lower than they'd be otherwise, to the benefit of its customers. In turn, Wal-Mart's success has redounded to the benefit of its investors. But most of us are *also* citizens who have ideas about fair play. And in this respect many of us are appalled at Wal-Mart's low pay and elusive benefits, its power to force suppliers to slash their own pay and benefits and to outsource abroad, and its decimating effects on Main Streets.

Yet the executives of Wal-Mart or any other large company are not brutally insensitive or ruthlessly greedy. They are doing what they're supposed to do, according to the current rules of the game – giving their customers good deals and thereby maximizing the returns to their investors. Just like players in any game, they are doing whatever is necessary to win. But just as all games require rules to define fair play, the economy relies on government to set the economic ground rules. If the American government wanted to do something about the means Wal-Mart employs, it could change the current rules. In theory, it could enact laws to make it easier for all employees to unionize, require all large companies to provide their employees with health insurance and pensions, enact zoning regulations to protect Main Street retailers from the predations of big-box retailers, and raise the minimum wage high enough to give all working people a true 'living' wage. All such measures would have the likely effect of causing Wal-Mart and other large companies across the board to raise their prices and reduce returns to investors.

Personally, I'd be willing to sacrifice some of the benefits I get as a consumer and investor in order to achieve these social ends – as long as I knew everyone else was, too. Yet how to create new rules of the game? The market is adept at catering to us as consumers and investors, but democracy has become less responsive to us in our roles as citizens seeking to make the rules of the game fairer. That's mainly because, as I will show in these pages, supercapitalism has spilled over into politics. The money Wal-Mart and other companies are pouring into Washington and every other major capital gets in the way.

The answer, I believe, is *not* to try to push companies to be more 'socially responsible'. Condemning Wal-Mart for not giving its employees better pay and health benefits may be emotionally gratifying but has little to do with the forces that have impelled Wal-Mart to keep wages and benefits low and bestow good deals on Wal-Mart's customers and investors. Wal-Mart, like every other capitalist player, is, as I have emphasized, following the current rules of the game. But *we* should make the rules – rules that reflect our values as citizens as well as our values as consumers and investors.

THE STORY I will tell is not technologically or economically deterministic. Our future is still very much in our hands. But to make the best choices we need to fully understand our past and present, and forsake mythic thinking. There is no prospect of returning to American democratic capitalism of the 1950s and 1960s – nor should we want to – but it is certainly possible to shape the future in ways that better serve our goals and interests as citizens.

The first and most important step is to have a clear understanding of the appropriate boundary between capitalism and democracy – between the economic game, and how its rules are set – so that the boundary can be better defended. Companies are not citizens. They are bundles of contracts. The purpose of companies is to play the economic game as aggressively as possible. The challenge for us as citizens is to stop them from setting the rules. Keeping supercapitalism from spilling over into democracy is the only constructive agenda for change. All else, as I shall make clear, is frolic and detour.

CHAPTER ONE

THE NOT QUITE GOLDEN AGE

ROUGHLY BETWEEN 1945 and 1975, America struck a remarkable accommodation between capitalism and democracy. It combined a hugely productive economic system with a broadly responsive and widely admired political system. America in those years achieved its highest degree of income equality (since measurements have been available). It generated a larger proportion of good-paying jobs than before or since, and more economic security than ever for more of its people. Perhaps not coincidentally, in those years Americans also expressed high confidence in democracy and trust in government, both of which sharply declined in subsequent years.[1] That singular success and that powerful promise extended the moral authority of the American system throughout the world. In contrast to Soviet communism, America became an exemplar of both political freedom and suburban middle-class affluence.

The economy was based on mass production. Mass production was profitable because a large middle class had enough money to purchase what could be mass-produced. The middle class had the money because the profits from mass production were divided up between the giant corporations and their suppliers, retailers, and employees. The bargaining power of these latter groups was enhanced and enforced by government action. Almost a third of the workforce belonged to a labor union. Economic benefits were also spread across the nation – to farmers, veterans, smaller towns, and small businesses – through regulation (of railroads, telephones, utilities, and energy supplies) and subsidy (price supports, highways, federal loans). Thus did democracy offset the economic power of large-scale production and widely disperse its benefits.

But it was not quite a golden age. Women and minorities still struggled for political equality and economic opportunity. Much of the nation's poverty was hidden away in rural hollows or black ghettos. Foreign policy, ostensibly shaped by the perceived threat of Soviet communism, all too frequently pandered to the needs of large American firms for cheap resources abroad, such as bananas, tin, and oil. Civil liberties were imperiled during Senator Joe McCarthy's anti-communist witch hunt. Much of American life was monotonous, conformist, and deadly dull. And yet for all its shortcomings, democratic capitalism seemed to be working remarkably well, and on the way to working even better.

In order to understand what happened to the Not Quite Golden Age, we first need to understand how it came about.

1

THE EVOLUTION began as the nineteenth century ended, when large corporations posed a profound challenge to American democracy. They brought a new level of prosperity to the nation but also sweatshops, child labor, and unsafe working conditions, and they monopolized whole industries. The unprecedented economic power of these giant companies made them politically unaccountable. America groped for a way to respond.

It started with outsized personalities whose footprints are still visible – J. P. Morgan, a banker's son who sold stocks for the railroads, engineered a huge rail combination, and became a wealthy financier (J. P. Morgan and Sons, which evolved into today's Morgan Stanley); Andrew Carnegie, who began as a telephone clerk, rose to the presidency of the Pennsylvania Railroad, and then made a fortune as a steel magnate (Carnegie Steel); John D. Rockefeller, who started as a bookkeeper in Cleveland, bought his first oil refinery in 1862, cornered the oil market in the 1890s with his Standard Oil Company (whose descendant is ExxonMobil), and then moved into coal, iron, shipping, copper, and banking (Chase Manhattan); and, subsequently, Henry Ford.

With these men and others like them flowed a stream of new inventions

– steam engines, railway locomotives, the telegraph, electric turbines, internal combustion engines, and iron and steel machinery with interchangeable parts – that allowed all sorts of things to be made and shipped in very large volume. Costs could be spread over so many units that each single one was cheap to produce. Procter & Gamble devised a new machine for mass-producing Ivory soap. Diamond Match used a machine that made and boxed matches by the billions. A cigarette-making machine invented in 1881 was so productive that just fifteen of them satisfied America's annual demand for cigarettes. Standard Oil, American Sugar Refining, International Harvester, and Carnegie Steel, among others, gained unprecedented efficiencies through giant furnaces, whirling centrifuges, converters, and rolling and finishing equipment.

Productivity surged. While the typical American worker in the early 1800s had produced a tiny .3 percent more each year (seeding and harvesting crops, logging, fishing, or applying his craft with hand tools), by the last decades of the century his productivity was rising at six times that rate.[2] Output also exploded. Iron production doubled in just a few years; steel production multiplied twenty-fold.[3] Railroad and telegraph networks expanded in tandem. Fast, regular, and reliable transportation and communication brought raw materials from far corners of the country into factories and sent finished goods out to wholesalers and retailers all over the nation.

An economic revolution on this scale inevitably had large social consequence. Supply outran demand, leading to a severe depression that jolted much of Europe and America in 1873. Another depression in the summer of 1893 impoverished thousands of farmers, closed banks, and left more than a quarter of America's unskilled urban workforce unemployed. A growing chorus of socialists in Europe and America proclaimed the imminent collapse of capitalism. A swelling cadre of western populists in deepening debt to eastern bankers demanded that currencies be converted from gold to silver. With silver far more abundant than gold, this would inflate currency values and thereby shrink the debts. Manufacturers on both sides of the Atlantic wanted higher tariffs to protect themselves from foreign imports. (Only Britain, whose advanced manufacturers were the primary beneficiaries of free trade, declined to raise its tariffs, resulting in what were seen there as German and American 'economic invasions'.)[4]

Hundreds of thousands of people moved from farms to factories. In 1870, fewer than 8 percent of America's adult population worked in a mill and only one in five lived in a place with 8,000 or more inhabitants; a half century later, almost a third were in factories and almost a half lived in cities. During this tumultuous span of time, New York City's population swelled fourfold; Chicago became ten times its former size. In the 1870s, 280,000 immigrants entered the United States each year. In the 1880s, 5.5 million came; in the 1890s, another 4 million. By the first decade of the twentieth century, the flow of immigrants, most of them destitute when they arrived, rose to a million a year. According to a 1908 government study, almost three-fifths of the wage earners in principal branches of American industry had been born abroad.[5] Immigrants then constituted a higher percentage of the total American workforce than they would a hundred years hence.

As America and every other manufacturing nation began scouring more backward regions of the globe for potential markets, the term 'imperialism' entered common speech. Teddy Roosevelt asserted America's imperial destiny in Latin America. 'Territorial expansion,' explained an official of the United States State Department in 1900, 'is but the by-product of the expansion of commerce.'[6] Britain and Germany equated their economic prowess with their nations' global spheres of influence. The British economist J. A. Hobson dourly predicted the logical end-point of such competition: Businessmen, he warned, opt for war when they have exhausted their home markets. Like John Maynard Keynes three decades later, Hobson urged instead that advanced nations increase their domestic markets by making more of their citizens rich enough to buy domestically produced goods. 'If apportionment of incomes were such as to evoke no excessive saving, full constant employment for capital and labor would be furnished at home.'[7] But the world war Hobson feared would occur before enough citizens had the wherewithal to buy a substantial portion of what they produced.

In the first decades of the twentieth century, productivity again surged. Sweatshops and mills were replaced by large manufacturing plants, inspired by Frederick Winslow Taylor's new theories of 'scientific management', which broke down every factory job into highly specialized and repetitive steps. Henry Ford's assembly line became the model. Not only could workers positioned along the line produce more cars in a shorter time but production could be concentrated in a few giant factories and materials could be bought in bulk at great savings. In 1909, Ford produced 10,607 cars; in 1913, 168,000; the following year, 248,000. By the beginning of World War I, much of American industry had consolidated into giant firms whose names became almost synonymous with America – Ford Motor, U.S. Steel, American Telephone & Telegraph, United States Rubber, National Biscuit, American Can, the Aluminum Company of America, General Electric, General Motors, and Rockefeller's Standard Oil.

The size of such enterprises became an almost impregnable barrier for smaller firms that might wish to enter the market. They dominated the American, and much of the world's, economy for most of the twentieth century. Of the Fortune 500 largest corporations in 1994, more than half were founded between 1880 and 1930.[8] A far smaller portion were founded during the long stable period between 1945 and 1975, an important fact to bear in mind as the story unfolds.

A SAMPLING OF 1994 FORTUNE 500 COMPANIES

FOUNDED IN THE 1880S (53 IN ALL)

Eastman Kodak
Johnson & Johnson
Coca-Cola
Westinghouse
Sears Roebuck (R. W. Sears Watch Company)
Avon Products (California Perfume Company)
Hershey Foods (Lancaster Caramel Company)
Chiquita Brands International (Boston Fruit Company)

1890s (39 IN ALL)

General Electric
Knight-Ridder (Ridder Publications)
Ralston Purina (Robinson Danforth Company)
Reebok International (J. W. Foster and Sons)
Harris Corporation (Harris Automatic Press Company)
Pepsico
Goodyear Tire and Rubber

1900s (52 IN ALL)

Weyerhaeuser
USX (United States Steel)
Ford Motor
Gillette (American Safety Razor Company)
Minnesota Mining and Manufacturing
UPS (American Messenger Company)
General Motors
McGraw-Hill

1910s (45 IN ALL)

Black & Decker
IBM (Computing-Tabulating Recording Company)
Merrill Lynch
Safeway (Skaggs United Stores)
Boeing (Pacific Aero Products)
Cummins Engine
Reynolds Metals

1920s (58 in all)

Chrysler
Time Warner
Marriott Corporation
Delta Air Lines (Huff Daland)
Ace Hardware
Walt Disney
Northwest Airlines
Fruit of the Loom (Union Underwear Company)[9]

2

BY THE FIRST decades of the twentieth century, capitalism seemed on its way to a stunning triumph. But its social consequences – urban squalor, measly wages and long hours for factory workers, child labor, widening inequality, the decline or abandonment of smaller towns and cities – distressed many people. Democracy seemed incapable of responding. The size and economic importance of giant corporations made them politically powerful and thus almost immune to any demand the public might make of them. American democracy had no experience dealing with anything on the scale of industrial capitalism. Democracy had been incubated in communities of the sort Thomas Jefferson had envisioned – in towns, villages, and small cities where the votes of average people (all of them white men) seemed to count – rather than the massively industrial and urbanized nation America was becoming. Voters felt powerless to affect these industrial titans.

The captains of industry did not exactly distinguish themselves as publicly spirited. A few, like Carnegie and John D. Rockefeller, established noted charities, but most echoed the sentiments of William H. Vanderbilt, the railroad tycoon, who, when asked by a reporter for the *New York Times* about keeping open the New York to New Haven line on the assumption that it was run for the public benefit, responded famously, 'The public be damned'. Vanderbilt proceeded to give the reporter a short lecture on capitalism. 'I don't take stock in this silly nonsense about working for anybody's good but our own because we are not. Railroads are not run on sentiment, but on business principles, and to pay.'[10]

The railroads and the rest of America's industrial colossus indeed existed to make profits. The public would benefit to the extent that the lure of profits caused owners to invest more money, create more jobs, and provide better products and services. But Vanderbilt left out a critical point. Because of the businesses' vast scale and the ruthless tactics he and others used to achieve that scale, these firms dominated their markets. Their ongoing strategy was to subdue all competition, which would allow them to charge the public high prices and do almost whatever else they pleased. In short, they were unaccountable.

The public was appalled; the unaccountable power of large corporations seemed inconsistent with democracy. The issue became a well-worn political theme for decades. Teddy Roosevelt decried the giant companies as 'malefactors of great wealth'. Woodrow Wilson fulminated against them. 'The masters of the government of the United States are the combined capitalists and manufacturers of the United States,' he thundered during the 1912 presidential campaign. 'The government of the United States at present is a foster-child of the special interests.'[11] Franklin D. Roosevelt sounded a similar note in 1936 when he blamed the nation's economic woes on 'economic royalists' sitting atop giant corporations who fixed prices and thwarted competition.[12]

The question of corporate accountability was raised everywhere capitalism surged forward, and it preoccupied much of the industrializing world. German economist and politician Gustav Stolper, writing in the late 1930s, noted that '[t]he trend of modern industrialization has been determined in all countries by two conflicting tendencies: the one toward liberation of the individual from ties and codes inherited from the Middle Ages and the mercantilist era; the other toward integration on a more or less monopolistic basis.'[13]

The challenge was how to ensure that capitalism served the people. Some supposed answers came from Europe and Russia. One was state ownership of monopolies and the largest enterprises – socialism, as it was

called. A more radical one was found in communism – common ownership of all 'means of production', in Karl Marx's words. A third was to turn
large corporations into extensions of government and to centralize
government authority in one person; hence, fascism. All were tried. All
ultimately failed.[14]

America flirted briefly with socialism but the flirtation was never con-
summated. At its height, just before World War I, America's Socialist Party
had 100,000 members and 1,200 officeholders in 340 towns and cities –
still far smaller than the Democratic Party or the Republican Party, but
large enough to gain national visibility. Half a million people subscribed to
its newspaper. In 1914, the biggest socialist stronghold was Oklahoma, with
12,000 dues-paying members and over 100 socialists in elected offices. The
movement died, however – socialism's aims seemed too vague; its
international ideals inconsistent with the fierce nationalism unleashed by
World War I; its methods too threatening to American individualism.

The nation chose a combination of more pragmatic techniques. One
was to break up conspicuously large monopolies into smaller, more competitive units. The Sherman Act of 1890 was the nation's first antitrust law.
Both Standard Oil and American Tobacco were disassembled by Supreme
Court decree. Other targets of antitrust prosecution in subsequent decades
were U.S. Steel, International Harvester, General Electric, and AT&T –
although antitrust proved a clumsy weapon. 'Monopolization' was difficult
to prove. Judges were reluctant to bust up well-established businesses.
More to the point, industrial giants could not be dismembered without
sacrificing the efficiencies of large-scale production. Antitrust began as a
political movement and ended as a technical legal specialty.[15]

Another idea emerged. In 1909, Herbert Croly, a young political
philosopher and journalist, argued in his best-selling book *The Promise of
American Life* that the large American corporation should not be broken
up but should be regulated in the public interest. 'The constructive idea
behind a policy of the recognition of the semi-monopolistic corporation is,
of course, the idea that they can be converted into economic agents …
unequivocally for the national economic interest,' he wrote. National
regulation would preserve the efficiencies of large scale and 'convert [the
corporation] to the service of a national democratic economic system'.[16]

It was to be a unique blending of capitalism and democracy. Independent regulatory agencies, headed by commissioners appointed to their positions by governors or presidents, would set rates and limit the number of competitors. That would assure companies a steady flow of profits and customers a steady price. Commissioners would also set industry standards – including ensuring railroad service to small towns and cities – and otherwise define the 'public interest' industries had to meet.

Few rewards are more comforting to a chief executive than a guaranteed stream of profits. The executives of many large corporations publicly objected to regulation but quietly welcomed government's help in preventing price cutting and keeping out potential rivals. The model was the Interstate Commerce Commission (ICC), established in 1887 to standardize railroad rates and in so doing secure the railroads healthy profits. Utility tycoon Samuel Insull urged state legislatures to treat electric power companies as regulated monopolies, too, arguing that competition subjected the public to much uncertainty. When AT&T's share of the telephone market began to drop, its president, Theodore Vail, launched a campaign for his company to become a state-regulated monopoly as well, saying it would give Americans cheaper and more reliable service. In 1914, Woodrow Wilson set up the Federal Trade Commission to prevent 'unfair' methods of competition, which sometimes meant unfairly low prices that might undermine some companies' profits.

By the middle of the twentieth century, around 15 percent of the nation's economy was directly regulated – the Civil Aeronautics Board setting airline rates and routes; the ICC overseeing railroads, trucks, and barges; the Federal Communications Commission in charge of telephone, radio, and the nascent television industry; the Federal Power Commission watching over natural gas pipelines, hydroelectric power, and nuclear energy; the Securities and Exchange Commission, over banking and finance; the Farm Bureau of the Department of Agriculture, agribusiness; the Federal Maritime Commission, shipping. Companies so regulated had significant influence over their regulators, to be sure. Political scientists subsequently spoke of regulatory 'capture' by the regulated. All such regulation reduced competition and thereby imposed higher prices on consumers than otherwise. But only the confirmed cynic would say regulators turned a blind eye to the public's broader interests. Regulation stabilized industry, maintained jobs and wages, and protected the economic bases of communities where regulated industries were headquartered or did business. It also sought to weigh industry's need for profits against the public's need for safe, fair, and reliable service.

For the other 85 percent, a less formal blend of capitalism and democracy involved voluntary industry associations and boards that worked closely with government agencies to set uniform industry standards. None dared call it 'planning', with that word's nefarious whiff of socialism. It was simply another means by which the largest firms in each industry coordinated prices, kept out rivals, and, on occasion, collected government checks. Many of these associations were formed in World War I. They continued, in various guises, for decades. A War Finance Board in World War I underwrote bank loans to war industries. It became the precedent for Herbert Hoover's Reconstruction Finance Corporation in 1932, and for various schemes of government-backed loans and loan guarantees that continued through the New Deal, the Chrysler bailout of 1979, the savings and loan bailout of 1989, and even the airlines bailout of 2001. Similarly, a War Industries Board during World War I (which one participant called the 'town meeting of American industry') morphed after the war into various trade associations and boards, which Herbert Hoover coordinated when secretary of commerce, and then into FDR's National Recovery Administration.

The NRA took industrial planning to a new level of explicitness. Every major industry was to establish codes of fair dealing, including prices and wages. The same business leaders who condemned socialism and communism were delighted. The Great Depression had left them with far more capacity than customers, resulting in a downward plunge in prices. The NRA offered a way to limit industry-wide capacity and stop the price cutting. The United States Chamber of Commerce enthused that the NRA was a 'Magna Carta of industry and labor'. Henry I. Harriman, its president, baldly stated that the free market 'must be replaced by a philosophy of planned national economy',[17] and that the NRA would allow industries to rid themselves of the 'industrial buccaneer' and the 'unscrupulous price-cutter'.[18] By enabling each industry to set prices and wages, the

NRA codes guaranteed a fair return to both capital and labor. Harriman waxed enthusiastic:

> We must take out of competition the right to cut wages to a point which will not sustain an American standard of living, and we must recognize that capital is entitled to a fair and reasonable return ... that ... goods must be sold at a price which will enable the manufacturer to pay a fair price for his raw material, to pay fair wages to his men, and to pay a fair dividend on his investment.[19]

The National Association of Manufacturers, no less enthusiastic, devised a model code for controlling prices and output, and offered it to all trade associations. While Europeans set up cartels and fussed with democratic socialism, America went right to the heart of the matter – creating democratic capitalism as a planned economy, run by business.

The NRA didn't make it past the Supreme Court, but trade associations continued to find ways to limit output and maintain prices, until World War II boosted demand so much that the nation's challenge was to keep prices down rather than buoy them up. Even under these more benign circumstances, the associations lived on. They advised the War Production Board and the Office of Price Administration, and in the 1950s and 1960s morphed into industry committees within the departments of Commerce, Interior, and Defense.

A final idea for reconciling democracy with large-scale capitalism was never realized but often discussed during the first half of the twentieth century, and it framed the way many Americans thought democratic capitalism would evolve. It was to make corporations themselves democratic. As early as 1914, the popular columnist and public philosopher Walter Lippmann called on America's corporate executives to be stewards of the entire nation. 'The men connected with [the large corporation] cannot escape the fact that they are expected to act increasingly like public officials ... Big businessmen who are at all intelligent recognize this. They are talking more and more about their "responsibilities", and their "stewardship".'[20] In 1932, Adolf A. Berle and Gardiner C. Means, lawyer and economics professor, respectively, published *The Modern Corporation and*

Private Property, a highly influential study revealing that top executives of America's giant companies were not even accountable to their own shareholders but operated the companies 'in their own interest, and ... divert[ed] a portion of the asset fund to their own uses'.[21] The only solution, concluded Berle and Means, was to enlarge the power of all groups within the nation who were affected by the large corporation, including employees and consumers. They envisioned the corporate executive of the future as a professional administrator, dispassionately weighing the claims of investors, employees, consumers, and citizens, and allocating benefits accordingly. '[I]t seems almost essential if the corporate system is to survive – that the "control" of the great corporations should develop into a purely neutral technocracy, balancing a variety of claims by various groups in the community and assigning each a portion of the income stream on the basis of public policy rather than private cupidity.'[22]

In the postwar years, as we shall see shortly, the top executives of America's largest corporations would indeed see themselves as 'corporate statesmen', responsible for balancing the claims of stockholders, employees, and the American public. The public would come to share this view.

3

ANY LINGERING DOUBTS about the compatibility of democracy with large-scale capitalism were erased by explosive prosperity in the 1950s, and the obvious fact of its being widely shared. David Lilienthal, a New Deal planner, rhapsodized over the giant American corporation in his popular 1953 book, *Big Business: A New Era*: 'Our productive and distributive superiority, our economic fruitfulness, rest upon Bigness.'[23] *Fortune* magazine, reporting on a 1953 public opinion survey that showed the vast majority of Americans approved of big business, concluded with its customary effusiveness that 'the huge publicly owned corporation ... has become the most important phenomenon of mid-century capitalism. Corporate bigness is coming to be accepted as an integral part of a big economy. Whatever attacks may be made against them in theory, the large corporations have met the test of delivering the goods'.[24]

They met the test only because government spending on an

unprecedented scale had pulled the nation out of the Depression and pushed companies to what before had seemed unimaginable feats of production. Now, at war's end, as government spending dropped, consumer spending kicked in. Millions of returning GIs swarmed back to set up families, get additional education (paid for by the government), and buy homes (with government-subsidized loans). In 1950, young families were moving into new houses at an unprecedented rate of four thousand a day, filling them with clothes dryers, electric skillets, air-conditioners, washing machines, baby carriages, and refrigerators – and at least one car in every drive-way. Auto ownership surged from 10 million in 1949 to 24 million in 1957. William J. Levitt bought hundreds of acres of Long Island potato fields and constructed a thousand homes from scratch, using a factory system that kept costs so low that the houses were priced at less than $10,000 – $1,000 down and $70 a month – for three bedrooms, a wood-burning fireplace, a kitchen with stove and fridge, and a landscaped lot seventy-five feet by one hundred feet. In Levittown and elsewhere across America, young families stormed to the suburbs.

Many other nations had succumbed to tyranny in the preceding decades. In America, democracy had prevailed, and the nation congratulated itself on the strength and durability of its system. Large-scale mass production was creating a large and stable middle class that was the bulwark of democracy. Here, finally, was the society J. A. Hobson had wished for a half century before, in which prosperity was so widely shared that the abundant fruits of mass production could find their market at home. Americans took it as their patriotic duty to consume. According to the chairman of President Dwight D. Eisenhower's Council of Economic Advisers, the 'ultimate purpose' of the American economy was 'to produce more consumer goods'.[25] It was well understood that the ultimate purpose of American democracy was to create a better standard of living for more and more Americans.

Large scale meant even fewer large players, but the contented public was no longer especially concerned about corporate economic power. Charles Erwin 'Engine Charlie' Wilson, president of General Motors when Eisenhower tapped him to become secretary of defense in 1953, voiced at his Senate confirmation hearing what was by then the conventional view.

When asked whether he would be capable of making a decision in the interest of the United States that was adverse to the interest of General Motors, he said he could. Then he quickly reassured the senators that the conflict would never arise. 'I cannot conceive of one because for years I thought what was good for our country was good for General Motors, and vice versa. The difference did not exist. Our company is too big. It goes with the welfare of the country.'[26]

With demand soaring, businesses argued that less regulation or government-industry planning was necessary. Besides, the largest companies had grown so vast that prices could be maintained and output controlled by the simple expedient of collusion among the two or three biggest ones in each industry (or, to use the more technical and less alarming language of economics, 'oligopolistic coordination'). Steel was controlled by three giants – United States Steel, Republic, and Bethlehem; the electrical equipment and appliance industry by two – General Electric and Westinghouse. In basic chemicals, there were three – DuPont, Union Carbide, and Allied Chemical. In food processing, three dominated – General Foods, Quaker Oats, and General Mills. In tobacco, three – R.J. Reynolds, Liggett & Myers, and American Tobacco; in jet engines, two – General Electric and Pratt & Whitney; in automobiles, three – General Motors, Ford, and Chrysler. In the new industry of television broadcasting, there were three networks – NBC, CBS, and ABC. This consolidation took place all across the vast expanse of American industry.

By 1950, most postwar reconstruction in Europe and Japan was completed. Even so, America still produced about 60 percent of the total output of the seven largest capitalist countries. America's manufacturing sector was about twice as productive (per employed person) as that of Britain, three times as productive as Germany, and nine times as productive as Japan.[27] Remarkably, fewer than five hundred American companies were responsible for almost half of the nation's entire industrial output (which then accounted for about a quarter of the industrial output of the entire free world) and employed more than a fifth of all American nonfarm workers.[28] These firms owned roughly three-quarters of the nation's industrial assets and accounted for about 40 percent of the nation's corporate profits. General Motors, the biggest manufacturing company on earth, itself generated 3 percent of America's entire gross national product in 1955, approximately equivalent to the entire gross national product of Italy at the time. Standard Oil of New Jersey (one of the pieces of the old Standard Oil Company) and AT&T each had revenues greater than Denmark's.

Arrayed around these giants and dependent on them as customers or suppliers were several thousand large but not immense industrial corporations and a few service firms that catered to their needs – banks, insurance companies, railroads, and mass retailers like Sears, Montgomery Ward, and J. C. Penney. Encircling these, in turn, were hundreds of thousands of smaller firms that filled specialized market niches. The remainder of the private economy was found on the Main Streets of America – local retailers, restaurants, barbers, hotels, hospitals, law firms – and a dwindling number of family farms. Unlike the giant oligopolies, these peripheral businesses were vulnerable to the whims of the marketplace. Coping with the continuous uncertainties of competition, their owners and employees lived far more precariously than the big corporations.

The largest corporations could not risk competition. Their output had to be planned far in advance with a high degree of confidence it could be sold at a predetermined price. Collusion and planning were essential. The '[t]echnology [of mass production], with its companion commitment of time and capital, means that the needs of the consumer must be anticipated – by months or years,' explained John Kenneth Galbraith, one of the few economists of the time who understood the corporate planning system. The large corporation, therefore, 'must exercise control over what is sold. It must exercise control over what is supplied. It must replace the market with planning … Much of what the firm regards as planning consists in minimizing or getting rid of market influences.'[29] The giant corporation of mid-century America necessarily possessed vast discretion and economic power.

To plan efficiently, the production process had to be organized precisely and predictably so every step could be synchronized with every other. The organization chart clearly delineated a chain of command. Key decisions descended from executive suites. Middle-level managers were to implement them, each within a limited span of control over his (almost always his, rarely if ever her) lower-level managers and division heads. Every major product had its own division and hierarchy. All clerical and blue-collar jobs were classified in rigid bureaucratic order. Rules and standard operating procedures determined who was to do what, and how. Most people were not supposed to think for themselves except in the most narrow of parameters. Original thought in most cases could imperil the entire plan.

Despite the careful preparation and execution, plans did not always succeed. Ford's Edsel was noteworthy because it so blatantly failed. But success was the norm and the norm was to avoid unnecessary risk, which typically meant eschewing novelty in favor of variations on products and services already proven popular. Such a system was not conducive to innovation. General Motors sold more than a million Cheverolet Impalas in 1965, for example, but the car contained almost nothing that prior models lacked or that competitors didn't also provide. While the basic technology of internal combustion remained the same for years, the Big Three emphasized style and comfort. They added power brakes, power windows, power steering, larger and more powerful engines, and air-conditioners. The tail fins got longer and headlights doubled. (One little-observed consequence was a drop in average gas mileage through the 1950s and 1960s.)

Although capitalism and communism were assumed to be direct opposites, the Soviets implemented their own form of planning with not dissimilar resolve and success. Vast economies of large scale fit snugly within Soviet five-year plans. As the American economy rebounded after the war, Russian industrial production also rose impressively. Steel output increased by about 9 percent a year through the 1950s. Between 1960 and 1973, per capita growth in the Soviet Union averaged 3.4 percent a year, while it averaged 3 percent in the United States and 4.4 percent in Europe.[30] When John F. Kennedy sat in the White House, Nikita Khrushchev could credibly boast that at the rate his economy was growing, it would overtake America's within twenty years.

4

BIG BUSINESSES found their correlate in big labor; the first begat the second. The bargains both sides struck over wages and working conditions established norms across the economy, spreading the benefits of high productivity and contributing to the growth of America's middle class. Their relationship was to be a central feature of democratic capitalism during the Not Quite Golden Age.

Labor's rise was not smooth. It had its fiery personalities – John L. Lewis of the United Mine Workers, Walter Reuther of the United Auto Workers, Philip Murray of the United Steelworkers. Yet as was the case with the rise of the giant corporation, structural changes in the economy accounted more for labor's rise (and subsequent decline) than the dominant characters who made the headlines. In the early twentieth century, the Supreme Court had determined that agreements among workers to form unions violated the nation's antitrust laws. Antitrust law did bar agreements that restrained trade, but the Court was acting cynically given the growing economic power of large corporations. As that power increased, labor nonetheless intensified its efforts to organize.

After the Wagner Act finally legitimized collective bargaining in 1935, unions grew considerably larger. General Motors recognized the United Auto Workers as bargaining agent for its workers, and United States Steel did the same for the United Steelworkers. They did so not just because the law now allowed for unions, but for much the same reason that they and other big businesses hadn't strongly opposed the Wagner Act in the first place. They saw in collective bargaining an efficient method for maintaining a stable workforce and minimizing unexpected disruptions – key preconditions for high-volume production.

During World War II, the ranks of organized labor swelled to 14 million. Big companies offered little resistance. They were raking in profits, mainly from government contracts. Open opposition to unions would have been unseemly under the circumstances. Labor, for its part, pledged not to strike; striking would have been seen as unpatriotic.

Soon after the war ended, though, labor demanded its share. American industry had grown fat on wartime profits, but American workers had not had a raise in years. An influential University of California study released in 1945 (authored by Dr. Walter Heller, who later chaired the Council of Economic Advisers in the John F. Kennedy and Lyndon Johnson administrations) found that the typical American family of four needed around $50 a week to maintain a 'decent standard of living', but the average factory worker earned only $40.98 a week (steelworkers were paid $45.60; autoworkers, $44.81; electrical workers, $41.25; garment workers $23.75).[31] William H. Davis, then director of the government's Office of Economic Stabilization, estimated that industry was so profitable it could raise wages as much as 40 to 50 percent without raising prices. President Harry S. Truman, who felt he had enough on his plate without getting involved in management-labor disputes, repudiated Davis's calculation and announced Davis was out of a job.

Steelworker president Philip Murray denounced the billion dollars big steel companies had raked in during World War II and the nearly $750 million they had distributed to their shareholders, compared to the paltry sums steelworkers had been paid. UAW president Walter Reuther demanded General Motors link autoworkers' paychecks to the auto giant's 'ability to pay'. At one noted bargaining session whose transcript became public, Reuther threatened, '[U]nless we get a more realistic distribution of America's wealth, we won't get enough to keep this machinery going.' His comment transcended the specific negotiation. He was referring to American workers in general, and the apparent urgency of spreading corporate wealth to them so they could buy the cars, kitchen appliances, radios, washing machines, and life insurance policies big business was now churning out. It was a signal moment in the history of labor and of democratic capitalism, but it did not elicit an especially constructive dialogue immediately thereafter:

GM: You can't talk about this … without exposing your socialistic desires.
REUTHER: If fighting for equal and equitable distribution of the wealth of this country is socialistic, I stand guilty of being a Socialist.
GM: You're convicted.
REUTHER: I plead guilty.

Reuther's threat – not only that the UAW would strike GM but that unless corporate profits were more broadly shared with American workers, they wouldn't be able to consume the output of American companies – struck a nerve. It prompted GM to run full-page advertisements in major newspapers setting out its philosophical view:

HERE IS THE ISSUE: Is American business to be based on free competition, or is it to become socialized, with all activities controlled and regimented? ... America is at a crossroads! It must preserve the freedom of each unit of American business to determine its own destinies. Or it must transfer to some governmental bureaucracy or agency, or to a union, the responsibility of management that has been the very keystone of American business![32]

Corporate America held fast. Labor acted: In 1946 more than 2 million autoworkers, steelworkers, meatpackers, and electrical equipment workers went on strike. Truman had no choice but to get involved. He set up a fact-finding panel that showed the cost of living had jumped about 33 percent since before the war, while the wartime wage freeze had limited pay increases of the typical workers to around 15 percent. The panel called on industry to raise wages 33 percent above what they had been in January 1941. Business leaders reluctantly agreed.

The results were not nearly as dire as they had feared. Because every large company in every major industry had to make the same concession, no single company or industry suffered a competitive disadvantage at home, and needn't yet fear competition from abroad. The biggest companies in each industry already coordinated prices and output; coordinating wages turned out to be a relatively simple matter. Labor had done it just right: In organizing itself by industry – including auto, aircraft, steel, rubber, shipbuilding, chemicals, electrical equipment – it mimicked the preexisting oligopolies, and therefore minimized the cost to any single firm of accepting union demands.

Moreover, markets were growing briskly. By virtue of ever greater economies of scale, productivity was rising, too, which meant that most items could be produced as cheaply as before even though workers got higher pay. Business leaders were also confident that, when necessary, extra labor costs could be passed along to consumers in the form of higher prices. Consumers, after all, didn't have much choice. Finally, and most important, business executives now appreciated what a toll strikes and work stoppages could take on large-scale production. It was often cheaper to give the unions what they wanted. 'Where you have a well-established industry and a well-established union, you are going to get to the point where a strike doesn't make sense,' wryly observed George Meany, the president of the AFL-CIO.[33]

By the 1950s the tumult was mainly over. Wages rose as did so-called fringe benefits. Indeed, benefits were becoming important features of pay packages. In 1950, 10 percent of union contracts offered pensions and 30 percent included health insurance. Five years later, 45 percent of medium-sized and large companies gave their workers pensions, and 70 percent provided a range of insurance – life, accident, and health that included hospitalization and maternity care. Such benefits were attractive both to employers and employees because, although equivalent to income, they weren't taxed as such, which meant American taxpayers as a whole in effect subsidized these benefits. Few understood at the time that the nation was thus embarking on a new form of publicly subsidized social insurance linked to employment. By the end of the twentieth century, its magnitude had reached astonishing levels. Corporate spending on employee pensions and health care, indirectly supported by government, was roughly as large relative to the overall economy as direct government spending on pensions and health insurance in most other advanced nations.[34] Other contract sweeteners were added through the 1950s and 1960s. Labor agreements came to include automatic cost-of-living adjustments by which wages rose with inflation. Paid vacations also became the norm. Supplemental unemployment benefits (beyond those provided by government unemployment insurance) guaranteed workers full income even when laid off during economic downturns.

By 1955, over a third of American workers belonged to a labor union. A large portion of those who did not got similar pay and benefit packages because their employers did not want to attract unions where none existed. Even smaller businesses aspired to give their employees what economists termed 'prevailing' wages and benefits in order to attract and keep the workers they needed.

Labor unions also became a powerful political force. Local chapters, joined together in state and national federations, grouped by industry and amalgamated together in the AFL-CIO, fought successfully to raise the minimum wage (thereby pushing upward all wages above the minimum), broaden Social Security, and create Medicare. 'The new labor leader is a member of the new class,' opined the editors of *Fortune*. 'His salary is high. He is a public figure. He enjoys a powerful place in society.'[35] Big labor thereby joined big business as integral to the American economic system. No longer a social movement, labor was by now an established part of democratic capitalism, sharing with business the credit and responsibility for ensuring the public's rising prosperity.

FIGURE 1.1

PRIVATE SECTOR UNION MEMBERS AS PERCENTAGE
OF PRIVATE SECTOR EMPLOYEES, 1929–1957

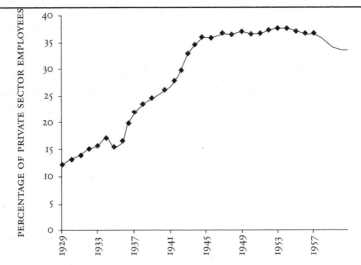

Sources: U.S. Bureau of Labor Statistics; Leo Troy and Neil Sheflin, U.S. Union Sourcebook *(West Orange, N.J.: IRDIS, 1985).*

5

AND RISE it did. From the end of World War II until the middle of the 1970s, the pay and benefits of the American workforce grew, on average, 2.5 to 3 percent each year, in tandem with productivity growth. Between 1947 and 1973, real median family income doubled, as did the value of what the typical American worker produced. If few became conspicuously rich, the great majority of Americans lived better than ever before. And they worked fewer hours, as the nation moved toward a five-day workweek.

The prosperity and growth of America's middle class was one of democratic capitalism's greatest triumphs. By the mid-1950s, almost half of all families fell comfortably within the middle range, defined as families earning between $4,000 and $7,500, after taxes, in 1953 dollars. Most such families were headed not by professionals or business executives but by skilled and semiskilled factory workers and clerks, who managed the flows of product and paperwork through the great corporations. Most breadwinners were men and husbands; most women in that vast and growing middle class did not work.

Americans were becoming more equal, economically. In 1928, the highest-paid 1 percent of earners had taken home 19 percent of total personal income, before taxes. By 1950, their share had plummeted to 7 percent.[36] After-tax income was even more equal. Under Republican president Eisenhower, top earners paid a marginal income tax rate of 91 percent. That dropped to a still significant 78 percent under Democratic president Kennedy. High taxes did not seem to constrain the economy, which continued to surge forward as productivity soared.

FIGURE 1.2

SHARE OF TOTAL INCOME RECEIVED BY RICHEST 1 PERCENT, 1913–1970

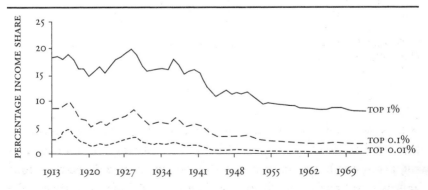

Source: T. Piketty and E. Saez, 'Income Inequality in the United States, 1913–1998', Quarterly Journal of Economics *118, no. 1 (February 2003).*

A college text of 1956 entitled *The American Class Structure* noted how far the nation had progressed from the class divisions of the 1920s. 'All are employees, not owners. Their places in the system depend upon the rules of bureaucratic entry and promotion.' The author, sociologist Joseph Kahl, noted how corporate bureaucracies were tending to level out incomes as pay at the bottom rungs on the corporate ladder moved upward while pay at the top rungs was constrained by civil service-like job categories. 'The trend of income distribution,' Kahl concluded, 'has been toward a reduction in inequality. Owners have been receiving a smaller share relative to employees; professionals and clerks have been losing some of their advantages over operatives and laborers.'[37]

Jobs were also more stable than they had been in previous decades – another by-product both of unionization and of the rigid oligopolistic structure that constrained competition and innovation in favor of economies of scale. In a 1952 survey, two-thirds of senior executives said they had been with the same company for more than twenty years.[38] The careers and pay of these 'organization men', to use the felicitous phrase of sociologist William H. Whyte, Jr., in a best seller of the era, came to be as ordered and predictable as those of their blue-collar counterparts. The young white-collar men he interviewed gave voice to the accepted view: '*Be loyal to the company and the company will be loyal to you*' (emphasis in the original). '[T]he average young man cherishes the idea that his relationship with The Organization is to be for keeps,' wrote Whyte. Mutual loyalty could be counted on because, it was thought, 'the goals of the individual and the goals of the organization will work out to be one and the same'.[39] More to the point (which Whyte missed entirely) was that the structure of the economy allowed and encouraged such lifelong loyalty.

The take-home pay of white-collar workers depended more on the number of years with the corporation than individual effort. Union contracts for blue-collar workers similarly stipulated that wages would rise with seniority. This predictably upward trajectory not only helped corporations anticipate their production costs; it also helped families plan their futures. One's pay 'grade' started at a modest level when household expenses rarely required more, and rose gradually as families grew.

Employees took out home loans and car loans with almost certain confidence they could be repaid. Starter homes and cars could be routinely traded up. At age sixty-five, after forty or more years with the company, the typical employee retired with a gold watch or pin and a company pension providing a modest but predictable sum thereafter.

FIGURE 1.3

REAL FAMILY INCOME GROWTH BY QUINTILE, 1947–1973

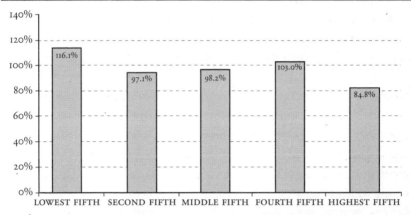

Source: Economic Policy Institute, The State of Working America, *2006/7, Chapter 1, Figure 11, from Bureau of the Census, CPS (all data deflated).*

'Thereafter' did not last especially long in those days. It was not a golden age in terms of longevity. Retirees could expect another five or six years of card games with old friends and visits from grandchildren before dying with the satisfaction of having lived an utterly predictable life.

Nor was it a golden age in terms of equal opportunity. America of the 1950s and 1960s still harbored vast inequalities. The very poor remained almost invisible to the rest of the nation. Blacks were overtly or covertly relegated to second-class citizenship and often inferior jobs. Few women dared aspire to professions other than teaching, nursing, or attending to airline passengers. It would be a while before such barriers began to fall, even as more and more Americans joined the stable, standardized bureaucracies of corporate America. Yet the nation had charted a new direction – toward steady jobs at good wages within a system that broadly shared the fruits of prosperity – and created a middle class sufficiently large to tilt democratic capitalism toward broader equality of opportunity.

6

POLITICAL SCIENTISTS of the time sought to describe the kind of democracy America had become with abstract terms like 'interest-group pluralism', to delineate a system that, while not conforming to the old textbook models of direct or even representative democracy, still managed to be responsive to the needs and aspirations of most citizens.[40] There was a degree of self-congratulation in this, but also a legitimate search for why American democracy had performed so well in the face of modern industrialization relative to socialism, communism, and totalitarianism.

Democratic government, in their view, was an ongoing negotiation among competing but intertwined groups. 'The principal balancing force in the politics of a multi-group society such as the United States,' wrote Columbia University political scientist David Truman in *The Governmental Process,* an influential 1951 treatise, consisted of '[o]verlapping membership among organized interest groups'.[41] According to Truman, most Americans belonged to several such groups (clubs, associations, political parties, unions) that conveyed their members' preferences to political leaders. These overlapping groups stabilized democracy while allowing for peaceful change. Yale political scientist Robert A. Dahl, in *A Preface to Democratic Theory,* published in 1956, added that democracy had succeeded in America while failing elsewhere by embracing a wide number of such groups, each of which was separately a political minority. Because they had to form coalitions with each other to get anything done, the overall system stayed flexible and responsive. The result was neither rule by majority nor by minority but 'minorities rule'.[42] When Dahl examined a typical American city (New Haven, Connecticut), he discovered, not surprisingly, that most citizens were uninvolved in day-to-day politics. Effective control was in the hands of competing elites who were largely self-selected. But unless they represented the interests of their broader constituents they risked losing out to other elites who did a better job of it.

It was a comforting theory that left out two discomfiting facts – interest groups did not automatically compete on equal terms, and they typically paid no attention to the poor. Yet it was undoubtedly true that elected leaders in the Not Quite Golden Age paid careful attention to local elites – small businesses that comprised the local chamber of commerce, for example, and to national organizations whose members were active in local chapters, such as the American Legion, the Farm Bureau, and union branches. Unlike many 'public interest' advocacy groups today – huddled in small offices in Washington, from which they routinely send out mailings soliciting contributions from true believers around the country – these groups had enough organizing heft at the grass roots to pressure legislators to do their bidding. The American Legion, for example, was singularly responsible for passage of the GI Bill of 1944, which guaranteed every returning veteran up to four years of post-secondary school education, subsidized home mortgages, and business loans.[43]

The political scientists left out something else, equally important to explaining how democratic capitalism distributed the benefits of a growing economy. By fits and starts, the federal government had created new centers of economic power that offset the power of the giant companies. Unions, as we have seen, pushed for and won legislation that legitimized collective bargaining. Small farmers got federal price supports and a voice in setting agricultural policy. Farm cooperatives, like unions, won exemption from federal antitrust laws. Small retailers obtained protection against retail chains through state 'fair trade' laws and the federal Robinson-Patman Act, requiring wholesalers to charge all retailers the same price regardless of size and preventing chains from cutting prices. (Wal-Mart would not have stood a chance.) The retail chains, meanwhile, were allowed to combine into large national organizations despite the antitrust laws, thereby countering the market power of the large manufacturers. Small investors gained protection under the Securities and Exchange acts. And so it went, across the economy. John Kenneth Galbraith approvingly dubbed it 'countervailing power'.[44] 'Given the existence of private market power in the economy,' he wrote, 'the growth of countervailing power strengthens the capacity of the economy for autonomous self-regulation and thereby lessens the amount of overall government control or planning that is required or sought.'[45]

In hindsight we now know that more than economic stability was at stake. These new centers of economic power gave the emerging system much of its political stability.[46] By spreading the gains of economic growth to groups that otherwise would have received little or none of them while also giving such groups a voice, the new power centers strengthened democratic capitalism. Political scientists of the era correctly noted that democratically elected representatives were sensitive to well-organized local interests (small businesses, veterans, doctors, and, increasingly, the elderly, for example). They just missed the bigger story: Democracy had made it possible for other groups (unionized workers, farmers, suppliers, retailers, and small investors) to look after their own economic interests directly.

7

AMERICA'S PREOCCUPATION with the Soviet Union during these years – a putative race between capitalism and communism that was more a contest between totalitarianism and democracy – served as ready justification for large-scale public investment. The adjectives 'national defense' when applied to almost any area of policy seemed automatically to justify large public expenditure. Sputnik's signal contribution to American education, for example, was dubbed the National Defense Education Act, whose avowed purpose was to ready more American scientists and engineers to compete with the Soviets. Its by-product was the grounding of a generation of researchers and teachers in many technologies that would be at the forefront of American industry. The National Interstate and Defense Highways Act – forty thousand miles of straight four-lane freeways to replace the old two-lane federal roads that meandered through cities and towns – was justified by Congress as a means of speeding munitions across the nation in the event of war. Its practical effects would be to spur national productivity by radically lowering the cost of transporting and distributing goods across the land, boost the sales of automobiles, and generate suburban sprawl.

Eisenhower warned the nation to beware the 'military-industrial complex', but he seems not to have understood how important that relationship was to jobs and the overall stability of the economy. Through the 1950s and 1960s, about one hundred corporations received two-thirds, by value, of all defense contracts. Most of these giant companies were unionized, which meant that their workers shared in the bounty. By 1959, 20 percent of California's nonagricultural workforce was employed directly or indirectly by major defense contractors. In Washington state, the comparable figure was 22 percent.

Defense contracts also helped spawn future technologies in aerospace and telecommunications. Billions of dollars dedicated to researching and developing complex weapons systems generated the first transistors that found their way into computers; hard plastics eventually used in automobiles and appliances; optical fibers that came to be the 'information highways' of the Internet; lasers that could eventually reshape eyeballs; jet engines that allowed commercial aircraft to travel ten thousand miles without refueling; and a vast array of precision gauges, sensing devices, and electronic gadgets that found their way into hundreds of thousands of commercial products and services. As we shall examine in the next chapter, many of these technologies, and the companies and industries that utilized them, contributed to the eventual shattering of the stable, oligopolistic American system.

AMERICA AT MID-CENTURY was not a trading nation. Few recently war-devastated economies were capable of selling Americans much of anything or buying much of what America might have had to sell. Even by 1960, only 4 percent of the automobiles Americans bought were built outside the United States, only 4 percent of the steel Americans used came from abroad, and less than 6 percent of televisions, radios, and other consumer products had their origins outside America's borders. Nonetheless, the nation in these years committed itself to an ambitious plan for extending the wonders of American capitalism to the rest of world, as a further bulwark against the spread of Soviet communism. This effort also contributed to the erosion of the stable oligopolistic system, as we shall see.

In the early postwar years, America championed a system of fixed exchange rates to minimize currency fluctuations, the International Monetary Fund to ensure world liquidity, the World Bank to direct development financing, the General Agreement on Tariffs and Trade to ensure an open trading system. The nation channeled billions of dollars to Western Europe and Japan to rebuild factories, railways, roads, schools. 'The old imperialism – exploitation for foreign profit – has no place in our plans,' said President Truman in announcing his Point Four program of technical assistance to developing nations. 'What we envisage is a program of development based on the concept of democratic fair-dealing.'[47] (He might have added: 'and the containment of the Soviet menace.')

By almost any measure, the effort was a large success. Between 1945 and 1970, real incomes tripled around the world and world trade quadrupled. Not coincidentally, America's foreign policy created new opportunities for America's largest corporations – then larger, richer, and more technologically advanced than anywhere else in the world – to expand their markets abroad. With the dollar as the currency on which the world's fixed-exchange system was based, America's bankers and large corporations could extend the reach of American capitalism at minimal risk. Under a World Bank controlled by Americans, development assistance could be focused around the globe precisely where large American corporations saw greatest opportunity.

The effect was not uniformly benign. With uncanny precision, the Central Intelligence Agency uncovered communist plots just where America's largest corporations wanted to ensure stable supplies of natural resources. When in 1953 an anti-colonial Iranian nationalist movement led by Mohammed Mossadegh challenged the power of the shah and seized the Anglo-Iranian Oil Company, the CIA secretly channeled millions of dollars to Iranian army officers dedicated to returning the shah to power. Once that objective was met, American oil companies were granted generous access to Iranian oil. The next year, Guatemala's democratically elected president, Jacobo Arbenz Guzmán, initiated land reforms that, along the way, confiscated the United Fruit Company's plantations. The CIA then bankrolled right-wing revolutionaries who, helped by CIA pilots and aircraft supplied by Nicaraguan dictator Anastasio Somoza, spared United

Fruit an otherwise dismal fate. Also in 1954, the United States became quietly involved in Indochina, another area rich in natural resources. In Latin America, Vietnam, and the Middle East, America's foreign policy sowed the seeds of profound problems for the future.

At home, Wisconsin senator Joe McCarthy fomented against alleged communists within the U.S. government and in the media and entertainment industries. Careers were wrecked; civil liberties compromised.

8

ONE LAST FEATURE bears mention because it serves as a particularly vivid point of contrast to where we are today. Sitting atop America's largest corporations were men who repeatedly stated (in words describing precisely the ideal propounded by Adolf Berle and Gardiner Means decades before in *The Modern Corporation and Private Property*) that their job was to balance the needs of everyone affected by the corporation, including the public at large. 'The job of management,' proclaimed Frank Abrams, chairman of Standard Oil of New Jersey, in a 1951 address that typified what other chief executives were saying, 'is to maintain an equitable and working balance among the claims of the various directly affected interest groups ... stockholders, employees, customers, and the public at large. Business managers are gaining professional status partly because they see in their work the basic responsibilities [to the public] that other professional men have long recognized in theirs.' *Fortune* lectured its executive readers on their duty to maintain a broad national perspective: 'To take the professional point of view, the executive must adopt a detached, reserved attitude toward the opportunities and tactics of the moment. He must become an industrial statesman.'[48]

The role came naturally to these men, many of whom had served at high levels of government during World War II and continued thereafter to serve on public advisory boards, panels, and commissions. (When 'Engine Charlie' Wilson brought with him to the Pentagon a platoon of GM executives, Democratic statesman Adlai Stevenson quipped that America had taken government out of the hands of the New Dealers and given it to the car dealers.) These self-described 'corporate statesmen' frequently testified before Congress. They were generous both with their time and with their opinions about what was good for the nation. A bipartisan group of them, led by Paul Hoffman, then CEO of the Studebaker Corporation, Bill Benton of Benton & Bowles advertising, and Marion Folsom of Eastman Kodak, formed the Committee for Economic Development. This was no business association in the modern sense, lobbying for narrow business interests. The committee pushed for the Full Employment Act of 1946, which committed the nation to full employment as an official goal of national economic policy. And it lobbied for the Marshall Plan to rebuild Europe, and helped sell the plan to the rest of America. (Hoffman himself became its first administrator.)

These business leaders could afford to be corporate statesmen – acting, in their view, for the betterment of the nation rather than *strictly* for the benefit of their own consumers and shareholders – because the oligopolistic system allowed them the license to be statesmen. Just as they could grant their blue-collar workers generous wages and benefits without worry that a competitor would undercut them, they could go to Washington to advocate the Marshall Plan without concern that a rival would steal away market share while their attention was elsewhere.

9

To SUMMARIZE: The central features of American democratic capitalism during the Not Quite Golden Age fit together into a remarkably coherent system, merging economics and politics. America's largest corporations would plan and implement the production of a large volume of goods, gaining significant economies of scale and thereby reducing the cost of producing each unit. By coordinating explicitly or implicitly with the handful of other giant companies in the same industry, they could set prices high enough to ensure substantial profits. A portion of those profits would be reinvested in new factories and machinery. Another share would go to executives and middle managers according to their rank in the organization. A portion would go to hourly workers, who were organized into industry-wide unions. Their hourly pay and benefits would be stipulated in contracts covering all workers in the industry; benefits would include tax-favored health insurance and pensions. In return, organized labor would, for the most part, forbear from strikes or work stoppages that would otherwise interfere with the smooth flow of high-volume production. Both sides would, for the most part, refrain from setting wages and prices so high as to spur inflation. These contracts would also, in effect, set prevailing wages and benefits for workers who were not unionized.

Regulatory agencies, meanwhile, would set prices and standards for key services that could be provided to the broad public on mostly equal terms through monopolies – utilities, airlines operating over specific routes, trucks, railroads, and the telephone. Legislators would pay particular heed to the interests of their local communities, including small businesses, local retailers, and farmers. The federal government would impose a high marginal tax on the wealthiest, and on companies. It would use much of the proceeds for national defense against Soviet communism, defined broadly to include a national highway system, higher education, the development of new technologies, large contracts for the aerospace industry, and foreign policies to expand markets and guarantee natural resources for the benefit of large American corporations.

Democratic capitalism of this era involved a complex and continuous set of negotiations – sometimes directly between key players, like big business and big labor; sometimes indirectly, within regulatory agencies and legislatures. There were several important consequences: first, large economies of scale, generating high productivity and hence significant profits; second, tens of millions of steady jobs; third, a wide distribution of the profits (downward to blue-collar workers and outward to smaller communities, farmers, and other constituents); fourth, millions of consumers who used this largesse to purchase the goods and services produced in ever larger quantities, thereby stabilizing the economy for large-scale production. The result was a large and growing middle class across the country that stabilized the political system. It was a full circle.

This was hardly the textbook model of democratic capitalism, which strictly separates the 'economy' from 'government' and believes capitalism occurs almost automatically through the workings of an idealized 'free market', while democracy happens because voters go to the polls to make

their selections as to who should oversee the public sector. In fact, much of
the government's unstated role was to *manage* the often untidy process by
which these economic and political negotiations took place. Only rarely
was this role perceptible, as it was when, in 1962, John F. Kennedy publicly
rebuked Roger Blough, then chairman of United States Steel, for raising
steel prices and thus violating the wage-and-price agreement that had been
worked out with the steelworkers union and other steel producers.

Efficiencies were sacrificed, to be sure. Consumers did not receive the
lowest possible price or best quality. They abided cars that became obsolete
a few years after purchase and telephone repairmen who showed up two
days late. Investors were similarly docile. Economist John Kenneth
Galbraith described the typical stockholder as a 'passive and functionless
figure'.[49] Average daily volume of traded shares was only 3 million by the
early 1960s; it did not rise above 10 million until 1970, and only thereafter
took off – as did share prices.[50] Across the economy, many assets failed to
be put to their most productive uses. The potent incentive of great wealth
was often absent. Innovation lagged. As we have seen, few major new
companies were founded during this period.

But most people enjoyed more security and stability, and a larger share
of the nation's income, than they ever had before or ever would again. The
average real wages of hourly workers continued to rise until the early 1970s.
Social tranquillity was preserved and protected. Something approximating
the common good was achieved. The trend toward equality would animate
the civil rights movement, culminating in the Voting Rights and Civil
Rights acts. The growing middle class would give voice to broad concerns
such as health insurance in retirement (resulting in Medicare) and clean air
and water (the Environmental Protection Act). It was not unusual for
noted chief executives, acting as 'corporate statesmen', to push for policies
that would be in the nation's interest even though not necessarily to their
own company's benefit. There was great pride in American democracy and
government. In a 1964 survey, three-quarters of the American public said
they trusted government to do the right thing most of the time,[51] a
percentage that in retrospect seems staggeringly high.

Europe and Japan followed somewhat different paths toward the same ends of high-volume, stable mass production and an increasingly equal distribution of its benefits. European governments took a more explicit role in industrial planning than did the United States; German 'co-determination' featured equal representation by employees and shareholders on the boards of iron and steel companies, and lesser representation on other boards. In Japan, huge industrial combines worked in close cooperation with government ministries to devise industrial policy. Because of its extraordinary size and political dominance, the American system led the way.

Much was still undone, but it seemed that America was moving past ideology and class division on its way toward solving its most pressing problems. In his 1962 commencement address at Yale University, John F. Kennedy sounded the prevailing theme. 'What is at stake,' he declared, 'is not some grand warfare of rival ideologies ... but the practical management of a modern economy. What we need is not labels and clichés but more basic discussion of the sophisticated and technical questions involved in keeping a great economic machinery moving ahead ... [T]echnical answers, not political answers, must be provided.'[52]

THEN SOMETHING HAPPENED that changed everything: America and the world got on the road to supercapitalism.

CHAPTER TWO

THE ROAD TO SUPERCAPITALISM

SINCE THE LATE 1970s, a fundamental change has occurred in democratic capitalism in America, and that change has rippled outward to the rest of the world. Capitalism has triumphed, and not simply as an ideology. The structure of the American – and much of the world's – economy has shifted toward far more competitive markets. Power has shifted to consumers and investors.

Meanwhile, the *democratic* aspects of capitalism have declined. The institutions that undertook formal and informal negotiations to spread the wealth, stabilize jobs and communities, and establish equitable rules of the game – giant oligopolies, large labor unions, regulatory agencies, and legislatures responsive to local Main Streets and communities – have been eclipsed. Corporations now have little choice but to relentlessly pursue profits. Corporate statesmen have vanished. In this way, the triumph of capitalism and the decline of democracy have been connected. Democratic capitalism has been replaced by supercapitalism.

How did it happen?

1

FEW QUESTIONS have generated more belligerently incorrect answers than this one. Some people insist that the catalyst was the runaway inflation of the late 1970s, fed by the Arab oil embargo, culminating with the decision by Paul Volcker, head of the Federal Reserve Board, and his colleagues, to break the back of inflation by raising short-term interest rates so high the economy was brought to a crawl. Others, who have made supply-side economics into a theology, are just as certain everything positive originated with President Ronald Reagan's tax cuts starting in the summer of 1981, which fed the animal spirits of capitalism. Others are sure the impetus was the wave of deregulation that began in the early 1970s. Others say globalization was responsible for the changes. Others find the root cause in a paroxysm of selfish greed that supposedly engulfed the executive suites of American business and finance in the 1980s. Others point to the writings of economic theorists who revivified Adam Smith. Others say political corruption, beginning with Watergate, should be blamed. Others point to a decline in civic life.

This is mostly nonsense. The shake-up began earlier than most of these theories suggest (the large productivity gains of the 1950s and 1960s slowed sharply in the early 1970s, for example, signaling something dramatic was happening), and escalated well into the present day – through the ups and downs of the business cycle, during Republican and Democratic administrations, in good times and bad, regardless of how brilliant or uncommonly stupid, rapaciously greedy or personally decent, the various leaders of business or government have been in the meantime. Surely deregulation and globalization have played a part, but this only begs the question of why both took hold so powerfully in the 1970s and not before. Moreover, none of these theories looks at the system as a whole – in which politics and economics are intertwined – and explains the shift of democratic capitalism in its entirety. Finally, most of these accounts are so American-centric they ignore the telling fact that a similar transition has occurred in Europe and Japan, and is affecting most other places on earth that profess to be capitalist democracies.

The real explanation involves the way technologies have empowered consumers and investors to get better and better deals – and how these deals, in turn, have sucked relative equality and stability, as well as other social values, out of the system. Let me explain.

Starting in the mid-1970s, the large oligopolies that anchored the American system began to teeter. Their sales, profits, and employment became far more volatile. For several decades before then, a firm that ranked in the top fifth of its industry was almost guaranteed to remain there. It had only a one-in-ten chance of losing that position within five years. But by 1998, the odds of losing top billing within five years had increased to one in four.[1] Large companies remained large – indeed, many became much larger. But their competitive position became far more precarious. Between 1970 and 1990, the rate at which companies disappeared from the Fortune 500 quadrupled.[2] And odd things started to happen. Very large companies increasingly became far more vulnerable. In 1993, for example, Microsoft's market capitalization surpassed IBM's, even though Microsoft's $3 billion in revenue that year was a tiny fraction of Big Blue's.

What happened is that consumers and investors gained more choice. The Big Three automakers that had quietly coordinated their prices, wages, and output during the 1950s and 1960s morphed into six North American car manufacturers, including three headquartered in Japan but with large assembly operations in America, and each was competing fiercely with all others. Three big television networks that in the 1950s and 1960s had turned the broadcast airwaves into a 'vast wasteland' (in the memorable words of FCC commissioner Newton Minow) of predictably dull soap operas and situation comedies eventually evolved into hundreds of channels specializing in everything from the weather to animals, with plenty of soaps and comedies in between, all furiously vying for viewers. A handful of big airlines that had owned major routes with established fares grew to dozens of carriers with routes and fares in constant flux, creating a frantic free-for-all. A motion picture industry ruled by a few big Hollywood studios became a Wild West shootout of giant media companies, independent production companies, cable companies, and Internet content providers. Ma Bell, the former AT&T monopoly, along with her Baby Bell progeny, came to compete with cell phones, cable, and voice-over-Internet services that threatened to charge nothing at all for making a call. Big Pharma, which had once carved up the drug market, was now squaring off against biotech firms with cutting-edge medicines. Chain stores were facing big-box retailers. Big boxes were facing online retailers.[3]

Entry barriers collapsed at an accelerating pace. Beginning in the 1990s, the digital revolution was even obliterating the borders between industries. When it came to services that could be offered online – news, e-mail, instant messaging, maps, search engines, movies, television, music, or online sales of almost anything – dozens of large companies from a range of industries were touting deals. What had been well-defined industries were turning into amorphous 'spaces' into which almost any seller could wander. What industry category defined the fusion of communication and content provided by Google, MySpace, MSNBC, AOL, YouTube, Yahoo, Microsoft, Disney, and Comcast? AOL thought it had a steady user base until Google invaded. Disney assumed it had cornered the market on animated films until Pixar began releasing its digital wonders. Newspapers thought they could milk their classified ads until Craigslist stole them. The blurring effect spread to finance and retail (Wal-Mart wanted to start a bank, credit card companies were moving into online sales), high-tech and consulting (IBM was selling management solutions), financial advice and entertainment (the new province of books, television shows, and celebrities). And as distribution channels moved well beyond Main Street and Wal-Mart into cyberdomains of virtually infinite shelf space (Netflix, iTunes, and Amazon, for example) where the cost of offering a new niche product approached zero, choices exploded even further.[4]

Size was no longer an entry barrier. By 2006, the median Fortune 500 company was three times larger than it was in 1980, in real terms. But that hardly mattered. Any company that raised its prices or reduced its quality risked invasion by a rival that would offer the same thing more cheaply or better. Financial pundits assumed eBay was impregnable because it had created an entire auction market of its own. But when eBay began raising commissions on trades, it discovered just how vulnerable it was. Customers who had been selling on eBay began setting up their own Web-based stores, using keywords they bought from Google to drive traffic to their sites. 'I think the rate of decline of the popularity of eBay's auction model has accelerated,' warned Safa Rashtchy, an analyst with Piper Jaffray & Company.[5] Like most analysts, Rashtchy saw only the numbers, not the underlying structure. There was nothing wrong with eBay's auction model, and it wasn't becoming unpopular. The error eBay made was to assume its customers had nowhere else to go, so they'd have to accept eBay's price increase. To the extent eBay had a problem, it was the company's hubris in thinking it had the power to set its own price – a power large oligopolistic firms forty years before had routinely exercised, but is now gone.

That old power, remember, had been based on vast economies of scale. Those firms could spread the fixed costs of expensive machinery and factories over many thousands or sometimes millions of almost identical items whose parts were spewed out of mass production machinery and mass-assembled in the factories. This dramatically cut the cost of each item. It meant the two or three dominant firms could confidently set prices, as well as determine output, style, and even quality, without fear of competition from new entrants.

Today, low costs can be matched by many potential rivals who don't produce in large scale. They use software to do their billing, procurement, and inventory controls; rely on the Internet for customer service; and depend on Internet auctions to subcontract production to the lowest-cost and most reliable bidders. Production is often cheap; high-quality movies and musical recordings, for example, can be made with equipment and software costing only a few thousand dollars rather than hundreds of thousands, as was the case decades ago. If scale economies are needed because equipment is just too expensive or cumbersome to rent, the budding entrepreneur can contract with suppliers anywhere around the world who are already making lots of the same stuff (possibly under contract to several competitors at the same time). If entrepreneurs actually have to make something, they can rent whatever space and computerized machine tools they need and hook them up to smart software from a wide choice of vendors. Services are even easier to replicate, as the eBay example makes clear. Moreover, lots of potential rivals have access to capital markets on almost equal terms, especially if they've already proven themselves good credit risks or worthy of private equity. Hence, all those old high fixed costs that had to be spread over many units can now be converted, at relatively low risk, into variable costs that rise or fall in direct proportion to the amount produced. The more readily the product or service can be reduced to digits, the tinier the added cost of producing another one.

As a result, large-scale production is no longer much of an entry barrier. The barrier started to erode in the 1970s, in several ways we'll examine.

The evidence was a steady decline in the pricing power of large companies at the center of the economy. The entire rationale for oligopolies and the planning system they constituted steadily disappeared. This disjuncture contributed to the productivity slowdown that began in the 1970s.[6]

LARGE SIZE can still be useful to a firm – but not because of production scale, and not to keep competition at bay so prices can be raised. It's useful if it enables a firm to aggregate the power of many separate buyers and thereby gain bargaining leverage over suppliers. The most notorious example is Wal-Mart, founded in 1962, along with Kmart and Target. Wal-Mart outgrew its rivals – indeed, it outgrew every other company in America – because Sam Walton focused relentlessly on one basic principle: getting low retail prices. The larger Wal-Mart grew, the more bargaining leverage it would have over the suppliers of products it carried in its stores. By passing such bargains on to its customers and keeping its own costs to a minimum, Wal-Mart could sell all sorts of things remarkably cheaply. This brought in more customers, which enabled Wal-Mart to grow even larger and get even better deals from suppliers.*

But, importantly, size has not given Wal-Mart the power to raise its retail prices. If Wal-Mart tried to do so, it would fall into the same trap eBay fell into. Customers would go elsewhere – to Target or another big-box retailer that offered them better deals. Instead, Wal-Mart's size has enabled it to get better deals from its suppliers, which it then passes on to its consumers. In effect, Wal-Mart aggregates the purchasing power of individual consumers, just as if consumers had formed a union to negotiate great deals on their collective behalf. As we'll see, big pension funds and mutual funds are doing something similar for investors – aggregating

---

* The Robinson-Patman Act of 1936, whose purpose was to protect small local retailers from large chain stores, posed no bar to Wal-Mart or any other big-box retailer. That's because by the time Wal-Mart grew very large, the act had been quietly whittled back by the federal courts, which, in a series of cases, came to see the act's purpose not as protecting competition but as protecting consumers from excessive market power that might drive up prices. According to this view, since most big chain stores offered lower prices than small independent retailers, they did not violate the act. See, for example, *United States v. U.S. Gypsum Company*, 438 U.S. 442 (1978), *Great Atlantic & Pacific Tea Company v. FTC*, 440 U.S. 69 (1979), *Falls City Industries v. Vanco Beverage* (1983). Here, another small but not insignificant step on the road to supercapitalism.

the purchasing power of individuals to get better returns for an entire group.

All across the American economy, the power of large corporations to set prices has dramatically declined. One by-product has been much tamer inflation. Alan Greenspan as chairman of the Federal Reserve Board in the 1990s got one thing exactly right. He understood that the economy could run at a faster clip and at a lower level of unemployment without igniting inflation than had previously been the case because companies no longer had as much power to raise prices. That is still the case.

The story of what transpired has no heroes or villains, and the plot runs in a fairly straight line. It starts in the 1970s with new technologies, most of them originating in the Pentagon, as I mentioned earlier. It then moves to supply chains that begin extending themselves in all directions, including across national borders, and to production systems that utilize the new software to drive down unit costs. Both reduce the need for economies of scale. It moves onward to entrepreneurs who push to deregulate markets because they can do things better, faster, or cheaper than firms that have been protected behind regulatory barriers. Technology, globalization, and deregulation – all of these intensify competition among companies to get or keep consumers, and to attract investors. The competition, in turn, pushes companies to cut costs. Since payrolls are the single largest cost, companies are under pressure to cut jobs and wages. The denouement is the demise of giant oligopolies, of labor unions, and of many communities; the end of the corporate statesman; and the unraveling of the kind of bargaining that characterized the American system of democratic capitalism. Consumers and investors gain power; citizens lose it.

2

MANY OF the inventions that shattered the stable oligopolistic system of the 1950s and 1960s emerged from the Department of Defense (and its closely allied institution, the National Aeronautics and Space Administration). Here, during the Cold War, was the innovative center of

American capitalism. At a time when the great oligopolies of America's private sector had no interest in devising any fundamentally new idea, competition with the Soviet Union inspired the Pentagon and NASA to great feats of technological boldness. These would eventually find their way into commerce.

It was not only Sputnik and the race to land on the moon that inaugurated the transformation, but the more prosaic, no less complicated challenges of designing a precision missile that could be launched from a submarine and reach targets ten thousand miles away, a bomber that could evade detection by radar, goggles that would allow their wearer to see almost perfectly at night, or a massive tank that could maneuver over almost any terrain. All such devices, and many more, were dreamed up by Pentagon planners or NASA futurists, and realized in the laboratories and development centers of America's giant defense contractors. The creative energies of tens of thousands of engineers were thereby focused on goals far more ambitious, and significant, than the design of a new toaster oven.

One such goal was to provide weapons with their own memories. Who had ever heard of such a thing? The engineers began with vacuum tubes and then invented semiconductors, which became tiny integrated circuits etched on silicon wafers, which in turn became the building blocks of computers. Because the Pentagon and NASA needed extraordinary precision and reliability, they were willing to pay almost any amount. They poured money into basic research. They underwrote failed experiments. They gave tens of thousands of engineers invaluable experience. And then, when the devices were ready, the Pentagon and NASA began purchasing them even though the cost of producing each one was still exorbitant. In 1962, a single integrated circuit cost $50. By 1968, after years of research and experimentation, its cost had dropped to $2.33, thereby transforming integrated circuits from exotic gadgets used in advanced weapons systems to potentially handy means of improving the performance of household appliances and automobiles. Not surprisingly, over that small interval of years the market for semiconductors burgeoned from $4 million to $31 million.[7] As the circuitry of semiconductors became smaller and more powerful, computers were reimagined. The typical mainframe computer in

1968 occupied a whole building. Only government, universities, and giant utilities could afford them. Twenty years later, computers were personal.

The Internet did not come out of Al Gore's head (he never quite said it did, in all fairness). It originated in the Pentagon's need for instantaneous real-time communication of complicated information. As the Web began to be spun, starting as a spider does with just a few threads, the Defense Department's Advanced Research Projects Agency dubbed it ARPANET. No one saw the vast web it would someday become. None foresaw its revolutionary impact on commercial life. Much the same could be said of new software programs developed for missile guidance and radar, with the hundreds of millions of dollars spent to develop fiber-optic cables and lasers, and the exceedingly strong but lightweight new alloys and composites for supersonic jets. Who would have imagined most would eventually find their way into industrial machines and consumer products? The Pentagon and NASA were busy fighting the Cold War, not designing a new economy.

The giant oligopolies of the private sector were equally ignorant of the commercial potential. Even the aircraft industry, whose military and commercial wings seemed so closely connected – planes are planes, are they not? – kept the two strictly separate, managed by entirely different bureaucracies, staffed by different managers and engineers. It was almost as if their top executives understood intuitively that the Pentagon and NASA were out to shake the very foundations of technology and production and to destabilize everything along the way in their fervid pursuit of ever more powerful and novel ways to wreak havoc on Soviet communism. Such undertakings were lucrative for the industrial giants, to be sure; Boeing and McDonnell Douglas welcomed military contracts with unbridled enthusiasm.

Despite the separation of interests, the discoveries of engineers working on military contracts gradually seeped over to commercial enterprise. Knowledge cannot easily be compartmentalized. Engineers talk. Enthusiasm can be infectious. McDonnell Douglas's popular DC-8 used many of the systems developed for Douglas's A-3D and A-4D military aircraft. The design of the commercially successful Boeing 707 can be traced directly to

Boeing's B-47 and B-52 bombers. Its 747 jumbo jet is based on the engineering work it did in its unsuccessful bid for the military's C-5 cargo plane. By the late 1970s, the Defense Department was underwriting 70 percent of the research and development funds of the nation's aircraft industry, a fact the Europeans repeatedly used – and continue to trot out to this day – in order to justify European taxpayer support for their own Airbus.

Look back on many other high technologies that took flight in the last decades of the twentieth century and you will see a similar pattern. In the late 1970s the United States government provided half the R&D funding of the nation's telecommunications industry – including fiber-optics, satellites, and automated switching equipment. Concerned that the nation's giant commercial oligopolies were using outdated production technologies that would retard military production, the Air Force and NASA even undertook a $75 million program to develop an automated 'factory of the future' built around integrated computer-aided manufacturing technology.[8]

All this research, all this engineering talent, all these newfangled inventions, would eventually shatter the stable oligopolistic system. The effect was neither immediate nor direct. It was more like a pebble hitting a car windshield at great speed, whose tiny divot causes a small crack to appear that eventually spreads until the glass is destroyed and must be wholly replaced. The commercial arms of the great oligopolies slowly found applications for the inventions. University research laboratories extended the discoveries. Entrepreneurs – engineers, financiers, errant professors, university dropouts – developed them further. Small businesses were founded. Niche markets were uncovered. Within a few years, the entire economy began to shift. Within two or three decades, a new economy was replacing the old.

Three developments bear particular mention. All were the indirect outgrowths of these Cold War innovations. The first is what's come to be known as 'globalization'. The second was the advent of new production processes. The third was deregulation. All hastened the demise of economies of scale and the mid-century form of democratic capitalism.

3

In the mythic and gratifying simplistic version of globalization, around the 1970s American corporations began to lose their international competitiveness. Exporters from other nations began invading America with products made by people content to work for a small fraction of prevailing American industrial wages, thus leading inexorably to the demise of well-paid blue-collar jobs in America. The story is largely incorrect. First, it fails to explain why the job losses began in the 1970s and accelerated thereafter. Second, American firms did not, in fact, lose their 'competitiveness'.

The timing was not accidental. Recall America's focused efforts to revive the economies of war-torn Europe and Japan. It took two decades before that mission was accomplished. But the critical ingredient igniting globalization was a raft of new transportation and communications technologies, mostly associated with fighting the Cold War – cargo ships and cargo planes, overseas cables, steel containers, and eventually satellites bouncing electric signals from one continent to another – that drastically reduced the cost of moving things from one point on the world's surface to another.

Containers – twenty- to forty-foot-long steel boxes, each capable of holding more than twenty-eight tons – could be shipped easily by train or truck and then lifted onto oceangoing vessels or planes and then placed back on railroad cars or truck beds to be taken to their final destinations, eliminating laborious loading and unloading, and possible theft or damage. Containers had been available since the mid-1950s but not widely used until the Vietnam War, when the U.S. military needed a huge supply system to meet its voracious needs in the jungles of Southeast Asia. Traditional shipping crates were too small and unreliable, so the Navy created a container port in Cam Ranh Bay, and American ports were upgraded to support container cargoes (with deep harbors, specially designed cranes, and giant loading decks).

One inadvertent result was to boost Japanese exports to the United States. Rather than return to America with empty containers, shippers discovered they could make more money by stopping in Japan on their way home and picking up tons of Japanese-made watches, televisions, and kitchen appliances for sale in the United States. In 1967, no commercial container service linked Japan and America. A year later, seven companies had entered the business.[9] From then on, container trade soared. By 2005, more than 3,500 cargo ships plied the seas, loaded with 15 million containers. Worldwide, between 1970 and 2000, the market for containers grew three times faster than the world economy.[10] As a result, the costs of transporting things from one spot on the globe to another plummeted.

Transportation costs also dropped as products became smaller and lighter. Tiny semiconductor chips took over more and more of the functions inside televisions, appliances, and other common consumer products. New lightweight plastics replaced steel and aluminum. Between 1970 and 1988, for every real dollar of imports, the number of pounds shipped to the United States by vessel and air declined by more than 4 percent a year.[11] The result was a surge of manufactured items into the United States from abroad. Between 1970 and 1980, the value of manufactured imports relative to domestic production skyrocketed from less than 14 percent to 28 percent. By 1986, for every $100 spent on goods produced in the United States, Americans were buying $45 worth of imports manufactured abroad.[12]

The surge generated a public outcry about American industry's so-called loss of competitiveness. Congress commissioned dozens of reports. Think tanks issued hundreds of white papers. Business associations organized task forces. Governors appointed advisory committees and blue-ribbon panels. The media went on a rampage. 'U.S. industry's loss of competitiveness over the past decade has been nothing short of an economic disaster,' wrote the editors of *BusinessWeek* in June 1980.[13] Universities assessed the extent of the damage. MIT's Commission on Industrial Productivity noted gravely in its 1989 report that '[c]ertain American industries that once dominated world commerce ... have lost much of their market share both at home and abroad; in a few industries ... the American presence in the market has all but disappeared.'[14]

Actually, American firms were doing fine. They had just become more global. They used the new transportation and communication technologies to set up factories abroad or to contract with foreign suppliers for the components they needed. To state it another way, they used containers and advances in telecommunications (including, eventually, the Internet) to create global supply chains. The old production system of the Not Quite Golden Age could now be fragmented and parceled out around the world to wherever pieces could be done best and most cheaply. Eventually, these supply chains would become so sophisticated that design engineers in one country could come up with three-dimensional prototypes of new products while manufacturing engineers in another country planned assembly lines and equipment needed to make and install them in a third country.

This was the real process of globalization, which the trade numbers by themselves hid from view. From 1969 to 1983, the total value of American imports from *American*-owned factories abroad rose from $1.8 billion to almost $22 billion, adjusted for inflation.[15] These were the same years American companies were supposedly suffering a 'loss of competitiveness'.

GLOBAL SUPPLY CHAINS continued to lengthen and deepen. By the 1990s, American companies with operations abroad accounted for about 45 percent of all American imports. By 2006, the portion was up to nearly 48 percent, according to Commerce Department data. Add in components they purchased from foreign-owned companies before assembling them in the United States and products they bought abroad that they then marketed in America under their own brands, and the percentage is much larger. Whirlpool's global supply chain included microwave ovens engineered in Sweden and fabricated in China. General Electric made small jet engines for the commuter planes that Bombardier produced in Canada; almost a quarter of the value of the engines came from components made in Japan. Dell linked its customers directly to its foreign suppliers; when a customer clicked on its Web site to purchase a laptop, the order appeared on a computer terminal in a factory in China managed by Quanta, a Taiwanese firm, where it was assembled and promptly shipped to the American customer who ordered it. The Eaton Corporation produced truck transmissions in Brazil, of which some were shipped to Ohio to be used in Navistar trucks. An increasing percentage of the Big Three's cars also came from abroad. Even if assembled in North America, a steadily larger portion of their innards came from elsewhere.[16]

More and more of what American companies sold abroad, they made in their factories there. Data on American exports therefore also dramatically understated the 'competitiveness' of American companies. At the same time, foreign supply chains found their way into America. More and more of what foreign companies sold in the United States was made in their factories here. Toyota, Honda, Nissan, and BMW built sprawling automobile plants in Kentucky, Tennessee, and Indiana. By 2006, they employed over 20 percent of American autoworkers.

Who was 'us'? Who was 'them'? Rather than American companies 'losing their competitiveness' starting in the 1970s, it is more accurate to say America started losing solely American companies. No longer was there an automatic connection between how well American-owned companies performed and how well Americans did. This marked a profound change. The old connection had been a basic premise of democratic capitalism during its Not Quite Golden Age. Recall 'Engine Charlie' Wilson's dictum about General Motors and the nation. The nation's large oligopolies had been embedded in a system of tight linkages to labor and government, so that as the economy became more productive, wages and benefits rose across the board. Now that old system was being transformed into something quite different. Those linkages were coming apart, and being newly forged outside America as well as in it.[17]

The media, political leaders, and even many CEOs continued to speak about the American economy as if it was a function of large firms headquartered in the United States – and as if the trade numbers signified something about the success or failure of both. 'Globalization' was understood as a competition between foreign companies and American companies. But it was nothing of the sort. The revolution that began around the start of the 1970s was technological, and its practical effect was to break down America's former oligopolistic production system into worldwide supply chains in which components or services were added depending on wherever they could be done best and most cheaply. These global supply chains terminated in places like Wal-Mart, which aggregated the bargaining power of American consumers to get the best possible deals from around the globe regardless of whose brand name appeared on the particular appliance, pillowcase, or whatever else was being sought.

4

HIGH-VOLUME PRODUCTION might have eroded anyway, even without the global supply chains. By the 1970s, gadgets dreamed up to improve military production were finding their ways into computerized machine tools, robots, and computer-aided design and manufacturing – all of which allowed things to be made at low unit cost even though not in great volume. Engineers sitting behind computer screens could alter designs in seconds, and instruct machines to mold or assemble however many units were needed. By the late 1980s, software even allowed purchasers to help participate in the design.[18] New technologies had similar effects on services. Banking, insurance, and telecom could be customized to the needs of particular users. By the 1990s, the Internet also vastly increased the number of ways services could be distributed, including advertising and marketing directed to specific groups of people who shared special tastes or interests. Consumers had access to search engines and online reviews that matched them even more precisely with sellers who would give them exactly what they needed at the best price. Any seller could likewise use software to create a virtual company consisting of little more than a chain of supply contracts with an auction held at each link in the chain designed to get the best deal every step of the way.

Oligopolies were no longer necessary; modest-sized businesses armed with the new technologies could match their economies of scale. Not surprisingly, every industry that had relied on stable high-volume production shifted toward more specialization and niche production. Standardized steel gave way to specialty steels (hot-dipped galvanized or electro-galvanized) for specific uses in automobiles, trucks, and appliances and to minimills that used electric-arc furnaces and scrap metal to serve the needs of particular customers. Other standard materials were replaced by polymers that could be molded into intricate parts (like those found in cell phones or computers) and withstand varying degrees of stress and heat. Uniform woolen or cotton fabrics were replaced by a huge variety of new synthetics that could be specially coated and finished to order. Standard telephone services fragmented into customized long-distance voice, video, and information processing, and private company networks linking employees in different locations.

Mass-marketers that assumed they had locked up their customers confronted a wide array of specialized competitors who lured customers away. Even Coca-Cola – whose secret formula, a giant system of syrup production and distribution to bottlers, and mega advertising budgets had made it almost impregnable (despite the Pepsi challenge) – was by the early twenty-first century losing out to a seemingly endless variety of specialized concoctions like bottled waters, sports drinks, carbonated juices, flavored iced teas, and vitamin-enriched energy drinks. Cheap broadband and digital storage had created almost limitless inventories and distribution channels – digital jukeboxes, Web-based movies, digital photo archives, art libraries – catering to connoisseurs of every taste.[19]

To summarize: Starting in the 1970s and accelerating over subsequent decades, countless new technologies replaced previously stable production systems with multiple sellers that could turn on a dime. The result was much the same as with global supply chains: Old stable oligopolies were undermined and competition for consumers intensified. By the first decade of the new century, according to a study by management consultants Bain & Company, the average American company was losing more than half its customers every four years, which meant it had to be continuously seeking new ones while doing everything possible to hold on to those who remained.[20]

5

THE PUSH for economic deregulation – the mirror image of the shift toward regulation that occurred between World War I and World War II, and which had been inspired by Herbert Croly and the Progressives of that era – is sometimes attributed to the free-market enthusiasms of Ronald Reagan. But by the time Reagan assumed the presidency in 1981, the move to deregulate had already been under way for a decade. It had started because even in the 15 percent of the economy where prices and the terms of entry were set by independent regulatory commissions, emerging technologies created new possibilities to make profits. Businesses that saw those possibilities wanted in. They pressured the commissions, lobbied Congress and state legislatures, hired professors to do studies showing the benefits of deregulation to consumers. They initiated lawsuits, arguing that regulated companies were stifling innovation and otherwise acting contrary to the public interest. As the pressure mounted, it was only a matter of time before the regulatory dams broke.

In telecommunications, for example, as early as 1968 companies producing new equipment saw a potentially lucrative market in selling that equipment directly to consumers. But the vast Ma Bell monopoly, officially named AT&T, wouldn't allow it. Sitting comfortably behind its protective shield of regulations, the company argued that non-AT&T telephones and components could not be connected with the AT&T system without jeopardizing the reliability of that system. The upstarts sued. The Supreme Court's *Carterfone* decision that year sided with the insurgents – the first crack in Ma Bell's windshield.

Then the cracks spread. New ways of transmitting information over long distances by satellite, cable, and fiber-optic cable created more opportunity. When MCI came up with a relatively inexpensive microwave repeater network that would cut the cost of long-distance phone calls, it wanted in, too. AT&T refused. After the Federal Communications Commission gave MCI the go-ahead to hook its long-distance network into local phone systems, AT&T dragged the FCC through the federal courts, until the company lost the battle. In 1974, the Justice Department filed an antitrust suit against AT&T, arguing that it constituted an illegal monopoly. Eight years and millions of dollars of legal fees later, AT&T settled the case and agreed to divest its Baby Bell regional phone companies. It probably settled because by then AT&T saw potential profits to be made in other areas of telecommunications – including data processing and computer interconnections, which had been out-of-bounds when it was a regulated monopoly.

Airline deregulation followed a similar pattern. Advances in telecommunications and aircraft design (high-strength materials, better aerodynamics, improved fuel economy) created new possibilities for profits outside the stable old regulatory system. In the early 1970s, upstart airlines that were not subject to federal regulation – Pacific Southwest flying routes in California, Southwest Airlines flying in Texas – found they could build profits with lower fares, smaller planes, and no-frills service. Charter carriers, also unregulated, were discovering the same thing. All wanted to expand. They pressured the Civil Aeronautics Board to deregulate fares and routes. Meanwhile, ailing Pan Am and TWA wanted more leeway to raise fares. United wanted the freedom to add more routes.[21] Academic studies seemed to confirm the benefits of airline deregulation. Few players wanted to keep the status quo. So in 1978, Congress deregulated the airlines, and began closing down the Civil Aeronautics Board.

Meanwhile, shippers that had been part of the container revolution also wanted more leeway to choose their routes, set rates, and consolidate their operations, anticipating large profits if they could overcome regulatory barriers. UPS and FedEx pushed in the same direction. In 1980, Congress deregulated trucking and railroads, and began shutting down the Interstate Commerce Commission.

Big banks and financial institutions took the lead in pushing for financial deregulation. By the 1970s, they had new electronic payment and computerized retrieval systems for both taking deposits and lending them out. But they couldn't get access to markets where local banks were protected from competition, so they pushed to deregulate. Meanwhile, pension funds, mutual funds, and insurance companies, armed with computers and software, saw potential profits in more actively managing people's savings but were likewise blocked by financial regulation. So they joined in the move to deregulate.[22]

One by one, financial regulatory walls came tumbling down. In 1974, after much debate, Congress passed the Employee Retirement Income Security Act (perhaps the single most complicated piece of legislation ever to be enacted, subsequently providing guaranteed livelihoods to thousands of lawyers and administrators). It allowed pension funds and insurance companies to invest their portfolios in the stock market, not just in high-grade corporate and government bonds. The next year, the Securities and Exchange Commission ordered stockbrokers to end their practice of fixing commissions on stock trades, thereby opening the way for brokers like Merrill Lynch to offer its customers mutual funds (dubbed Cash Management Accounts) on which checks could be written.[23] In

1980, the government allowed commercial and savings banks to set their own interest rates on deposits and loans. Banks were given permission to merge and consolidate, and open branches wherever they wanted. In 1982, even savings and loan banks – the mainstays of local home mortgage markets (remember *It's a Wonderful Life?*) – got wide leeway to invest their deposits.

It is fashionable among economists to judge deregulation an unmitigated success – apart from unfortunate isolated incidents like the savings and loan fiasco. (No one should have been surprised that savings and loan bankers used their new freedom to invest in junk bonds and other risky ventures that would yield high returns since their deposits continued to be insured by the government – at a final cost to taxpayers of some $600 billion. Arrangements that confer all upside benefit on private investors and all downside risk on the public are bound to stimulate great feats of entrepreneurial daring.) Overall, deregulation was successful in terms of economic efficiency. Looked at through the wider lens of democratic capitalism, however, the issue is more complicated. The regulatory systems that were dismantled included all sorts of cross-subsidies, reflecting delicate balances among various interests. After deregulation, those cross-subsidies disappeared. Most consumers ended up with better deals than they had before. Yet some consumers ended up worse off, as did many small communities, middle-level managers in large monopolies or oligopolies, and their blue-collar employees.

Before the Bell System was broken up, for example, profitable phone services subsidized unprofitable ones. Customers in the city subsidized customers in the country. Users of long-distance service subsidized those who stuck to local service. Business customers subsidized residential customers. People who rarely used the telephone subsidized more frequent users. Cornell economics professor and onetime regulator Alfred Kahn described the Bell System as 'a welfare state with the power to tax and use the proceeds to do good things'.[24] After the breakup, when competition heated up, all such subsidies ended, as did the 'good things'.

Airline deregulation in 1978 also redistributed the benefits. By 1983, service to hundreds of smaller communities had either been lost or greatly reduced. Braniff and a number of smaller airlines had gone under. Down with them (unless or until they found new jobs paying as well) went their employees and many others in the communities where they had been headquartered. Continental, meanwhile, was operating under bankruptcy protection and had received permission from the court to disavow its labor contracts, a tactic other airlines would replicate over the next quarter century. Eastern and Republic were struggling to survive. United was operating at almost the same capacity as before, but now with 20 percent fewer employees. Across the industry, pilots, flight attendants, and mechanics unions agreed to more flexible work rules. Fourteen new airlines were launched, most of them nonunion, and none burdened by the costs of employee pensions and health care in retirement.

In the first three years after trucking deregulation, some three hundred trucking companies went belly-up. Many of them had been sizable. Their dissolutions also had ripple effects, affecting many people who had been dependent on them. On the other hand, ten thousand new small trucking operators entered the industry. Before deregulation, most rates had been set by the ICC. Now, 90 percent were negotiated between individual shippers and carriers. Before deregulation, most drivers had been members of the International Brotherhood of Teamsters union. In the first years after deregulation, about a third of them lost their jobs. At small trucking companies, Teamster affiliates accepted wage cuts averaging between 10 and 15 percent. The national union signed off on a contract that raised pay and benefits only half as fast as inflation.

Trucking and airline deregulation created new opportunities and new forms of competition. UPS had been a trucking company – for decades its familiar brown trucks cheerfully signaled the arrival of packages to the front doors of America. Once under competitive pressure to make deliveries faster and more efficiently, it bought a fleet of cargo planes and became an airline, too. FedEx, by contrast, had been an airline. Competitive pressures to do more door-to-door deliveries moved FedEx to buy a fleet of trucks and it became a trucking company as well. Head-to-head combat between these two systems (and others, like DHL Worldwide Express, eager to grab a larger share of this lucrative market) generated increasing improvements, such as UPS's decision to do overnight deliveries. They even forced innovations on the hidebound U.S. Postal Service.

The consequences of financial deregulation had a huge impact on democratic capitalism as a whole. For our purposes here, though, it is sufficient to note that in the three years after 1980, when banks were allowed to open branches wherever they wished, approximately 22,000 automatic teller machines were installed in banks, airports, and storefronts – the terminals of a vast and fast-growing network of electronic payment and computer retrieval systems. The technology revolutionized the way average people finance their everyday lives. It also cost thousands of bank tellers and clerks their jobs.

The computers and software behind all of this were to have far larger consequence. In 1983, banking consultant Edward E. Furash predicted the nation was on the verge of a financial revolution. Deregulation had 'changed the psychology of people, particularly the younger generation', changing the individual from 'being a simple saver to becoming an investor. We are going to have an economy of intense competition for funds from investors'.[25] He was remarkably prescient.

6

BEFORE FINANCIAL DEREGULATION, America's savers had been a docile lot. Most kept their savings in a bank where they earned, by law, 5.25 percent interest. Mutual funds seemed exotic; 401(k)s and money market funds had not yet been invented. Few Americans paid attention to the Dow Jones Industrial Average. Even fewer put their savings into shares of stock. As recently as 1970, only 16 percent of Americans owned stock. Corporations were owned mostly by wealthy individuals who tucked their stock certificates into safe deposit boxes. Big companies did not, as a rule, distribute their oligopolistic profits to individuals as dividends. Companies tended to retain profits and reinvest them in plant and equipment for even larger economies of scale – yielding capital gains for individual shareholders – and distribute much of the rest to employees. This, as we have seen, was part of the social bargain during the Not Quite Golden Age.

But then everything changed. During the 1970s, savers turned into investors, and investors turned active. The percentage of Americans owning stock rose to 20 percent in 1985, and then took off. By 2005, a majority of households owned some stock. (Of course, most of the value was still owned by the very richest.)[26] The average daily volume of trades on the New York Stock Exchange went from 3 million shares in the 1960s to 60 million in the early 1980s, and escalated sharply thereafter.

Americans' interest in the stock market was stimulated by the longest and most energetic bull market in American history, from the early 1980s to 2000 (with one small, terrifying pause in October 1987). What caused that bull market is of large economic and political importance.

There was, as in any bull market, the self-fulfilling process of speculative aspiration. As more Americans bought shares of stock, they bid up their prices, causing investors to want to buy more shares of stock in the expectation that prices would continue to rise. To that extent, the market turned into a bubble, which burst in 2000. Yet by 2006, the Dow Jones Industrial Average had resumed its upward trajectory. So something other than speculation must have been responsible, something related to a shift in the structure of American corporations toward generating high returns for shareholders.

JUST AS Wal-Mart and other big-box retailers aggregated the bargaining power of individual consumers, so did mutual funds and pension funds aggregate the power of individual investors. To lure or keep these collections of shareholders, CEOs had to do everything possible to raise the value of their companies' shares. They had no choice but to focus ever more intently on creating 'shareholder value'. (In 2002, investors discovered that some of that value had been manufactured by clever accountants and chief financial officers deficient in scruple; but most of it was real.) And just as consumers kept the pressure on companies by moving (or threatening to move) with ever greater ease to a competitor with lower prices or better quality, so did investors – aided by fund managers – become more agile in hunting for bargains. In the 1990s, the average investor held on to a share of stock for a little more than two years. By 2002, the average holding period was less than a year. By 2004, it was barely six months, a new record.[27]

If money managers failed to deliver high returns, investors might abandon them, too. Since bonuses for money managers typically exceeded 50 percent of their salaries, they were amply rewarded for keeping investors happy, and attracting more.

Just as Wal-Mart has squeezed its suppliers for better deals, so have the managers of America's largest pension funds and mutual funds squeezed companies for higher profits, which translate into (not always directly, but with sufficient predictability that such squeezes are typically rewarded) higher share prices. Before 1980, Wall Street had been the handmaiden of industry, helping large oligopolies raise capital when necessary. After 1980, industry became the handmaiden of Wall Street.

It has been said by many that the 1980s launched an era of greed in America, as though that particular trait was somehow lacking before. In fact, as we now see, the change occurred not in human nature but in the structure of the capital market. The combination of new technologies and deregulation created abundant ways for Wall Street to make bundles of money helping individuals move their money where it could earn higher and higher returns. Americans eagerly bought in – through Merrill Lynch's Cash Management Accounts, Peter Lynch's popular Fidelity Magellan mutual funds, Charles Schwab's online system for investors to buy and sell stocks on their own, or through thousands of other mutual funds, pension funds, newfangled instruments, junk bonds, tax dodges, and day trading schemes.[28]

The financiers who invested and moved all this money on behalf of individual investors took a generous cut for themselves to make their bundle. As a result, America's financial sector has become one of the most profitable industries in the world. Its total profits rose from about one-fifth as big as the total profits of America's nonfinancial firms during the 1970s and 1980s to about half as big after 2000.[29]

To reiterate my point, it was not greed that stimulated the hostile takeovers, corporate raiders, junk bonds, proxy fights, and leveraged buyouts of the 1980s; or created the hedge funds, private equity firms, 'minority activists', and another round of leveraged buyouts and proxy fights in the 2000s. Nor was it greed that inspired some of America's most aggressive and talented young men and women, starting in the 1980s, to

FIGURE 2.1

U.S. FINANCIAL SECTOR CORPORATE PROFITS RELATIVE TO NONFINANCIAL SECTOR

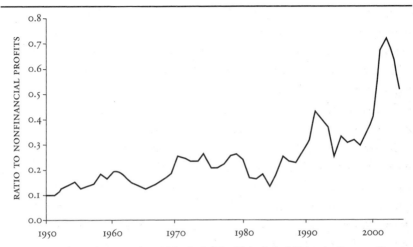

Sources: Andrew Glyn, Capitalism Unleashed *(New York: Oxford University Press, 2006), p. 52; Bureau of Economic Analysis (BEA), National Income and Product Accounts (NIPA), Table I.14, line 27, at http://www.bea.gov/bea/dn/nipaweb/TableView.*

seek admission to prestigious business schools in order to get jobs at investment banks, financial services companies, hedge funds, and private equity funds, or rise to the ranks of chief financial officers at large corporations. Nor was it greed that focused so much intellectual energy onto the arid field of corporate finance. Nor did greed link executive pay to share prices through bounteous stock options and generous bonuses.

In all these cases the motivating factors were opportunities that had not presented themselves before. To confuse greed with opportunity is to confound desire with availability. The libidos of college students are not higher than they were forty years ago; the ease with which they can exercise them, however, is arguably more bounteous.

Chief executives who failed to use every opportunity to maximize shareholder returns created opportunities for financial entrepreneurs who would eagerly exploit them. During the 1970s, there were 13 hostile takeovers of companies valued at $1 billion or more; during the 1980s, the number soared to 150. As the stock market slowed in the first decade of this century, similar strategies emerged. Hedge funds, private equity firms, and shareholder activists initiated another round of takeovers and leveraged buyouts. Sometimes they involved the same players, the sharpness of whose elbows did not dull over time. In 2006, Carl Icahn, who in 1987 forced Texaco and TWA into bankruptcy, launched a proxy fight to gain board seats and control over lackluster Time Warner. 'I never called Dick Parsons [CEO of Time Warner] a moron,' Icahn protested.[30]

You might say aggressors saw possibilities that escaped the notice of comfortable executives accustomed to the tame old world of stable oligopolies. Or you might say they were willing to be more ruthless – not more 'greedy' – by borrowing to the hilt in order to mount their raids, then getting costs down by squeezing suppliers, fighting unions, slashing wages, and subcontracting to lower-cost producers all over the world. Both descriptions would be equally accurate. The result was higher profits, which meant higher share prices.

Several of the warriors and junk bond kings condemned in the 1980s for their ruthlessness are today lionized for improving the performance of American business. It's a fair point, although their strategies did not always work as planned. When the prices of junk bonds plummeted in the late 1980s, many small investors lost their shirts. RJR Nabisco, the largest of the leveraged buyouts of the 1980s, was unceremoniously dismembered in 1999. Moreover, there were (and continue to be) discomfiting conflicts of interest when top executives who join in leveraged buyouts subsequently take initiatives to raise share prices they could have undertaken before the buyout, at substantial gain for themselves rather than their former shareholders. More generally, the obsessive drive among CEOs to meet or exceed Wall Street's estimates of pending quarterly earnings – a direct legacy of what began in the 1980s – has undoubtedly led to excessively short-term thinking in executive suites, as well as a string of abuses and distortions. As Kathryn Ruemmler, the prosecuting attorney in the government's case against Enron's Ken Lay and Jeffrey Skilling, told jurors: 'They can make the numbers say whatever they want to say.'[31]

Yet there is little doubt that investors have benefited greatly. Consumers have benefited, too, as America's giant corporations cut costs and became far more efficient and innovative than before. After all, their continued profitability, to which their stock prices were connected, has depended fundamentally on a growing stable of satisfied customers. Finally, it could be argued – and has been, with relish, by American economists lecturing Europeans, the Japanese, and the Chinese – that the discipline imposed on the large American corporation by the large and transparent capital market of the United States has improved the efficiency and sped the growth of the overall American economy. But even if these benign economic effects are granted, they do not necessarily settle the question of whether the growth and dominance of the financial sector has been a good thing for democratic capitalism.

7

THERE WAS no longer a place for corporate statesmen who viewed their role as balancing the interests of all parties, including their employees, the citizens of communities where they did business, and the nation as a whole. Roberto C. Goizueta, former CEO of Coca-Cola, stated the new logic with particular clarity. 'Businesses are created to meet economic needs.' he said. When they 'try to become all things to all people, they fail… We have one job: to generate a fair return for our owners … We must remain focused on our core duty: creating value over time'.[32] In other words, maximize the price of shares.

Today's CEOs do not have the luxury to do otherwise. If they fail to meet the 'number' – a certain level of earnings per share expected by the managers of the mutual funds, pension funds, hedge funds, and private equity partnerships that preside over their investors' money – they will be replaced. The CEOs of the 1950s and 1960s had no particular need to meet with shareholders or institutional investors. Their jobs were secure. Annual shareholder meetings were perfunctory affairs where CEOs offered well-scripted little presentations, took a few questions, and departed. Today's CEO engages in an ongoing effort – in person, on the phone, in meetings and formal presentations – to reassure major investors, impress Wall Street analysts, and assuage any worries of bankers and credit-rating agencies.

Researchers Margarethe Wiersema of Rice University and Mark Washburn of the University of California at Berkeley looked at what happened to the top executives at Fortune 500 companies between 1996 and 2000, after analysts covering a company downgraded their recommendations about buying its stock. Wiersema and Washburn found that when recommendations dropped by just one notch – from, say, a 'buy' to 'hold' – the odds increased by nearly 50 percent that the CEO would be fired within the following six months. The impact of such downgrades on CEO tenure was even greater than the impact of declining profits or even falling share prices.[33]

Chief executives are turning over at a faster clip, and a record number are being forced out. The consulting firm Booz Allen Hamilton found that the rate of CEO turnover in the world's 2,500 largest corporations increased from 9 percent in 1995 to 15.3 percent in 2005 – and not because CEOs wanted to leave. Turnover increased largely because CEOs failed to perform up to expectations. In all these companies, performance-related firings quadrupled over the ten-year period. In 2005, 'performance-related turnover set a new record in North America, where 35 percent of CEOs who left office were forced out, and both Europe and Japan experienced near-record levels'.[34]

You could see the trend in 1990, as the economy slowed. That year, high-priced heads rolled at AT&T, GM, Xerox, Coca-Cola, Aetna, and other blue-chip American companies. Such decapitations often occurred quickly and bloodlessly, sometimes after a tenure of only a few months. As the stock market struggled to regain its footing during the early to mid-2000s, executive firings resumed apace. Between 2004 and 2006, top bosses were sent packing at AIG, Pfizer, Boeing, Fannie Mae, Hewlett-Packard, Kraft, Disney, Merck, Morgan Stanley, and Bristol-Myers Squibb. The trend in unceremonious sackings was accompanied by a decline in the average number of years a CEO remained in office. By 2006, some 60 percent of the top executives at Fortune 500 companies had held their jobs for six years or less, a record low.

Some CEOs dug in their heels, like Pfizer's Hank McKinnell, a venerable figure who had chaired the Business Roundtable, the Washington-based association of CEOs. But after several years of declining share prices (during which he pocketed $148 million), even he was told his time was up in the summer of 2006, nineteen months ahead of when his tenure was due to end. There was a limit to what major investors would tolerate.[35]

By 2006, a majority of boards met regularly in executive session without the CEO. This was not a function of law but of the increasing power of investors, aggregated through large funds. As investors grew more demanding, fund managers became steadily more active. As funds became more active, boards had to become more independent in order to satisfy them.

By the same token, CEOs who raised share prices received no end of praise. Jack Welch, the legendary former chief executive of GE, named by *Fortune* 'manager of the century', had the good luck to become CEO in 1981, near the start of the long bull market. But he did his bit to cut costs and add to GE investors' good fortunes. At the start of his reign, the company was valued by the stock market at less than $14 billion. When he retired in 2001, it was worth about $400 billion. Its stock price had grown three times faster than the overall stock market.

Before Welch arrived, most GE employees spent their entire careers with the company and knew they'd be looked after when they retired. Welch put an end to that. Between 1981 and 1985 he laid off one in four GE employees – more than 100,000 in all, earning him the now familiar moniker 'Neutron' Jack. Even when times were good – and for most of Welch's years, they were – he encouraged senior managers to replace 10 percent of their subordinates every year in order to keep GE competitive. 'Some think it's cruel or brutal to remove the bottom 10 percent of our people,' he wrote. 'It isn't. It's just the opposite. What I think is brutal and "false kindness" is keeping people around who aren't going to grow and prosper.' He rated his managers A, B, or C players, and routinely culled the Cs.[36]

Welch fought to cut or limit every extra expense at GE, including the cost of retrieving the toxic chemical polychlorinated biphenyls (PCBs) that GE had dumped into the Hudson River. He led a lobbying effort in Congress to weaken environmental rules for cleaning toxic sites and to limit what polluters had to pay in cleanup costs. In 1997, residents of Pittsfield, Massachusetts, learned that the soil around homes near a GE factory there was contaminated with PCBs. They also learned that GE had known of the problem since the 1980s, but had not told them.[37] But, hey, Welch's job was to maximize shareholder value, not be a corporate statesman. That's why he was anointed 'manager of the century'.

Other CEOs tried to outdo even 'Neutron' Jack. As CEO of Scott Paper for two years, 'Chainsaw' Al Dunlap laid off eleven thousand workers and fired 71 percent of headquarters staff. Wall Street was obviously impressed; the company's stock rose 225 percent. Dunlap's next move, to Sunbeam, proved to be less auspicious for investors, although his reputation for being a tough guy sent Sunbeam's stock upward as soon as he arrived there. Andrew Shore, a stock analyst at PaineWebber, upgraded the stock to a 'buy' in October 1997, telling investors that 'Sunbeam possesses an intangible asset, the Dunlap factor'. Dunlap proceeded to lay off half of Sunbeam's six thousand employees. William Kirkpartrick, an operating manager who worked with Dunlap at both Scott and Sunbeam, explained Dunlap's management theory. 'If you didn't hit your numbers, he would tear all over you.'[38] Unfortunately, Sunbeam's board learned in 1998 that Dunlap hit the numbers by manipulating them – a practice that the executives of Enron and WorldCom would later adopt with relish – causing Sunbeam an actual loss that year of $898 million. They sacked Dunlap, who left for Australia to give a series of lectures on business leadership, offering the Aussies trenchant one-liners such as 'If you want a friend, you get a dog. I've got two'.

Between the legal aggressiveness of 'Neutron' Jack and the illegal excesses of 'Chainsaw' Al were more moderate approaches, but all involved slimming down and cutting costs. Carlos Ghosn became nearly legendary as Nissan's chief executive. When he took the reins in 2001, Nissan was $20 billion in debt, and its global market share had declined for twenty-seven consecutive years. Ghosn embarked on a very un-Japanese strategy. He closed plants and laid off thousands of workers. Within a year, Ghosn had increased Nissan's operating margin to a record 10.6 percent.

'GOING PRIVATE' did not shield a chief executive from pressure. Private equity partners who took a company private expected top executives to cut costs and add value with no less alacrity. In fact they expected more, because they intended to resell the company later at a much higher price.

If the deal was highly leveraged, the CEO was under added pressure – to generate enough profit to meet interest payments as well.

Not even traditional family firms were immune. Malden Mills in Lawrence, Massachusetts, had been in Aaron Feuerstein's family for three generations. It was one of New England's last textile manufacturers. After a fire destroyed most of its factory in the winter of 1995, Feuerstein could have taken the insurance money and rebuilt in North Carolina where wages were lower, or subcontracted to China. But he opted instead to spend about $450 million to rebuild in Lawrence and continued to pay salaries of his then four thousand workers while they were idled, at a total additional cost of some $15 million. As he later said, 'The workers are depending upon me. The community is depending upon me. My customers are depending upon me. And my family.' Peter Jennings, then the anchor of ABC News, named Feuerstein 'Person of the Week'. Tom Brokaw called him 'a saint for the 1990s'. President Clinton recognized him in the State of the Union address a few weeks later. Feuerstein seemed a modern example of a corporate stateman who cared deeply about his workers and his community.

But the effort saddled Malden Mills with a $150 million debt. A consortium of banks, along with GE Capital, set a rigid repayment schedule for Feuerstein at high interest rates because they had lots of other places to park their money that were less risky and promised a better return. Feuerstein struggled to meet the payments, but fell behind. Finally, in November 2001, Malden Mills reorganized under Chapter 11 of the bankruptcy law. After it emerged in 2003, its creditors sacked Feuerstein and appointed a new CEO, who proceeded to set up two manufacturing plants in China. Although the new CEO promised to maintain some manufacturing presence in Lawrence, it seemed doubtful that Lawrence would produce more than the 15 percent of Malden Mills's $175 million annual sales that went to the United States military – which is required by law to buy uniforms made in America.[39]

Do not be overly concerned about the plight of modern CEOs, however. Notwithstanding the pressure on them to show results, despite the greater risk that they will lose their jobs, regardless of the continuing danger that rivals will erode their markets, their lives are, for the most part, comfortable. Their private jets are well maintained; their golf club and spa memberships automatically renewed; their pay, as we shall examine in the following chapter on the social consequences of supercapitalism, far beyond that of mere mortals. And should they be fired, their consolation prizes are wondrously generous.

8

In 1955, more than a third of American workers in the private sector belonged to a labor union. By 2006, fewer than 8 percent did. The practical consequence was a sharp decline in the bargaining power of American workers to get higher wages and benefits. From 1945 to 1980, union wage agreements almost always involved wage increases; afterward, union agreements frequently involved giveback concessions on both wages and benefits. Nonunion workers were also affected. Organized labor no longer had enough clout for its wage agreements to raise prevailing wages across an industry.

A view widely held among those in organized labor attributes the decline in membership to a riptide of virulent anti-union activism by American corporations and their CEOs set loose by Ronald Reagan after he fired the nation's striking air traffic controllers (who had no legal right to strike in the first place) on August 5, 1981, and banned them from ever returning to work. According to this view, America's big corporations took Reagan's act as a sign that it was now okay to fight unions – which they began to do with a vengeance.

One problem with this theory is its timing is off. As you can see from Figure 2.2, union membership actually started its rapid descent in the mid-1970s, when Jimmy Carter was president. By the time Reagan fired the air traffic controllers, the slide had already turned into an avalanche.[40] CEOs did indeed become more aggressively anti-union but their anti-union behavior began in the 1970s, not the 1980s. In 1962, 46.1 percent of union elections occurred with the complete consent of employers. In the 1970s, employers began challenging them. By 1977, only 8.6 percent of elections were uncontested by employers.[41] Companies also started replacing striking workers in the 1970s, and even more threatened to do so if

FIGURE 2.2

PRIVATE SECTOR UNION MEMBERSHIP IN THE UNITED STATES, 1929–2005

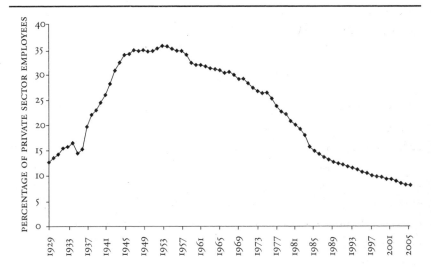

Sources: U.S. Bureau of Labor Statistics; Leo Troy and Neil Sheflin, U.S. Union Sourcebook *(West Orange, N.J.: IRDIS, 1985).*

their workers dared go on strike. They also began firing workers who engaged in union organizing, which workers had a perfect right to do. In the 1950s, the National Labor Relations Board chronicled illegal dismissals in one of every twenty union elections. The rate increased in the 1970s. By the 1990s, there were illegal dismissals in one out of every four union elections.[42]

There's another problem with this view. Union membership declined not only in the United States but also in Europe and Japan. To understand why, review this chapter. The structure of all advanced economies began to shift, as the system of stable mass production started to crack. The shift came first to the United States. Oligopolies had once been able to absorb wage increases or pass them on to consumers in higher prices, but as competition intensified and the old oligopolies came apart, this was no longer possible.

Consumers had far more choice. They didn't have to pay prices that

FIGURE 2.3

TRADE UNION MEMBERSHIP AS PERCENTAGE
OF EMPLOYEES IN OTHER ADVANCED NATIONS

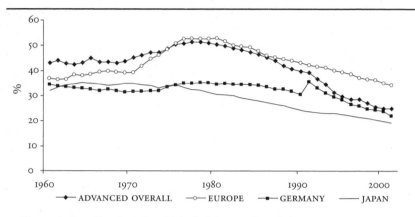

Sources: Andrew Glyn, Capitalism Unleashed *(New York: Oxford University Press, 2006), p. 121; Organization for Economic Cooperation and Development; Dean Baker et al., 'Labor Market Institutions and Unemployment: A Critical Assessment of the Cross-Country Evidence', in David R. Howell, ed.,* Fighting Unemployment: The Limits of Free Market Orthodoxy *(New York: Oxford University Press, 2005).*

reflected generous union contracts. They could scour the world for better deals. Meanwhile, a growing chorus of investors began demanding that CEOs boost share prices. Otherwise they would put their money into more profitable companies whose shares would become more valuable. With all the new mutual funds on the market and the increasing ease of trading, these investors also had more choices.

As CEOs scrambled to meet the demands of consumers and investors, they were under unrelenting pressure to cut costs. And because wages and benefits were their single largest cost – typically accounting for 70 percent of total expenses – top executives began to chop payrolls. This often entailed tough bargaining with unions, and even launching anti-union campaigns. Ronald Reagan probably signaled to companies that these strategies were legitimate, but Reagan wasn't the reason they occurred.

Moreover, while CEOs of big companies did take on their unions, this wasn't the main reason unions began to lose members and decline in influence. From the 1970s onward, the nonunionized sector of the American economy grew faster than the unionized sector because consumers and investors steadily shifted their dollars to where they could get the better deals.[43] In much of the American economy, and, increasingly, in other advanced economies, consumers and investors would no longer abide unionized wages and benefits. Unionized companies that failed to trim payrolls lost market share to unionized companies that did. And both lost consumers and investors to companies that were nonunionized from the start.

After airline deregulation, big carriers faced intense competition from low-cost upstarts who were either nonunion or, even if unionized, did not have the costly pension and retirement health benefits the old carriers had agreed to. In what would become a repeating nightmare for unionized airline workers, Frank Lorenzo, who was CEO of Continental Airlines in 1982, took the cash-strapped carrier into bankruptcy. He ripped up its labor contracts, laid off thousands of workers, and hired replacements for striking pilots and flight attendants. He then paid his new employees half what he had paid his old unionized employees and demanded they work longer hours. Lorenzo was vilified, of course, but he got Continental flying again. In 1993, Northwest Airlines threatened bankruptcy and insisted on wage concessions from flight attendants and mechanics. A decade later, when more than four thousand Northwest mechanics went on strike, the airline outsourced most of their jobs. Some five hundred union members crossed picket lines to keep working. In 2002, United Airlines entered bankruptcy. Its pilots and flight attendants were forced to accept pay cuts ranging from 9.5 percent to 11.8 percent. United emerged from Chapter 11 in 2006. Most Wall Street analysts thought it hadn't yet cut its payrolls enough to remain competitive.

THE SLIDE was most dramatic in the nation's biggest industrial unions. Before the late 1970s, the United Auto Workers' industry-wide contract with the Big Three had been the gold standard – the most generous and the most secure, flush with the highest pay and best benefits of any union contract in the country. A job in an American auto plant was a ticket to middle-class prosperity. The UAW was king of the road, with one and a half million members. But starting in the late 1970s, everything changed.

The Big Three lost their ability to set prices. Many consumers could get better deals from Toyota or Honda or other foreign automakers, even when the foreign cars were made on American soil with American workers. As the Big Three's profits were squeezed, investors became unhappy. To be sure, the Big Three's problem wasn't just high wages and benefits. Years within a stable oligopoly had generated somnolence in executive suites. Management had grown lazy. Too many of the cars they made were clunkers. Yet by the late 1980s they had awakened and were learning from the Japanese; by the early 1990s they had just about closed the quality and reliability gap. Even so, they still couldn't compete. Their costs were still too high. The UAW had focused on keeping as much of the pay and benefits of existing members as possible, especially of older members who were protected by seniority rules from being fired.

In 2006, each of the Big Three's unionized blue-collar workers was earning around $60 an hour in wages and benefits – still very high relative to nonunionized autoworkers in America. Japanese automakers in the United States were paying their nonunionized employees around $40 an hour. The Big Three were also burdened with promises they'd made to their unionized employees years before to pay them generous pensions and health care benefits during retirement. The Japanese automakers in the United States didn't have this cost. So it's not surprising the Big Three continued to shrink and the Japanese Three – Toyota, Honda, and Nissan – continued to grow in America.

By 2006, the Big Three's American workforce was less than half what it had been in the glory days. And further shrinkage was coming. GM announced plans to close a dozen more plants and trim another 30,000 workers; Ford said it would trim 75,000; Chrysler wasn't even part of the Big Three any longer – it had become Daimler Chrysler, with headquarters in Stuttgart, Germany. In 2006, Toyota had fifteen assembly and parts plants in North America, employing 38,000 American autoworkers, and was well on the way to exceeding the number of Americans working for Ford. Only 60 percent of American car buyers were choosing Big Three cars, and young Americans were hardly choosing them at all. Wall Street, meanwhile, was unwilling to invest more in them. It rated GM's and Ford's bonds as junk. The plans to further shrink payrolls still didn't satisfy the

Street. 'How many times in the last twenty years has GM had a meaningful restructuring announcement, but it hasn't been followed up by higher stock prices?' asked David Sowerby, portfolio manager for Loomis Sayles, a money management fund with $70 billion in assets.[44]

Other industries with unionized employees were following the same downward path. Delphi, a huge auto parts company that was spun out of GM, in 2006 paid its unionized workers $27 an hour – $65 including benefits. In China, where Delphi also had a plant, its workers received roughly $3 an hour. Robert 'Steve' Miller, Jr., a 'turnaround specialist' who became Delphi's CEO in 2005, committed himself to cutting two-thirds of Delphi's 34,000 hourly workers in the United States and reducing wages to as little as $10 an hour. The UAW wouldn't hear of it. So Miller put Delphi into bankruptcy and sought to end existing labor contracts. Miller warned that to do otherwise would put all of Delphi's remaining jobs at risk.[45]

It didn't matter that a company was profitable; if investors could get higher profits and higher stock prices elsewhere, the company was still under the gun. Nor did it matter that a product was relatively cheap and of fair quality, if consumers could get better deals elsewhere. In 2006 Caterpillar Tractor was profitable, but it was under pressure from investors to show better earnings. Its union wanted to preserve the good wages and benefits of its current members. To satisfy Wall Street and accommodate the union, Caterpillar decided to split its workforce. Current employees would continue to receive about $42 an hour in wages and benefits. But new hires would get just $22 an hour. 'There is a balance that must be struck,' Caterpillar group president Douglas Oberhelman told the *New York Times,* 'between being competitive and being middle class.'[46]

Workers who inhabited the local service economy – retail, restaurants, custodial, hotel, elder and child care, hospital, transportation – faced a different challenge from their counterparts in big industry. Their jobs weren't in danger of disappearing. They couldn't be outsourced abroad and most wouldn't be automated. In fact, the number of local service jobs in America kept growing. The real problem was these jobs tended to pay very low wages, rarely included any benefits, and provided little chance of advancement. Significantly, most of them were not unionized. Had they been, these workers might have had more bargaining clout with their employers. Unions looking out for these workers – the Service Employees International Union (SEIU), the Teamsters, the Hotel Employees and Restaurant Employees International Union, and the United Food and Commercial Workers – left the AFL-CIO. The split was more about strategy than it was any clash of personalities, although the popular press played up the personal angle. The service unions saw their mission less as preserving good jobs in danger of disappearing and more as boosting the prospects of people trapped in poor ones. Their future depended on how many other local service workers became union members, and how quickly. Organizing was of central importance to them.

But it would be a hard slog because consumers still had lots of choice even at the local level, including everything from online retailers to discount big boxes like Wal-Mart. Wal-Mart is aggressively anti-union, even going so far as to close a Canadian store whose workers had voted a union in. As Wal-Mart moved into groceries and pharmaceuticals, chain groceries and pharmacies clamped down on their own wages. This elicited a predictable reaction: In 2003, some sixty thousand grocery workers in California went on strike against three major supermarket chains. After suffering through a long lockout, they won few gains. In the summer of 2005, more than a thousand Chicago pharmacists went on strike against Walgreens. The strike collapsed when half of the pharmacists crossed picket lines to return to work.

In these ways, the decline of unions has been driven by consumers and investors intent on getting the best possible deals. The result has not been especially good for people in their capacities as employees, however.

9

A SUMMARY is in order. The road to supercapitalism began with technologies that emerged from the Cold War – containers, cargo ships and planes, fiber-optic cables, and satellite communications systems. They allowed the creation of global supply chains. They also spurred the commercial development of computers and software that could produce items at low cost without large scale, and eventually distribute services over the Internet. All this shattered the old system of large-scale production and dramatically increased competition. It allowed big-box retailers to aggregate consumer buying power and push companies even harder for bargains. It also created profitable opportunities for entrepreneurs to knock down regulatory barriers in telecommunications, airlines, trucking, shipping, and financial services – which also increased competition. Together, emerging technologies and financial deregulation opened the way for investors to put their savings into giant mutual funds and pension funds that pressured companies for higher returns. CEOs who delivered were generously rewarded. Those who didn't were sacked. Finally, intensifying competition for consumers and investors put pressure on companies to cut payrolls, hitting unionized workers especially hard.

The central institutions of democratic capitalism in the Not Quite Golden Age – big oligopolistic companies, big labor unions organized by industry, and government representing communities and local interests through regulatory agencies – came undone. So-called corporate statesmen lost whatever capacity they had to weigh the interests of their communities and employees. Power shifted to consumers and investors. Supercapitalism replaced democratic capitalism.

Do we approve of what has occurred? Most of us, if we are candid with ourselves, are of two minds.

CHAPTER THREE

OF TWO MINDS

I N RECENT YEARS, the cheerleaders of American capitalism – denizens of Wall Street, lobbyists on Washington's K Street, the inhabitants of top executive suites and New York penthouses, most Republicans, many economists, editorial writers for the *Wall Street Journal*, free-marketeers around the world – have had difficulty containing their enthusiasm about the economy. America's gross national product has virtually tripled since the 1970s! The Dow Jones Industrial Average has risen from 1,000 to over 13,000 today! Behold the wondrous innovations and inventions, and the plethora of new products and services! The cheerleaders disdain what they consider to be constraints on further capitalist exuberance – taxes and regulations, labor unions, 'Old Europe's' inefficiencies, anything that retards consumer well-being and investor gain.

But other trends have worried labor leaders, community activists, most Democrats, some economists, many sociologists, editorial writers for the *New York Times,* trade protectionists, and left-wing populists. Look at all the workers who are falling behind! The widening inequalities of income and wealth! The instability of jobs! The loss of communities! The destruction of the environment! The trampling of human rights abroad! Conservatives will sometimes join this chorus, especially with regard to the so-called coarsening of American culture and the entertainment industry's seeming obsession with lurid and titillating sex and violence. For these critics, the villains are often greedy CEOs, immoral corporations, and a cabal of wealthy global elites.

The two stories – Oh the wonder of it! Oh the shame of it! – both describe aspects of twenty-first-century supercapitalism. But considered separately, each is seriously misleading. Each leaves out the other, which is actually its flip side. Each disdains or blames imaginary forces in opposition when the qualms are actually inside almost every one of us.

The awkward truth is that most of us are of two minds: As consumers and investors we want the great deals. As citizens we don't like many of the social consequences that flow from them. The system of democratic capitalism in the Not Quite Golden Age struck a very different balance. Then, as consumers and investors we didn't do nearly as well; as citizens we fared better.

What's the right balance? Are our gains as consumers and investors worth the price we're now paying for them? We have no real way to tell. The old institutions of democratic capitalism, and the negotiations that took place within them, are gone. But no new institutions have emerged to replace them. We have no means of balancing. Our desires as consumers and investors usually win out because our values as citizens have virtually no effective means of expression – other than in heated rhetoric directed against the wrong targets. This is the real crisis of democracy in the age of supercapitalism.

1

IT HAS BECOME fashionable in progressive circles to bash Wal-Mart. 'My problem with Wal-Mart is that I don't see any indication that they care about the fate of middle-class people,' shouted Senator Joe Biden from the rooftop of the State Historical Society of Iowa building in Des Moines. It was a little more than two years before the 2008 presidential election, and Biden was among a number of Democratic hopefuls who wanted to burnish his credentials as someone who cared about what was happening to American jobs and wages. 'They talk about paying them $10 an hour ... How can you live a middle-class life on that?'[1]

Wal-Mart has become the poster child for all that's wrong with American capitalism because it replaced General Motors as the avatar of the economy. Recall that in the 1950s and 1960s GM earned more than any company on earth and was America's largest employer. It paid its workers solidly middle-class wages with generous benefits, totaling around $60,000 a year in today's dollars. Today, Wal-Mart, America's largest company by revenue and the nation's largest employer, pays its employees about $17,500 a year on average, or just under $10 an hour, and its fringe benefits are skimpy – no guaranteed pension and few if any health benefits. And Wal-Mart does everything in its power to keep wages and benefits low. Internal memos in 2005 suggested hiring more part-time workers to lower the firm's health care enrollment, and imposing wage caps on longer-term employees so they wouldn't be eligible for raises. Also, as I said earlier, Wal-Mart is aggressively anti-union.

Wal-Mart's CEO in 2007 was H. Lee Scott, Jr. Scott was no 'Engine Charlie' Wilson, who as GM's top executive in the 1950s saw no difference between the fate of the nation and the fate of his company. Scott has a far less grandiose view of Wal-Mart's role. 'Some well-meaning critics believe that Wal-Mart stores today, because of our size, should, in fact, play the role that is believed that General Motors played after World War II. And that is to establish this post-World War middle class that the country is so proud of,' he opined. 'The facts are that retail does not perform that role in this economy.'[2] Scott was right. The real problem – not of his making – is that almost nothing performs that role any longer.

The rhetorical debate over Wal-Mart is not nearly as interesting as the debate we might be having in our own heads if we acknowledged what was at stake. Millions of us shop at Wal-Mart because we like its low prices. Many of us also own Wal-Mart stock through our pension or mutual funds. Isn't Wal-Mart really being excoriated for our sins? After all, it is not as if Wal-Mart's founder, Sam Walton, and his successors created the world's largest retailer by putting a gun to our heads and forcing us to shop there or to invest any of our retirement savings in the firm.

Wal-Mart could afford to give its employees better pay and benefits, but would it remain competitive if it did? In 2005 its profit margin on sales was around 3.5 percent. This came to about $6,000 per employee. So at least in theory, Wal-Mart has some maneuverability. If it boosted wages and benefits of all full-time employees by $3.50 an hour, the extra cost would still total less than 3 percent of Wal-Mart's sales in the United States. It could absorb that cost by raising its prices a bit or settling for somewhat lower profits. But few of us as Wal-Mart consumers would be happy to pay the higher prices. We might go elsewhere in search of better bargains. Certainly, few of us as Wal-Mart investors would be pleased with lower profits. We might move our money to where it could earn a higher return. In fact, by 2006, Wal-Mart's profits were showing signs of wearing thin. In the second quarter of 2006 the company reported the first drop in profits in a decade. Apparently, customers were finding better deals at some of Wal-Mart's competitors and shareholders were finding better investment opportunities elsewhere. Wal-Mart's stock price, which had risen 1,100 percent in the 1990s, dipped in the 2000s.

The issue of Wal-Mart's comparatively low pay and benefits – and our tacit complicity as Wal-Mart consumers or investors – pales in importance beside Wal-Mart's effect on the wages and benefits of tens of millions of other workers across the larger economy. Here our complicity is more significant. Recall that Wal-Mart gets great deals for us as customers by squeezing its suppliers. As the biggest single company in the world, Wal-Mart has huge bargaining power. 'We expect our suppliers to drive the costs out of the supply chain,' a spokesman for Wal-Mart said.[3] Translated: We demand our suppliers squeeze the wages and benefits of the millions of people who work for them in the United States and abroad. If they don't, we'll buy from their competitors who will.

Wal-Mart suppliers could reduce their prices by inventing new products and services that are better than the old, while keeping their payrolls as before. But because payrolls are 70 percent of a typical business's costs, it's almost inevitable that wages and benefits will also be affected. If jobs cost too much here, suppliers will outsource them to China, Southeast Asia, or Mexico; or they'll substitute computers and software for human beings.

How else do you suppose Wal-Mart can sell detergent at a fraction of the price of a box of Tide? Or televisions for $50 and printers for $30? Or a gallon jar of Vlasic dill pickles – twelve pounds, an entire year's supply – for $2.98? Think of Wal-Mart as a giant steamroller moving across the global economy, pushing down the costs of everything in its path – including wages and benefits – as it squeezes the entire production system. It's because of this big squeeze that bargain hunters who throng Wal-Mart save at least $100 billion a year. Some studies put the savings closer to

$200 billion.[4] That comes to more than $600 per family – no small change for the typical Wal-Mart shopper with an average family income of $35,000 in 2005.

Wal-Mart is the biggest steamroller but there are lots of others. Because of our increased power as consumers and investors to choose the best and lowest-cost products from a wide array of alternatives, almost every company has had to become its own steamroller. That's why so many prices are lower in real terms and so many products and services are better than they were several decades ago, and why so many more Americans have access to so much more bounty.

Consumer markets are still far from perfect, of course. Some big companies temporarily preserve monopolies through patents and copyrights or predatory strategies to intimidate competitors. Consumers sometimes find it difficult to compare prices or are manipulated into buying things they don't really want – which is why the advertising industry is such a massive part of our economy and why 'buyer's remorse' is such a common predicament. Yet, these imperfections notwithstanding, over the last several decades the market has become more responsive to what consumers want than ever before.

The proof is in the numbers. (To make the following comparisons meaningful, I've used the value of a dollar in the year 2000.) A color television that cost $2,227 when color TVs were first introduced in the late 1950s cost half that by 1967. By 2000, its cost had dropped to just $175, making it affordable to virtually all American families – including over 90 percent of families with incomes under the poverty line.[5]

Microwave ovens have followed the same trajectory. In 1955, you had to pay $1,300 for one. By 1967, a standard microwave cost $495. By 2002, it was $208,[6] putting microwaves within easy reach of almost all American families, including 73 percent of the poor. The price of a VCR has dropped at roughly the same pace, eventually allowing some 78 percent of poor families to own one. The price of a transistor radio plunged from $228 in 1962 to $15 by 2000; the price of a refrigerator, from $2,932 to $1,000.[7]

The standard personal computer went from $1,300 in 1998 to $770 in 2003. (Dell Computer, like Wal-Mart, rates each of its suppliers weekly in a cutthroat search for better and cheaper parts.) All the while, PCs have grown more powerful. In 1996, you couldn't do much better than a desktop with a one-gigabyte hard drive. (One gigabyte is roughly the amount of words and data in all the books that can fit into a pickup truck.) Ten years later, one gigabyte could be stored in a portable USB flash drive the size of your index finger. Meanwhile, starting in the 1990s, digital cameras, flat-paneled TVs, external hard drives for backing up data, DVD players, iPods, and wireless routers all emerged and then continued to improve. At each level of quality, they also became cheaper.

A generation ago, the typical American family owned one car. By 2006, that family had two. A third of American families own three cars or more. This is not particularly good news for the environment or the cause of energy conservation, but it is welcomed by members of a household who no longer have to wait to borrow the family car. The average automobile cost less in real-dollar terms in 2006 than it did in 1982, despite being equipped with air bags, CD players, antilock brakes, and other items considered luxury options in the early 1980s.[8] As we have seen, the Big Three have had to compete harder, and consumers have had many other automakers to choose from.

IN DEREGULATED INDUSTRIES, consumers have done especially well.[9] Trucking rates dropped 30 percent in real terms between 1980 and 2000 – a savings that affected almost every item shipped long-distance. The cost of long-distance air travel also sank in real terms, making it possible for millions of Americans to fly who couldn't afford to before. The average cost of every hundred passenger miles flown (still using the value of the dollar in year 2000 as a comparison point) was about $35 in 1960. By 1980, the price had dropped to about $20; by 2000, under $15. In 2005, the average 1,000-mile, one-way flight cost 20 percent less than it did in 2000.[10] One recent study found that in the year 2000, travelers would have paid $20 billion more in higher airfares and less frequent service if Southwest Airlines didn't exist.[11]

Take a look at your telephone bill and adjust for inflation (still using the dollar's value in 2000). The average monthly base rate for residential phone service remained around $35 through the 1950s and 1960s, but in

1980 was down to $18. In 1983, in the wake of deregulation, MCI charged 37 cents for a one-minute call between St. Louis and Atlanta, while the Bell System was still charging its old rate of 62 cents; Bell's rates dropped to meet the competition. The price of telephone equipment also dropped. After AT&T wrung wage concessions out of Western Electric Company employees in 1983, the cost of a standard phone fell by nearly a third. Long-distance rates also took a dive. In the 1950s, it cost about $15 to make a ten-minute daytime phone call to someone over two hundred miles away. By 2000, that same call cost $8.50. Telecom revenue per minute plummeted from almost $1.50 in 1980 to less than 25 cents in 2003.[12] I now call friends in Europe and Asia over the Internet for free.

Not everything has become cheaper in real terms, of course. The price of health care has skyrocketed. But that's partly because competition for consumer and investor dollars has unleashed a wave of medical devices and new drugs. The result is better health for most people. When I was born in 1946, the typical American was expected to live 66.7 years. (Hence, Social Security, which kicked in at sixty-five, was not such a great deal.) Someone born in 2006 can expect to live eighty years. Old age is not what it used to be, either. Forty years ago, people in their sixties spent their days in rocking chairs and at card tables. Today many people in their seventies and eighties travel, enjoy an active sex life, and play sports. My father, at the age of ninety-three, plays golf three times a week.

Surgery has become easier and more successful. Twenty years ago I could hardly walk; then I had both hips replaced, and now walking is a cinch. The incidence of heart disease leading to death is 60 percent lower than it was in 1950 (adjusted for the increased size of the population). Cancer mortality is also down. Infant mortality has dropped 44 percent since 1980, according to the Centers for Disease Control. Through new drugs, millions of people who suffered from chronic pain have found relief, millions more have been lifted out of depression, people with AIDS have been given their lives back.

The health care system still has problems, of course. It is wildly ineffi-cient. Our bad eating habits have created an epidemic of obesity. Forty-seven million Americans have no health insurance and have to use hospital emergency rooms when something goes seriously wrong. Nonetheless, most of us are still far healthier than we were four decades ago.

Homes are more expensive, too, but generally larger and better equipped. Air-conditioning is standard in warm climates; central heating, in cool ones.[13] The cost of a college education is sharply up, but I cannot justify the increase, although I have taught in several fine institutions of higher learning. Higher education is a uniquely hidebound industry whose economics largely defy rational explanation.[14]

2

CAPITAL MARKETS – including stock exchanges, banks and other financial institutions, and money market funds – are far more efficient than they were decades ago, though still far from perfect. Stock prices reflect anticipated earnings rather than present ones, and investors sometimes make large collective mistakes – as many of us did at the end of the 1990s by investing in the Internet bubble and then suffering the consequences when it burst in 2000. Companies can mask problems through fancy accounting, at least for a time, as did the executives of Enron. The mutual funds and pension funds we entrust our money to don't always represent our best interests, especially if they have lucrative relationships with the same companies they invest in on our behalf. And Wall Street takes a famously myopic view of the future, looking at quarter-to-quarter results rather than longer-term performance.

Yet for all of this, investors have triumphed, just as consumers have. Capital markets are the most sensitive barometers available for gauging how well executives are squeezing value out of what they control in order to reward us as investors. Again, the proof is in the numbers. As the old oligopolistic system gave way to competition – allowing financial entrepreneurs to squeeze companies for higher profits – share values took off. The Dow Jones Industrial Average reached 1,000 on November 14, 1972. On January 8, 1987, it reached 2,000. On April 17, 1991, it broke 3,000. It hit 4,000 on February 23, 1995; 8,000 on July 16, 1997; 11,000 on May 3, 1999. It dropped when the Internet bubble burst but then bounced back and reached 12,000 on October 19, 2006, then 13,000 on April 25, 2007. Even though each milestone became progressively easier to reach and even though some investment proved to be speculative, investors nonetheless have become far wealthier.

FIGURE 3.1

THE RISE OF THE DOW

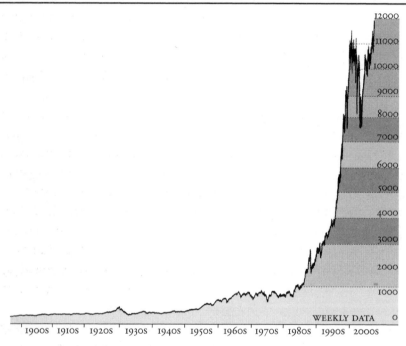

Source: Dow Jones Indexes.

This colossal increase in wealth was not the result of Ronald Reagan's supply-side tax cuts, as some conservative economists continue to believe. The Dow accelerated after the first George Bush and Bill Clinton both raised taxes. It has mostly reflected the increased capacities of companies to generate profits, as they have moved along the road to supercapitalism. Top executives have had strong incentives to be more efficient: We as consumers have threatened to take our business elsewhere unless they do things as efficiently as possible, and we as investors have threatened to take our money elsewhere unless they show a good return on our investments. The pressure we have applied – through consumer intermediaries like Wal-Mart or investor intermediaries on Wall Street – has resulted in remarkable wealth for successful CEOs and financial entrepreneurs, as we shall examine, or sudden job loss for the unsuccessful, as we have already seen.

By the late 1990s, most American households had become shareholders, putting retirement savings into the stock market or within 401(k) plans or other pension savings plans. The typical shareholder only owns roughly $5,000 worth, but that is enough to get her to pay exquisite attention to whether the Dow is trending up or down. The financial pages, which used to be read exclusively by the very rich, now rival the sports pages in provoking general interest.

Intensifying competition for us as consumers and investors has made the entire economy more productive. In order to be successful, CEOs and financiers have had to move money, machinery, factories, and other assets to where they can be most valuable. They've also had to invest in better products and services, and cheaper ways of making or delivering them. And of course they have moved, demoted or promoted, or laid off millions of people. As a result of all this, between 1973 and 2006, the gross domestic product of the United States tripled in size, adjusted for inflation. Economists calculate that during these years productivity increased by roughly 80 percent. In 2006, American workers were producing over 30 percent more every hour than they did only a decade before.

As economic power has shifted to consumers and investors, and away from large corporations and unionized workers, inflation has become far tamer. In the Not Quite Golden Age, big business and big labor negotiated pay packages that set prevailing wages throughout much of the economy. Now, hourly workers have little power to demand and get more pay, and most companies likewise have little power to raise prices. That means the entire economy can run faster and at a lower level of unemployment, without much risk that wages and prices will spiral out of control. The overall economy is sufficiently productive and flexible so that there's less risk of inflation when demand picks up. Alan Greenspan, as has been noted, understood this reality earlier than most.

3

BUT MOST of us are not just consumers and investors. We also work for a living. If our wages and benefits are not growing at the same rate the economy is growing overall, we are likely to feel we're not making progress.

Unless we are committed narcissists, our concerns are not limited to our *own* jobs, wages, and benefits. Many of our parents work or our children work, as do our siblings and their children, our friends and colleagues and their parents or children. Economics, as a discipline, focuses on a domain of personal concern strictly bounded by what analysts in government statistical agencies define as one's 'family' or 'household'. But such categories are arbitrary. The capacity of human beings to empathize – to feel responsibility, loyalty, and simple human connection – extends far beyond them.

We're also members of communities, participants in the life of our neighborhoods, members of a democracy, patriots. Some of us would willingly die for our country. Standard economic models have little to say about any of these altruistic sentiments. Yet as citizens we may care a great deal if most people's jobs are insecure and wages are stagnant, and if a relatively small number of people have cornered most of the nation's wealth. We may also worry that our Main Streets are disappearing because small retailers can no longer compete with big-box retailers. We may be upset that companies are spewing gunk that causes global warming, or trampling human rights abroad, or pandering to our basest instincts for sexual titillation and violent thrill, or trying to fill our children's stomachs (and perhaps our own) with junk food.

Here, too, the boundary between enlightened self-interest and broad empathy is blurry. For example, I want to see poor people educated and part of the workforce – if they are not, crime will rise and more likely threaten my loved ones; one of my grown children or I could be mugged by a poor kid who thinks he has no future in the legitimate economy. Similarly, I'm concerned about the loss of Main Street not only because I care about small retailers but because I used to enjoy strolling along it. Global warming not only threatens the planet but it also threatens to erode the beaches I love to walk on. I don't want the Internet to carry so much easily accessible pornography because I don't want my grandchildren watching it.

These issues of economic security, social equity, community, our shared environment, and common decency were central to democratic capitalism as we knew it in the Not Quite Golden Age. They were – and still are – concerns to us in our capacity as *citizens*. But as power has shifted to us as consumers and investors, these issues have been eclipsed. We've entered into a Faustian bargain. Today's economy can give us great deals largely because it punishes us in other ways. We can blame big corporations, but we've mostly made this bargain with ourselves.

After all, where do we suppose the great deals come from? In part they come from lower payrolls – from workers who have to settle for lower wages and benefits, or have to get new jobs that often pay less. They also come from big-box retailers that kill off Main Streets because they undercut prices charged by independent retailers there. They come from companies that shed their loyalties to particular communities and morph into global supply chains paying pennies to twelve-year-olds in Indonesia. They come from CEOs who are paid exorbitantly; from companies all over the world who wreak havoc on the environment; and, in some instances, from companies that pump out violence or porn or nutritionless foods and beverages.

You and I are complicit. As consumers and investors, we make the whole world run. Markets have become extraordinarily responsive to our wishes – more so all the time. Yet most of us are of two minds, and it is the citizen in us that has become relatively powerless. Supercapitalism is triumphant. *Democratic* capitalism is not.

4

WHEN WE FIND great deals on cars, refrigerators, picture frames, or almost any other manufactured item, it's often because the Americans who molded, fit, clamped, or bolted these things have either accepted cuts in pay and benefits or lost their jobs altogether. Their pay dropped or their job vanished along the road to supercapitalism because, as we saw in the last chapter, software or a foreign worker or a nonunionized worker in the United States could do it more cheaply. Most of the displaced workers have found new jobs, but often in the local service economy – in retail stores, restaurants, hotels, and hospitals – which pay less, with fewer benefits. According to the 2002 Displaced Workers Survey of the Department of Labor, manufacturing workers who lost their jobs due to competition from imports found new jobs paying an average of 13 percent less than the jobs they lost. Manufacturing workers who lost their jobs for other reasons – say, because their employer substituted automated machinery and software – obtained jobs that paid an average of 12 percent less than the old ones.[15]

When we find good deals on services, chances are we're also indirectly holding down someone else's wages and benefits in America. Say we go to the Internet to find a low-cost airfare. Similar moves by millions of travelers have affected people like Shannon Wareham, twenty-nine, a Northwest flight attendant who was interviewed by the *New York Times* in 2006, just as a bankruptcy judge was deciding whether to allow Northwest to impose more wage cuts and bar strikes. After working for Northwest for seven years, Wareham finally earned more than $30,000 in 2005. But in 2006 she expected to make closer to $21,000, given the cuts Northwest was demanding. 'I am an expert at living within my means,' she wrote in a letter to the judge. 'I have no air-conditioning, cable, call waiting, high-speed Internet or car. I live in a 230-square-foot studio on 142nd Street in Harlem. Yet over the last couple of months, I have had no money left after paying my bills to buy food, and have had to resort to using my credit card to eat.'[16]

We also indirectly push salaries and benefits downward when we move our savings from one fund to another to get a higher rate of return. Among the voices demanding companies make bold cost-cutting moves are the managers of large charitable foundations, retirement funds of university teachers, and union pension funds. Competition for the pool of money they invest on behalf of their beneficiaries acts as a kind of flywheel for everything else. And who's pushing them to get higher returns? I am, and probably you, too. If a portfolio manager in charge of my teachers' retirement fund doesn't get the best possible return on my savings, I'll switch funds. I can switch more easily now than ever before. All I need do is click on another fund that's showing higher returns. Every fund manager knows that and acts accordingly. So indirectly *I'm* pushing CEOs to squeeze wages and benefits. I may even be pressuring CEOs to fight their unions.

CEOs do occasionally upgrade the skills of their employees in order to make them more productive and worth every penny of good wages and benefits. Big-box retailer Costco carefully trains its personnel to know merchandise and help customers, and pays them well. In 2005 they averaged $17 an hour, more than 40 percent higher than employees at Wal-Mart's Sam's Club receive. Costco also offers a generous health plan. Some observers assume that if Costco can do it, Wal-Mart can, too. But the better training justifies higher wages and benefits only if consumers are willing to pay for them in the form of higher prices. Costco and Wal-Mart are not really direct competitors. The average Costco customer earned $74,000 in 2005, more than twice the income of the average Wal-Mart customer.[17] Costco's prices are generally higher than Wal-Mart's. Costco customers receive better service, and presumably they are willing to pay for it.

For many years I've spread the gospel of treating employees as valuable assets, and I still believe it. But how much a company can afford to spend on workers depends on how much value those people generate. If Costco couldn't pass the higher wages and benefits on to its customers in the form of higher prices, it would have to take the money out of its profits, which would upset investors. As a matter of fact, Wall Street has not been terribly happy about Costco CEO Jim Sinegal's beneficence toward his employees. As one analyst put it in 2004, 'From the perspective of investors, Costco's benefits are overly generous. Public companies need to care for share-holders first.'[18] An analyst from Deutsche Bank complained that at Costco 'it's better to be an employee or a customer than a shareholder'. When analysts objected that Sinegal was asking workers to pick up only 4 percent of their health costs, he raised it to 8 percent, still well below the retail average of 25 percent. This prompted Emme Kozloff, a stock analyst at Sanford C. Bernstein & Co. to conclude that Sinegal 'has been too benevolent.

He's right that a happy employee is a productive long-term employee but he could force employees to pick up a little more of the burden.'[19] Kozloff, let me remind you, isn't telling Sinegal what to do. She's advising the people who manage stock funds what steps to take to maximize the value of our shares of stock – and that is putting pressure on Sinegal. So indirectly, here again, *we're* telling Sinegal to be less generous.

Our pursuit of great deals is also affecting middle-level managers and software engineers. In September 2006, for example, Intel announced it would cut 10,500 jobs, about 10 percent of its workforce. Analysts described the cost-cutting measure as essential if Intel had any hope of taking market share back from its rival, Advanced Micro Devices, in sales of microprocessors used in computers. In fact, many analysts were disappointed Intel didn't cut more jobs, and its stock price sank on the news. By 2007, after a bruising price war, AMD was on the defensive and Intel was regaining market share. Relentlessly pursuing good deals on ever more powerful computers, we have put pressure on both AMD and Intel.

The overall result is that America is far more productive than it was twenty or thirty years ago, but most people haven't shared much in the bounty. Had median household incomes continued to grow at the same rate productivity grew over the last thirty years, the typical household would have earned around $20,000 more in 2006 than it actually did.

Meanwhile, employer-provided benefits have gone into free fall. Recall that full health coverage was the norm in wage contracts of the Not Quite Golden Age. But as the economy shifted, the proportion of large and medium-sized companies offering full coverage steadily dropped from 74 percent in 1980 to 18 percent in 2005.[20] As recently as 1988, two-thirds of large and medium-sized employers (with two hundred or more workers) provided health insurance to their retirees. By 2005, the portion had fallen to around a third.[21]

In 1980, more than 80 percent of large and medium-sized firms provided their employees with a traditional defined benefit pension, which guaranteed them a fixed amount of money every month after they retired. By 2006, only slightly more than a third did. Hewlett-Packard, Verizon, Motorola, and IBM all terminated their traditional pensions, replacing

FIGURE 3.2

PRODUCTIVITY VS. COMPENSATION, 1950–2005

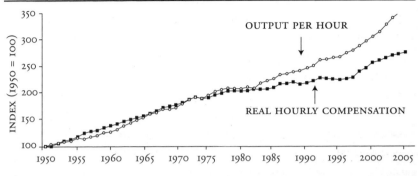

Source: U.S. Department of Labor, Bureau of Labor Statistics.

them with defined contribution plans that offer no guarantee at all. At best, employers put some money into a kitty depending on how much an employee contributes. A third of all workers contribute nothing, which means their employers don't, either.

The main culprit has not been corporate greed or CEO insensitivity but rather the increasing pressure on companies from consumers like you and me who want better deals, and from investors like us who want better returns. You or I did not *intend* this outcome, and we may not like what's happened to the wages and benefits of so many people – perhaps including ourselves or our children – as a result. But we can safely ignore these developments as long as we don't connect the consumer and investor half of our brain with the citizen half. It's easier to cast rhetorical blame on the intermediaries between the two halves – corporations, CEOs, Wall Street, Wal-Mart.

Another consequence of our actions is less economic security. In the Not Quite Golden Years, breadwinners held steady jobs and their pay increased gradually and predictably over time. But since the old system crumbled, jobs and incomes have become less predictable. Factories have closed, new ones have appeared elsewhere – usually far away. Companies have disappeared, sometimes reemerging in a different form after a bankruptcy or reappearing as a subsidiary of another company. Old product lines or standard services have been terminated, new ones introduced. Novel software with 'killer' applications have wiped out older rivals, and sometimes undermined entire industries. Economist Joseph Schumpeter called it 'creative destruction' – the result of untrammeled competition, the essence of economic dynamism. The creative destruction that has occurred since the 1970s has undoubtedly benefited consumers and investors. But along the way, many families' earnings have been created and destroyed as well.

The Panel Study of Income Dynamics at the University of Michigan has tracked 65,000 people since 1968. The researchers have found that over any given two-year stretch about half of all families experience some decline in earnings, then often make up for it later on. Yet the swings have become progressively larger as the decades have passed. In the 1970s, a typical decline was about 25 percent. By the late 1990s, it was 40 percent. By the mid-2000s, family incomes rose and fell twice as much as they did in the mid-1970s, on average.[22]

Polls show a substantial increase over recent decades in the number of people worried about losing their jobs.[23] During the first nine months of 2006 – the fifth year of a so-called economic recovery – some 4.5 million Americans, on average, left their jobs or were fired every *month,* and some 4.8 million people started new jobs every month. Presumably some of these people relished the change of pace, the new opportunities, the excitement of it all. Some would have preferred the status quo. A not insignificant number, we can assume, fell on their faces. Upheaval can be stimulative when the electricity bill can be paid and there's enough food in the refrigerator. It is considerably less welcome when the kids have to go hungry, even temporarily.

Here again, we are of two minds. We're eager to comparison-shop and discover the newest, coolest, most powerful, and cheapest stuff. But the citizen in us worries about the stress and insecurity that is the inevitable consequence. In the Not Quite Golden Age, consumers and investors had little choice but to hang in there with the same company. During the last three decades we've gained access to a steadily widening range of choices, many offering better deals than the ones we have at the moment. And we've become ever more facile at severing economic relationships in pursuit of better deals. The result has been lots of creative destruction, including some of the jobs in the relationships we abruptly terminated.

Are the benefits we accrue from the creative destruction worth the price? Other capitalist societies are moving in our direction, as we'll see, but still provide their citizens more security. Great Britain's economy is not markedly less successful than America's, although its citizens tend to live in smaller houses and drive less. But people there still remain in their jobs longer, and if they lose them they have more generous unemployment insurance than in the United States. Sir Michael Marmot, a professor of epidemiology and public health at University College in London, and his colleagues compared the health of Americans and Britons, and published the findings in 2006 in the *Journal of the American Medical Association*. At every level of wealth and family income, more illness was found in the United States than in the United Kingdom. Marmot hypothesized the difference was related to heavier stresses in the United States.[24]

But it's our choice, isn't it?

5

IF REAL median household income has gone nowhere over the last three decades while the overall economy has grown exuberantly, where has all the wealth gone? Mostly to the very top. Professors Emmanuel Saez of the University of California at Berkeley and Thomas Piketty of the École Normale Supérieure in Paris examined tax records and found that by 2004, America's top 1 percent of earners received 16 percent of the nation's total income – double their 8 percent share in 1980.[25] The share going to the top .1 percent more than tripled since 1980, to 7 percent. Wage inequality has also increased in Europe and Japan, although not by as much. College graduates and professionals in the top 20 percent of America's income ladder pocketed some, but a college degree has offered no assurance of that. Even the incomes of people in the ninety-fifth percentile – those earning more than nineteen out of twenty Americans – rose less than 1 percent a year, on average, between 1978 and 2004.[26]

FIGURE 3.3A

REAL FAMILY INCOME GROWTH BY QUINTILE, 1947–1973

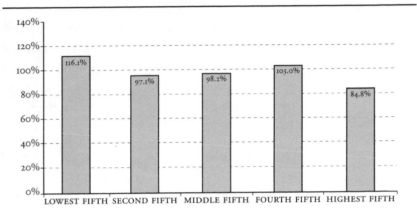

FIGURE 3.3B

REAL FAMILY INCOME GROWTH BY QUINTILE, 1974–2004

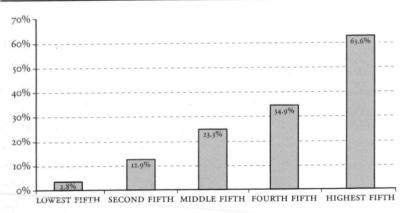

Source: Economic Policy Institute, The State of Working America, 2006/7, *Chapter 1, Figure 11, from Bureau of the Census, CPS (all data deflated).*

The very top hasn't been occupied by precisely the same people over the entire stretch, but that's not the point. The fact is, a very few have pocketed most of the bounty, and the trend has been in the direction of a smaller and smaller number pocketing more and more. This trend, too, began in the

1970s and has accelerated since. It's a significant reversal of the move toward income equality that began in the early part of the twentieth century and culminated during the Not Quite Golden Age. By 2005, the top 1 percent got a larger share of total income than at any time since 1929 (except, briefly, during the stock bubble of 2000).

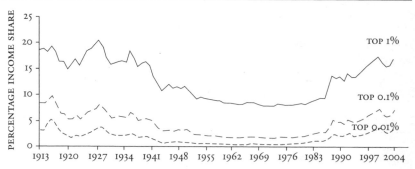

FIGURE 3.4

SHARE OF INCOME GOING TO THE HIGHEST EARNERS, 1913–2004

Source: T. Piketty and E. Saez, updated version of 'Income Inequality in the United States, 1913–1998', Quarterly Journal of Economics 113, no. 1 (February 2003), with tables and figures updated to 2005, http://elsa.berkeley.edu/~saez/TabFig2005prel.xls.

Much of this has accrued to people who were already rich, in the form of investment income. Rich people own far more shares of stock than do middle-class investors, so the increasing returns on capital have disproportionately benefited them. But that alone is not the most significant aspect of recent developments.

PROFESSORS LUCIEN BEBCHUK of Harvard and Yaniv Grinstein of Cornell took a close look at the $83 billion the top .1 percent of earners reported on their 2001 taxes and found that more than half that sum $48 billion – was the combined incomes of the top five executives at American companies. Executive pay averaged $6.4 million, including stock options and perks; CEO pay, $14.3 million. When the researchers compared

executive pay to the firms' total earnings year by year, they saw a pro-
nounced upward trend. In the mid-1990s, the typical firm paid its top five
executives 5 percent of total earnings. By the start of the 2000s, top executives were getting 10 percent.[27] By 2006, CEOs were earning, on average,
eight times as much per dollar of corporate profits as they did in the 1980s.

The trend line is the same when you compare CEO pay to that of
average workers. During the Not Quite Golden Age, the CEOs of major
American companies took home about 25 to 30 times the wages of the
typical worker. After the 1970s, the two pay scales diverged. In 1980, the
big-company CEO took home roughly 40 times as much; by 1990, it was
100 times. By 2001, CEO pay packages had ballooned to about 350 times
what the typical worker earned.[28] To make the comparison especially vivid,
the CEO of General Motors took home about $4 million in 1968
(translated into today's dollars), which was around 66 times the pay and
benefits of the typical GM worker at the time. In 2005, Wal-Mart's CEO,
Lee Scott, Jr., took home $17.5 million, some 900 times the pay and bene-
fits of the typical Wal-Mart worker.

What explains this impressive trajectory? Have top executives become
greedier? Have corporate boards grown less responsible? Are CEOs more
crooked? Are investors more docile? Is Wall Street more tractable? There's
no evidence to support any of these theories. Here's a simpler explanation.
Forty years ago, everyone's pay in a big company – even pay at the top –
was affected by bargains struck among big business, big labor, and,
indirectly, government. Oligopolies and their industry-wide unions
directly negotiated pay scales for hourly workers, while white-collar
workers understood that their pay grades were indirectly affected. As we've
seen, large corporations resembled civil service bureaucracies. Top
executives in these oligopolies had to maintain the goodwill of organized
labor. They also had to maintain good relationships with public officials in
order to be free to set wages and prices; to obtain regulatory permissions on
fares, rates, or licenses; and to continue to secure government contracts. It
would have been unseemly of them to draw very high salaries.

Since then, competition has intensified. Oligopolies are mostly gone
and entry barriers are low. With ever greater ease, rival companies can get
access to similar low-cost suppliers from all over the world. They can

FIGURE 3.5

RATIO OF AVERAGE TOP EXECUTIVE AND CEO COMPENSATION TO AVERAGE WORKER'S PAY

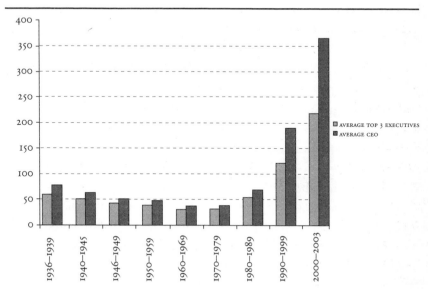

Source: Carola Frydman and Raven E. Sakes, 'Historical Trends in Executive Compensation, 1936–2003', Working Paper No. 15, November 200 , at http://tinyurl.com/f3pzz.

streamline their operations with the same information technology; they can cut their labor force and substitute equally efficient software culled from many of the same vendors. They can just as readily outsource hourly jobs abroad. They can get capital for new investment on much the same terms. They can gain access to distribution channels that are no less efficient, some of them even identical (Wal-Mart or other big-box retailers).

The dilemma facing so many companies is therefore how to *distinguish* themselves: how to offer products or services superior to rivals' – cheaper, faster, or otherwise more riveting – so as to attract and keep consumers who have better and better comparative information; how to make larger profits than rivals (or create expectations of larger profits) so as to attract investors and gain higher share price. They need the right person at the helm.

The CEO of an oligopoly during the Not Quite Golden Age did not have to be especially clever or even particularly bright. He did not need to be ruthless or compulsively driven to succeed. Success was almost assured because profits were almost assured. Rivals did not impinge. He was mostly a bureaucrat in charge of a large production system whose rules were so standardized he did not need to break a sweat. The CEO of a modern company is in a different situation. Rivals are impinging all the time – threatening to lure away consumers all too willing to be lured by a better deal, threatening to hijack investors eager to jump ship at the slightest hint of an upturn in a rival's share price. The modern CEO must therefore be sufficiently ruthless and driven to find and pull the levers that will deliver competitive advantage. There are no standard textbook moves, no well-established strategies to draw upon. If there were, rivals would already be using them.

Boards of directors well understand this, which is one reason why executive talent is in such high demand. The pool of proven talent is small because so few executives have been tested and succeeded at the job of running a company. Moreover, boards of major companies do not want to risk error. The cost of recruiting the wrong person can be very large – and readily apparent in the deteriorating value of a company's shares. It is an elemental principle of economics: When demand rises while the supply remains limited, prices soar. Boards are willing to pay more and more for CEOs and other top executives because their rivals are paying more and more for them. And all are willing to pay more because, in effect, consumers and investors are pressuring them to.[29]

Of course, some CEOs reap giant rewards even as their share prices plummet, and some pocket huge goodbye gifts even if they're sacked. But this is unlikely to last long. Only the rare company today can remain competitive headed by a CEO who is unworthy of his pay, including exit bonuses. A CEO who keeps his job because of clubby relationships on the board won't succeed as well in satisfying consumers and investors as one who occupies the corner office because of proven talent. Consumers and investors won't stick around because of friendship, loyalty, or sentiment. Consumers, as we know now, want great products and great service, and if they don't get them they'll leave. Investors want high returns, and if they don't get them they'll leave.

Once again, the proof is in the numbers. Between 1980 and 2003, as the average value of America's largest five hundred companies rose by a factor of six, adjusted for inflation, average CEO pay in those companies also rose roughly sixfold.[30]

In 2005, ExxonMobil reported $36 billion in profits. Its former chairman, Lee R. Raymond, retired comfortably that year with a compensation package worth approximately $140 million. According to a proxy statement filed by the company with the Securities and Exchange Commission, Raymond was also entitled to stock, stock options, and long-term compensation worth another $258 million. That seems outrageous until you consider Exxon's shareholders did exceedingly well during the decade over which Raymond presided – enjoying a return of 223 percent, including the benign effects of Exxon's 1998 takeover of Mobil. Although the shareholders of almost every large oil company also did well because oil prices were rising, other large oil companies delivered lower returns by comparison – on average, 205 percent. That 18 percent difference, according to Fadel Gheit, senior energy analyst with Oppenheimer & Company as reported by Alan Murray in the *Wall Street Journal,* was worth a total of about $16 billion to investors who had bought Exxon stock at the start. In this context, Raymond's compensation seems economically reasonable: He took home just 4 percent of the $16 billion bonanza.

In economic terms, CEOs have become less like top bureaucrats and more like Hollywood celebrities or star athletes, who take a share of the house. Hollywood's most popular celebrities now pull in around 15 percent of whatever the studios take in at the box office, and athletes are also getting a growing portion of sales.[31] As *The New Yorker*'s James Surowiecki has reminded us, Mickey Mantle earned $60,000 in 1957. Carlos Beltran made $15 million in 2005. Even adjusting for inflation, Beltran got forty times as much as Mantle. Clark Gable earned $100,000 a picture in the 1940s, which translates into roughly $800,000 today. Tom Hanks, by contrast, makes closer to $20 million per film.[32] Movie studios and baseball teams find it profitable to pay these breathtaking sums because they're still relatively small compared to the money these stars bring in and the profits they generate. Today's big companies are paying their CEOs mammoth sums for much the same reason.

This economic explanation for the startling level of CEO pay does not justify it socially or morally. It only means that as *consumers and investors* we think the CEOs are worth it. As citizens, though, most of us disapprove. About 80 percent of Americans polled by the *Los Angeles Times* and Bloomberg in early 2006 said CEOs are overpaid. The reaction was roughly the same regardless of the income or political affiliation of the respondent.[33] The Securities and Exchange Commission has recently required companies disclose to investors more information about the compensation of their top executives. Given the economic realities I've just discussed, however, the disclosures are unlikely to hold back the meteoric rise in such pay. Disclosure may make it harder for a CEO to claim to be worth it if his company's shares have lost ground during his tenure or risen no more than the average share prices of other companies in the same industry. But disclosure might also intensify competition for star CEOs, with the result that CEO pay soars even higher.

Top investment bankers and traders take home even more than CEOs. They make their money by raking off small percentages of huge transactions, here again taking a share of the house. In 2006 – a big year for giant mergers and acquisitions – senior investment banking executives collected bonuses of $20 to $25 million, while traders got checks of $40 to $50 million.[34]

Even these sums pale by comparison with what hedge fund managers take home. In 2005, James Simons of Renaissance Technologies reported earning $1.5 billion, mostly on management fees; T. Boone Pickens, Jr., of BP Capital Management, was awarded $1.4 billion; George Soros of Soros Fund Management, $840 million; Steven Cohen of SAC Capital Advisors, $550 million. The *average* take-home pay for the twenty-six managers of major hedge funds in 2005 was $363 million, a 45 percent increase over their average earnings the year before.[35] These funds are so large (totaling hundreds of billions of dollars) and their average returns to investors so good (averaging 12 to 20 percent in 2005, far better than an equity index fund) that a typical management fee of 2 percent of assets and 20 percent of profits is trifling by comparison. Again, the stars get a share of the house, but here the houses are immense. Among investors who have benefited – in the form of infinitesimal fractions of the large pension funds and mutual funds that poured money into these giant hedges – were, very likely, you and me.

We, as I've said, are of two minds. Star CEOs, investment bankers, and top hedge fund managers have delivered us great bounty. But as citizens, many of us are appalled by the sums they pocket – especially as most other workers are stuck in neutral or losing ground. Every two weeks Lee Scott, Jr., of Wal-Mart rakes in roughly the same amount his average employee earns in a lifetime. Continental Airlines provides health care for retired chairman Gordon Bethune and his dependents, according to Continental's proxy statement, on top of the lump-sum pension payout of $22 million Continental bestowed on Bethune on his retirement at the end of 2004. Meanwhile, Continental's employees have to settle for lower pay and skimpier benefits.[36]

In September 2006, the ailing Ford Motor Company lured a new chief executive, Alan Mulally, with a $2 million 'base salary'; a $7.5 million signing bonus; options and stock units valued at more than $15 million; $11 million to offset options he forfeited by leaving his former employer, Boeing; and undisclosed perks and benefits, for a grand total of somewhere around $36 million. Ford, of course, has been busily slashing its payrolls. While at Boeing, Mulally had cut the workforce by almost 60 percent – 'a sign,' according to the *Wall Street Journal,* that 'he is able to make the kind of painful choices that are clearly needed at Ford.'[37] ('Painful choices' is Street-speak for deeper cuts that will inflict further pain on employees, not shareholders. In fact, on news of Mulally's appointment, Ford's stock shot up 2 percent.)

The citizen in us may also be concerned that the nation's wealth is becoming even more concentrated at the top. It is the financial equivalent of hydrodynamics: Large streams of income create even larger pools of wealth. The family of Wal-Mart founder Sam Walton has a combined fortune estimated to be about $90 billion. In 2005, Bill Gates was worth $46 billion; Warren Buffett, $44 billion. By contrast, the combined wealth of the bottom 40 percent of the United States population that year – some 120 million people – was estimated to be around $95 billion.[38]

Since the 1970s, the nation's richest 1 percent – comprising roughly

FIGURE 3.6

AVERAGE HOUSEHOLD WEALTH BY WEALTH CLASS, 1962–2004

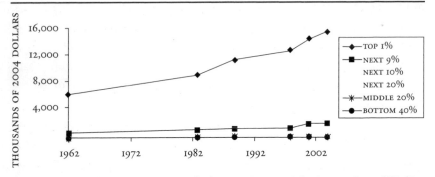

Sources: Survey of Consumer Finances, Federal Reserve; Economic Policy Institute, State of Working America 2006/07, *Chapter 5, Table 5.9; see Edward N. Wolff, 'Recent Trends in Wealth Ownership,' New York University Working Paper, updated 2006.*

one and a half million families in 2004[39] – have more than doubled their share of total national wealth. In 1976, they owned about 20 percent of America. By 1998, the latest data available, they had accumulated over a third of the nation's wealth – more than the entire bottom 90 percent put together.[40]

As citizens, we may feel that inequality on this scale cannot possibly be good for a democracy. It undermines solidarity and mutuality on which responsibilities of citizenship depend. It creates a new aristocracy whose privileges perpetuate themselves over generations. It breeds cynicism among the rest of us. But the super-rich are not at fault. By and large, the market is generating these outlandish results. And the market is being driven by us as consumers and investors. That does not make it right, however.

6

WE ARE ALSO OF TWO minds about other consequences of modern capitalism – its effects on the environment, on our communities, and on common decency. Three or four decades ago, democratic capitalism had protected these. Laws were passed to guard the environment; companies were not yet financially pressured to abandon their hometowns; codes governed what could be said or done on television, radio, and in the movies; and laws banned obscenity. But since then, we newly empowered consumers and investors have gotten access to much better deals.

I know many boomers who profess to be worried sick about the effects of increasing levels of carbon dioxide in the atmosphere. They're furious at big power companies that continue to spew it into the air, and at politicians who refuse to act. But some of these same boomers tool around in SUVs or four-wheel-drive trucks. A few of the richer ones drive Humvees and have second and third cars for their families. Their lifestyles require kilowatts of energy whose production spews even more gunk into the atmosphere – homes of four thousand or more square feet maintained year-round at comfortable temperatures, and filled with thin-screen televisions, wireless sound systems, massage recliners, and whirlpool spas. They also invest wherever they can get the highest return, regardless of how much of the environment is destroyed along the way. As citizens they are sincerely concerned about global warming; as consumers and investors they are actively turning up the heat.

Similarly, most of us value the ideal of the traditional community even while we help it wither away. Those of us old enough to recall the traditional Main Streets of America's towns and cities may remember a variety of independently owned stores, maybe even some friendly relationships our parents struck with shopkeepers, and small talk with neighbors and friends along the way. In recent years, architects and urban planners across America have been trying to re-create the ambience and charm of these almost-forgotten American byways. You can find their handiwork inside gated communities, within gentrified downtown condominium complexes, in 'new urban' townscapes, even in some airport malls and public housing complexes. New Orleans's old St. Thomas public housing site, once one of the city's most intractable slums, has been converted into 'River Garden', a mixed-income development that approximates a late-nineteenth-century New Orleans neighborhood. Celebration, Florida, the Disney Corporation's contribution to the current wave of nostalgia, mimics 'a community rich with old-fashioned appeal', according to

Celebration's Web site, with 'a unique collection of charming shops and tempting eateries nestled around a dazzling lakeside promenade'.

Yet none of this quite works. Regardless of how quaint, independent shop owners are rarely to be found along these ersatz Main Streets. Most of the stores are outlets of national or global chains whose brands and ambiences are identical to those in every one of their other outlets around the nation or even the world. As consumers, we don't really spend many dollars along these fake boulevards anyway. Most of our spending these days is in big-box retailers like Wal-Mart or in factory outlets in super-sized malls. Or, with ever greater ease, we're ordering merchandise online via our asocial personal computers. Some towns, such as Berkeley, California, don't allow big-box retailers. But just beyond Berkeley's city limits lies Emeryville, whose zoning laws apparently beckon virtually every big box in the world. Emeryville is jammed on weekends. The developers of River Garden had no such qualms; they allowed a Wal-Mart right at the center.

Critics charge Wal-Mart with sucking the lifeblood out of the nation's Main Streets, but Wal-Mart isn't the motivating force. That giant sucking sound you hear is the consumers who flock to Wal-Mart. Wal-Mart's Lee Scott, Jr. – whose office, incidentally, is in Bentonville, Arkansas, a small Republican town with small-town values – thinks Main Streets are anachronisms. 'There are people who care about sprawl and envision a life that's more like where I grew up, a life where people park and walk down Main Street and shop store to store to store,' he told John Heilemann of *New York* magazine. 'I actually have respect for those people. I think their intentions are good. But they have a view of life which I don't think is coming back. And I don't think society should protect that view of life.'[41]

Whether society should protect that view of life is at least debatable – the old Robinson-Patman Act of 1936, you recall, protected small retailers from chain stores before the courts whittled it down. Yet there's often something odd going on when so-called community groups fight to keep Wal-Mart out. Late in 2004, after Wal-Mart announced it aimed to open its first store in the New York City metropolitan area, in Rego Park, Queens – in a 135,000-square-foot mall where Queens Boulevard intersects with the Long Island Expressway – 'community groups' fought the project until Wal-Mart abandoned the plan the following year. But who did the fighting, and what exactly did they preserve in Rego Park? Within blocks of where Wal-Mart's store would have stood was already a Bed Bath & Beyond outlet, a CVS, a Pizza Hut, and a Payless, as well as a Baskin-Robbins, Old Navy, Dunkin' Donuts, Subway, Circuit City, Sears, and Marshalls. Perhaps Wal-Mart's presence might have caused several of these giant chain outlets to leave, but it seems doubtful anyone would have grieved much for their passing.

The real objection to Wal-Mart locating in Rego Park probably had more to do with the fears of these chains, and of people working in them. While average citizens may support their efforts, the 'community groups' that fight to keep Wal-Mart out are often headed by chain stores and labor unions. The reason is straightforward. Wal-Mart's low prices force the chains to lower their prices. That means their profits get squeezed, and they have to lower their wages, too.[42] Researchers examined detailed jobs data in regions before and after a Wal-Mart opened its doors and found that afterward, retail workers earned 3.5 percent less. Again, consumers get great deals largely because workers get shafted. The irony of it is they're often the same people.

Meanwhile, the people who work on the Main Streets of truly charming places like Nantucket, Massachusetts, or Berkeley – as cashiers, waitresses, schoolteachers, police, or firemen – often can't afford to live there because the cost of living in these towns is so high. Housing costs are high because these places are zoned to be charming, at a price that includes the extra cost of shopping on a Main Street without easy access to a big box or mall. Nantucket even bans chain stores, making its Main Street especially charming and dazzlingly pricey. Citizen and consumer values are easily reconciled when one is rich enough to afford both.

The tension between the consumer-investor and the citizen in us can be quite personal and even alarming. For years I patronized a local independent bookstore on Harvard Square, located about ten blocks from where I lived. I liked the particular store, and I still worry about the dwindling number of owner-operated bookstores. The big chains make their money off blockbusters, which means new authors often have to rely on independents to find and promote them. But one day I discovered, much to my chagrin, that a steadily larger portion of the books appearing on my home bookshelves came from the airport outlets of Borders or Barnes & Noble, and from Amazon.com. Apparently I didn't have – or hadn't made – the time to walk down to the Square. Last time I looked, that independent bookseller had closed. I wasn't singlehandedly responsible, of course; a few thousand others joined me, probably with similar good intentions to the contrary notwithstanding.

The conflict is typically impersonal and routine, as when big companies uproot themselves from the communities where they were founded and turn themselves into global supply chains. They do so in order to satisfy consumers and investors, some of whom ironically live in the very communities that are becoming economically stranded. Boeing began in Seattle, where its sprawling factories created tens of thousands of jobs. GE was Schenectady, New York; General Motors was Detroit; Kodak, Rochester, New York; Alcoa, Pittsburgh; Procter & Gamble, Cincinnati; Gillette, Boston. These companies erected baseball stadiums and sponsored local charities. Regulatory agencies ensured sufficient public subsidy to maintain good airline, bus, railroad, and phone service to these locales. Legislators ensured a flow of government contracts to these companies back home.

As power has shifted to consumers and investors, the linkages between company and place have been weakened if not severed. Over the last three decades, Pittsburgh, for example, has lost all its mills, nearly half its population, and much of its downtown commercial district. Some would say it's now a more attractive place to live in than when it was a mill town, but far fewer people live there and the median age of its voters is approaching seventy. Alcoa still maintains its official corporate headquarters in Pittsburgh, in a six-story city landmark. But soon after Alain Belda became CEO in 2001, he set up offices in the Lever Building on Park Avenue, in New York, bringing with him Alcoa's other top brass. No Alcoa signs or logos announce the fact, but, as a practical matter, it's where the company has moved. In a speech to the New York City Business Summit, Belda explained: 'We need access to the best and the brightest. We need it when we need it, not a week from today when they can lose a whole day to come and meet with us in Pittsburgh. We need them for breakfast meetings, for just a five-minute break, when the idea or the need comes. We need it every day.'[43]

Pittsburgh once housed the mills and blue-collar workers Alcoa then needed. But now these sorts of assets can be found anywhere because Alcoa's global supply chains provide them effortlessly. Alcoa's executives routinely deal all over the world. Alcoa's new needs are met in New York City, where Alcoa executives can get immediate access to the 'best and brightest' financiers, lawyers, business consultants, and media professionals. They, along with Alcoa's executive team, deploy Alcoa's global supply chains and market Alcoa's products and services in such a way as to satisfy Alcoa's worldwide investors (as represented by Wall Street) and Alcoa's worldwide consumers (as represented by Wal-Mart and other big boxes) in their ongoing scramble to get great deals.

7

As CITIZENS, we may also be concerned about the erosion of common standards of decency. Entertainment companies now spew out a sulfurous geyser of sex and violence. Movies are more lurid and gorier than ever; musical lyrics, more raunchy and provocative; cable television, more squalid; the Internet, a virtual repository of filth; video games feature exploding heads and severed body parts.

Conservative pundits thunder about the 'coarsening' of American culture and blame it on their universal demon, liberalism. 'In keeping with the progress of liberalism,' writes Robert Bork, the conservative jurist turned moral crusader, 'popular entertainment … celebrates the unconstrained self, and savages those who would constrain … What America increasingly produces and distributes is now propaganda for every perversion and obscenity imaginable.'[44] To Bork and many other social conservatives, the heart of the liberal beast lies in Hollywood. 'Many in Hollywood insist upon a liberal lacing of foul language in their films because they regard brutality and obscenity as signs of "authenticity".'[45]

Personally I hate how popular culture turns women into sex objects, celebrates bloodthirsty aggression, and sends this garbage into our homes. But Hollywood is not responsible, and the rot has nothing to do with liberalism. The descent of popular culture is being financed by America's giant media conglomerates, among them Fox Entertainment (owned, incidentally, by right-wing billionaire Rupert Murdoch), distributor of such banal vulgarities as *Melrose Place* and *Beverly Hills 90210*. Other large corporations are using ads featuring sex or aggression to sell everything from sportswear to kitchenware.

These companies do this not to corrupt anyone's morals but because there are lots of profits to be made by peddling sex and gore. Consumers want sex and gore, and investors in companies that give it to them couldn't be happier. If the hundreds of millions of people in the United States and elsewhere who lap it up decided they didn't want it, there wouldn't be any market for it. If consumers didn't respond so enthusiastically to advertisements featuring butt-naked actors and actresses, such ads wouldn't exist. Here again, we have met the enemy and it is us.

Many of the advocates of 'family values' who are in high dudgeon about the media are the same people, by the way, who celebrate the free market and are deeply suspicious of government regulation. Unfortunately for them, they cannot have it both ways. Either they favor freedom of choice or they favor government paternalism. If they don't like what America's media giants are dishing out to consumers who are eager to buy it, these defenders of morality have to get government to stop the sellers and block the buyers – and do it without violating the First Amendment of the Constitution.

It was simpler in the Not Quite Golden Age when each of a handful of broadcasters had to be licensed by the Federal Communications Commission, which made sure they didn't stray too far beyond predictable family fare; when movies had to pass Hollywood's board of censors; and when the Supreme Court enforced laws banning pornography. (Justice Potter Stewart famously declared that although he could not define obscenity, he knew it when he saw it.) Then, consumers and investors had to take a back seat. Power was in the hands of regulators and a few big oligopolies – three big television networks, a few major movie studios and record companies, and a handful of big, nationally distributed magazines. Modern conservatives need to be reminded that democratic capitalism in those days enforced middle-class norms of common decency.

Now thousands of entertainment companies are in furious competition to lure consumers and investors. Even large television networks that still decorously bleep offensive words do end-runs around their internal censors and FCC commissioners by placing uncensored versions of the same shows on their Web sites.[46] Now that media competition has been unleashed, capitalism inevitably panders to our baser instincts. This doesn't make it right, which is exactly the point.

You might also blame the interplay between supercapitalism and our baser instincts for the new plague of obesity. Americans and many others around the world now have easier access to massive infusions of calories and junk food than ever before. Intensive competition among fast food companies has unleashed a torrent of sugary cereals, fatty snacks, jumbo portions of deep-fried meats, sugar-intensive soft drinks, and horrible bread made from refined carbohydrates. Competition among specialty foods manufacturers, dairies, and bakeries has generated super-thick premium ice creams, endless variations on chocolate brownies, and a cornucopia of cakes, pies, croissants, and candies, made with confectioner's sugar, granulated sugar, refined sugar, brown sugar, and raw sugar. Our intake of soft drinks rose from 24.3 gallons per person a year in 1970 to 53 gallons in 1997. Fat in our food supply increased by 25 percent from 1970 to the late 1990s. Total calories increased from an average of 3,300 per person per day in 1970 to 3,800 in the late 1990s – twice the amount needed to meet the energy requirements of most adult women, a third more than needed by most men, and far more than needed by children or the elderly.[47]

The Not Quite Golden Age had its junk foods as well, of course. I spent many afternoons after school gorging on Hostess cupcakes with creme filling. Yet there was nowhere near the current variety or accessibility, nor the incessant marketing that characterizes supercapitalism. The demand for 'organic' and 'natural' foods is growing, but not as fast as the demand for junk. In 1998, food manufacturers introduced slightly more than eleven thousand new products; more than two-thirds were condiments, candy and snacks, baked goods, soft drinks, cheeses, and ice cream novelties.[48] That we know we should limit our intake of such delectables has not made much difference, especially in light of intensifying competition for the limited but growing space in our bulging stomachs and hips. That we so choose does not make it right – which is, again, the point.

8

SUPERCAPITALISM'S consequences don't end at America's borders. A few years ago when Alcatel, a mostly French-owned telecom company, announced its annual profit would be less than had been forecast, its share price dropped. It bounced back a few months later after the firm took the distinctly un-French steps of cutting twelve thousand jobs and leaving several French communities stranded. French president Jacques Chirac explained in his next Bastille Day address what had triggered the crisis: 'California retirees suddenly decided to sell Alcatel,' he noted testily, referring to California's giant public employee retirement fund.

California's public employees – tens of thousands of granola-munching souls who probably do not view themselves as rabid promoters of free-market capitalism – park their retirement savings in a giant pension fund called CalPERS that is busily severing links between companies and their employees and communities around the world. Like all fund managers, those who run CalPERS understand their job is to maximize the value of their retirees' portfolios. CalPERS had invested in Alcatel because it was a good bet – if Alcatel slimmed down and cut unnecessary costs, as seemed likely. But when Alcatel's executives wouldn't cut their payrolls quickly enough, CalPERS forced Alcatel's hand by threatening to sell. CalPERS wasn't singling out the French. A few years ago it complained that a German utility, RWE, gave the cities it served too much control over its board and thus diminished the value of RWE shares. The utility argued that the arrangement represented an important bond with its customers. Apparently unimpressed, CalPERS threatened to dump its RWE shares, leading RWE to scrap its system of city representation.[49]

In this way, California's gentle public employees are ruthlessly bringing supercapitalism to Old Europe. New York City's public employees are bringing it to Indonesia in more dubious form. As of January 2006, they owned some $37 million of Freemont Mining Company's giant open-pit gold mine in Papua that has been dumping billions of tons of toxic waste into what had been a pristine river system crucial to the area's food chain. Despite the suffering of local inhabitants, the company contended its methods of waste disposal were approved by provincial authorities – an approval perhaps related to the nearly $20 million Freemont paid into the personal bank accounts of Indonesian military and police officials between 1998 and 2004, as reported by the *New York Times*. Yet with gold prices surging to a twenty-five-year high of more than $550 an ounce, New York City's pension fund trustees seemed in no hurry to dump Freemont's stock. Their only qualm, according to city comptroller William C. Thompson, Jr., was that Freemont might be found to have violated the Foreign Corrupt Practices Act, in which case the value of the shares might be jeopardized.[50]

Supercapitalism is also being spread by American consumers, with similar consequences. A job in an Indonesian textile factory is undoubtedly better than subsistence farming in Indonesia, but the real wages of Indonesian textile workers have been declining in recent years as Americans have become better and better at finding bargains. Because of intensifying competition, big manufacturers like Nike and major retailers like Foot Locker, Intersport, and J. C. Penney have been pressuring their foreign suppliers and subcontractors to lower their costs. As a result, the price paid for T-shirts produced overseas for a well-known sports brand dropped from $3.70 per dozen in 2000 to $2.85 in 2003. A factory in Sri Lanka that supplies Nike reported a 35 percent drop in unit prices during a more recent eighteen-month period. J. C. Penney paid its foreign supplier $5 for a two-piece toddler's outfit it bought five years before for $5.75. As one worker in an Indonesian factory said, 'The manager in our division often uses [this drop in prices] as a reason why our standard monthly wages can't be increased.'[51]

AMERICAN CONSUMERS and investors may be in the vanguard but consumers and investors elsewhere are discovering they also like the great deals the global economy can provide them, even at the cost of their own social values. Inequality has widened in almost all advanced economies, even those that call themselves 'social democracies'.[52]

The major impetus behind the wave of corporate restructurings that hit Europe beginning in the late 1990s – including mounting unfriendly takeovers, sacking executives who don't make the grade, and moving operations to lower-wage nations – has been Europeans themselves. Daimler Chrysler CEO Dieter Zetsche, for example, faced mounting financial losses as Europeans abandoned the company in favor of competitors; Zetsche cut 26,000 jobs and closed six European factories in an effort to cut costs and get customers and investors back. When the union representing Volkswagen's assembly workers balked at the company's plan to extend hours at its plants without increasing wages, CEO Wolfgang Bernhard warned if Volkswagen couldn't bring down labor costs the company would move its operations to Eastern Europe or Asia.[53] 'We ... thought in Western Europe that because of our high productivity and flexible workforce we could demand higher wages,' Bernhard explained. 'Now, with the emergence of Eastern Europe and some Asian competitors we see that they can get to the same productivity levels with a much lower hourly wage base.'[54] Even profitable German companies are feeling pressure to cut costs. In 2005, Deutsche Bank chairman Josef Ackermann simultaneously announced an 87 percent increase in net profits and a plan to cut 6,400 jobs in Germany and move 1,200 of them to low-wage nations.

Meanwhile, the pay of European CEOs is escalating rapidly toward American levels. In 2005, Jan Bennink, CEO of Royal Numico, a Dutch food manufacturer, got $13.4 million; Lord Browne of BP took home $18.5 million; Antoine Zacharias, former chairman of the French construction giant Vinci, raked in $22 million in compensation and severance.[55] Some Europeans worry that their Catholic, social democratic tradition of equity is eroding, but the reason for the rise in CEO pay is more prosaic. As large European corporations become global, their executives are in the same talent pool as Americans. Simply put, global consumers and investors are demanding the best talent money can buy.

CEO salaries in Japan are still much lower than in the United States or Europe, but they're on the rise as Japanese companies also feel pressured to recruit talent worldwide. In 2005, for example, Howard Stringer was named Sony's first American CEO. And as Japanese consumers and investors become more demanding, inequalities of income and wealth are rising across that nation that once prided itself on being a 'one hundred million, all-middle-class society'.[56] Most companies have abandoned lifetime employment, begun to lay off large numbers of employees, tied promotions to performance, and closed down unprofitable lines. Just months after he arrived, Stringer announced Sony would trim ten thousand employees, or 7 percent of its workforce. The shift toward supercapitalism has benefited Japanese consumers and investors – by 2006 the Japanese stock market had reached a fourteen-year high, and commercial land prices in large cities were rising – but many Japanese workers have not enjoyed the benefits. Between 2001 and 2006, the number of Japanese without savings doubled.

China has become a model of rapid economic development, growing about 10 percent a year since the early 1980s. That's been good news for Chinese consumers and people who invest in China, but the social consequences have been decidedly mixed. In recent years, income inequality has been widening sharply. China's new business elite lives in the equivalent of gated suburban communities replete with McMansions and swimming pools; they give their children lessons in golf and water polo, and send them to study abroad. At the same time, many of China's coastal cities have become crowded with peasants from the countryside who have sunk into urban poverty and unemployment. According to the World Bank, even as China's total income rose sharply between 2001 and 2003, the average income of the poorest 10 percent of its households fell 2.5 percent.[57] Pollution has become so bad that inhabitants of certain industrial areas routinely wear masks in order to breathe outdoors. Some 24 million acres of cultivated land there – a tenth of China's arable land – is so polluted it reportedly threatens food safety.[58] Inequality is also rising in India, along with rising prosperity.[59] Much the same thing is happening throughout Latin America, contributing to class tensions. Ten years after joining the North American Free Trade area, Mexico's national product is considerably larger than it was before but earnings inequality is much wider, too. Mexico's upper middle class has grown, but so have the number of Mexicans in poverty – a contentious issue in the close 2006 presidential elections there.

Supercapitalism is generating unimagined prosperity around the world, a great accomplishment. But it is also fomenting social discontent as inequality widens, jobs become less stable, old ties are severed, older communities are abandoned, air and water quality deteriorates, and traditional cultures are offended by commercial prurience. That all of this is being driven by global consumers and investors – some of whom are themselves deeply troubled by these social consequences – does not diminish the sting.

<h1 style="text-align:center">9</h1>

IF MOST people are of two minds about supercapitalism, why does the consumer-investor side almost always win out? The answer is that markets have become hugely efficient at responding to individual desires for better deals, but are quite bad at responding to goals we would like to achieve together. While Wal-Mart and Wall Street aggregate consumer and investor demands into formidable power blocs, the institutions that used to aggregate *citizen* values have declined. No longer do negotiations between big oligopolies and industry-wide labor unions have much significance in the wider political economy; no longer do local voluntary associations have much effect on legislators; no longer do regulatory agencies with broad reach define the public interest; no longer do CEOs have leeway to be 'corporate statesmen'.

There is an irony here. Precisely because supercapitalism is so efficient and dynamic, citizen needs are arguably greater than they were before. As companies drop health insurance and pension coverage, for example, public provision of them becomes more important. As jobs and incomes grow less secure, public safety nets become more essential. As companies are pressured to show profits, tougher measures are needed to guard public health, safety, the environment, and human rights against the possibility that executives may feel compelled to cut corners.

So what should the citizen do? We cannot resurrect the democratic capitalism of the Not Quite Golden Age, and should not even try. We as consumers and investors may have sacrificed too much then. But there is reason to think we have inadvertently swung too far in the other direction – toward a society driven mainly by consumers and investors, one in which the idea of the common good has all but disappeared.

The problem is that the choices we make in the market don't fully reflect our values as citizens. We might make different choices if we understood and faced the social consequences of our purchases or investments *and* if we knew all other consumers and investors would join us in forbearing from certain great deals whose social consequences were abhorrent to us. But we are unlikely to make the sacrifice if we think we'll be the only consumer or investor who refrains. Lonely forbearance can be the last refuge of a virtuous fool.

The only way for the citizens in us to trump the consumers and investors in us is through laws and regulations that make our purchases and investments a social choice as well as a personal one. A change in labor laws making it easier for employees to organize and negotiate better terms, for example, might increase slightly the price of products and services I buy – especially in local services sheltered from global competition. My inner consumer won't like that very much, but the citizen in me thinks it a fair price to pay. I'd also support a small transfer tax on sales of shares of stock, in order to slow the movement of capital ever so slightly so people and communities have a bit more time to adapt to changing circumstances. That might reduce the return on my retirement fund by a small fraction, but the citizen in me thinks it worth the price. For much the same reason it seems to me there should be 'circuit-breakers' that prevent a large, profitable company from laying off more than a certain proportion of the workers in a particular community during the course of a year.

I wouldn't go so far as to re-regulate the airline industry or hobble free trade with China and India – that would cost me as a consumer far too much – but I'd support extended unemployment insurance combined with wage insurance and job training to ease the pain for workers caught in the downdrafts of deregulation or trade. And I believe trade treaties should require all participating nations to allow their citizens to organize unions and establish minimum wages that are half their median wages. I'd also support paid family leave, so workers can upgrade their skills or take the time to attend to a newborn or sick parent without sacrificing pay. These provisions might end up costing me some money, too, but the citizen in me thinks they are worth the price. I don't see how we're ever going to create good middle-class jobs again unless our schools are far better –

which will require paying teachers enough to attract talented young men and women into our nation's classrooms (the law of supply and demand is not repealed at the schoolhouse door) and hiring more of them so that fewer children are in each room. How to afford this? Through a more progressive tax system. The take-home pay of CEOs, investment bankers, hedge fund managers, and celebrities has reached such astronomical heights that a higher tax on such pay seems unlikely to discourage talented people from pursuing these lines of work.[60] Finally, I'd decouple health care from employment, and use the tax savings – recall that employer-provided health care is a tax-free benefit – to give everyone access to no-frills health insurance. More on this later.

You might think differently about these issues – that is, the consumer-investor in you may strike a different balance with the citizen in you than *my* consumer-investor strikes with the citizen in me. The problem is that as a nation we rarely have this sort of discussion. Instead, our debates about economic change tend to occur between two warring camps representing the extreme positions: those who want the best consumer and investor deals, and those who want to preserve jobs and communities much as they are. Instead of finding ways to soften the blows, compensate the losers, or slow the pace of change – so the consumer in us can enjoy lower prices and better products, and the investor can enjoy higher returns, without wreaking too much damage on our values as citizens – we go into battle. Consumers and investors almost always win, but sometimes citizens get so riled up they temporarily put a stop to things – blocking a new trade agreement or blocking a Wal-Mart.

It's much the same when it comes to stricter environmental laws, more ambitious health and safety regulations, broader social insurance, and more potent rules governing international human rights. Because many of these would increase consumer prices or reduce investor returns, they're often politically difficult to achieve. But the material well-being of consumers or investors should not be the sole criterion. A dramatic cut in greenhouse gases seems worth the economic sacrifice if it's necessary to save the planet. By the same token, a case could be made that affordable health insurance is a basic common good. Or that human rights around the world are intrinsically important. I don't want American high-tech companies giving Chinese authorities tools to suppress free speech, for example, even if that means a small diminution in the value of my retirement earnings from Yahoo, Google, or Microsoft.

OUR DEMOCRACY as a whole seems incapable of having these debates, though we very much need them. Instead, citizen initiatives occur at the margin, often at the state or local level, and are killed off or whittled back without full public knowledge or discussion. California passes strict emissions controls for cars and then slugs it out in the federal courts. Maryland passes a law requiring Wal-Mart to spend 8 percent of its payroll on health care and a federal judge strikes it down. The Chicago City Council raises the minimum wage for its big-box retailers, but the proposal is vetoed by the mayor, who worries it will make Chicago less competitive.

Democracies abroad seem no more capable of hosting these debates. Wanting the great deals the global economy offers but reluctant to give up the job security they've traditionally enjoyed, Europeans are stymied. Their democracies are so paralyzed that Europeans often express their views as citizens through massive boycotts and strikes. By 2006, Germany had adopted new rules making it easier for employers to fire workers during the first two years of employment, but Chancellor Angela Merkel's efforts to further deregulate labor markets ran into a wall of opposition. Jacques Chirac floated a law allowing employers to fire workers under twenty-six years of age in their first two years of employment, but had to revoke it in response to public uproar. In Italy, Romano Prodi's left-of-center 'union' alliance eked out a narrow victory over Silvio Berlusconi, whose conservative reform agenda was frustrated. 'The old heartlands of the Eurozone are clogged by high unemployment and starved by low growth,' London's *Independent* editorialized, smugly, 'and yet the political systems of France, Germany and now Italy are failing to produce the necessary solutions.'[61] But Britain is suffering rising inequality and declining job security, and not even its phlegmatic democracy is deliberating meaningful solutions.

Japan is also moving toward supercapitalism but with a democracy too enfeebled to face its negative social consequences. China is surging toward supercapitalism without democracy at all – just demonstrations and riots that are put down by force. In October 2006, China's ruling elite pledged to bring 'social harmony' back to the nation by, among other things, narrowing the wealth gap and protecting the environment – but it remained unclear if and how China would accomplish either. In Mexico and parts of Latin America, democracies are not strong enough to spread prosperity and soften supercapitalism's harsher blows, which is breeding a reaction against it. Parts of the Muslim world are in outright revolt against the culture of supercapitalism in a fundamentalist backlash that's returning them to premodern times; democracy in these domains is still a vague aspiration, at best.

Why is it so hard for democracy to rise to the challenge supercapitalism poses? Why are citizen values barely represented in politics? Why is it so difficult to create a new, updated democratic capitalism? It is to these questions that we now turn.

CHAPTER FOUR

DEMOCRACY OVERWHELMED

A MERICANS ARE losing confidence in democracy, as are many of the inhabitants of other democracies. As I observed at the outset of this book, thirty-five years ago the vast majority of Americans thought our democratic government was run for the benefit of all the people. But over the intervening decades, that confidence has steadily declined. Now the vast majority thinks it is run by a few big interests looking out for themselves. Surveys done in other democracies show a similar pattern of declining trust and confidence in government.[1] What happened?

None of the conventional explanations, as noted, is persuasive. A more likely cause, in America and to a lesser but increasing extent elsewhere, is the expanding role of money in politics – especially money coming from large corporations.[2] As I shall argue, that money is a by-product of the very feature of supercapitalism that has led to its economic triumph – intensifying competition among firms for consumers and investors. That competition has spilled over into politics, as corporations have sought to gain competitive advantage through public policy. The perverse result has been to reduce the capacity of democracy to respond to citizens' concerns.

1

THERE IS little debate over what has happened. The ever-rising flood of corporate money into Washington and other capitals is apparent. The confusion is over why it has happened. An important clue is found by looking at when the escalation began.

Before the corporate money poured in, Washington was a rather seedy place – 'a city of Southern efficiency and Northern charm', as John F. Kennedy put it.[3] Even by the mid-1970s, when I worked there as a political appointee at the Federal Trade Commission, much of the downtown was still run-down. I'd take any lobbyist who insisted on lunch to a cockroach-infested sandwich shop on the other side of Pennsylvania Avenue, after which I would never see the lobbyist again. But when I returned to Washington in the 1990s, the town had been transformed. The sandwich shop was long gone; the avenue now glittered with the polished facades of refurbished hotels, fancy restaurants, and trendy bistros. The dazzle stretched from Georgetown to Capitol Hill – office complexes of glass, chrome, and polished wood; well-appointed condominiums with doormen who knew the names and needs of each inhabitant; hotels with marble-floored lobbies, thick rugs, soft music, and granite counters; restaurants with linen napkins, leather-bound menus, and heavy silverware, which served $75 steaks and offered $400 magnums of vintage French wine. Charlie Palmer Steak, at the base of Capitol Hill, featured a ten-thousand-bottle wine cellar. The Bistro Bis, attached to the Hotel George, offered lightly breaded, crisply fried frogs' legs and sweetbreads Zingara. The Palm, on 19th Street, offered more expensive fare, designed to impress even the most jaded public official.

The flow of money had inflated everything in its path – not only hotel and restaurant tabs, but the compensation of powerhouse Washington lawyers, lobbyists, and public relations professionals; the price of Washington real estate; even home prices in surrounding counties. By 2005, Washington's seven suburban counties were listed by the Census Bureau as among the nation's twenty with the highest per capita incomes.[4]

Political contributions to candidates for elective office escalated significantly after the 1970s. As the flow of money increased, each candidate became acutely aware of how much money might flow to a challenger – unless the candidate's own campaign chest was so large as to scare challengers off. As a result, the attentions of senators and representatives who at one time had been particularly solicitous toward local 'pluralistic' interest groups in their home states or districts – especially those that organized themselves into national federations – have become increasingly

FIGURE 4.1

THE GROWTH OF CAMPAIGN SPENDING, IN REAL 2000 DOLLARS

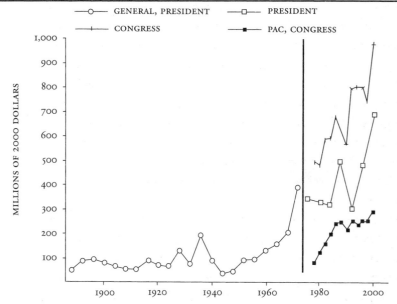

Source: Stephen Ansolabehere et al., 'Why Is There So Little Money in U.S. Politics?' Journal of Economic Perspectives *17, no. 1 (Winter 2003), pp. 105–30.*

focused on soliciting potential cash. And the largest single source of potential campaign money has been found in corporate political action committees (PACs), corporate executives, and corporate lobbyists who 'bundle' contributions from executives and their business associates.

Direct contributions are only the visible tips of vast influence-peddling icebergs that have also grown over the last several decades, as the following charts make clear.[5]

This is not merely a bloated and expensive form of the interest group pluralism that captivated political scientists in the middle of the twentieth century. Almost all of this vast increase in lobbying has been financed by businesses. Lobbying by nonbusiness groups has been paltry in comparison. For example, in 2005, the AFL-CIO had only six paid lobbyists on Capitol Hill. Of the one hundred organizations that spent the most on

FIGURE 4.2

NUMBER OF REGISTERED LOBBYISTS IN WASHINGTON, D.C.

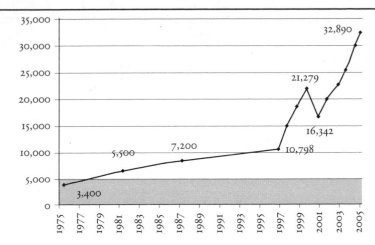

Sources: Congressional Budget Office, Political MoneyLine.com, Senate Office of Public Records. Note that registration requirements were strengthened in 1995.

FIGURE 4.3

MONEY SPENT ON LOBBYING (IN MILLIONS OF DOLLARS)

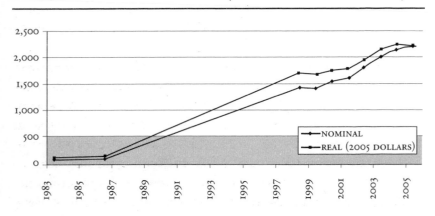

Sources: Congressional Budget Office, Senate Office of Public Records.

FIGURE 4.4

NUMBER OF LAWYERS REGISTERED WITH THE D.C. BAR

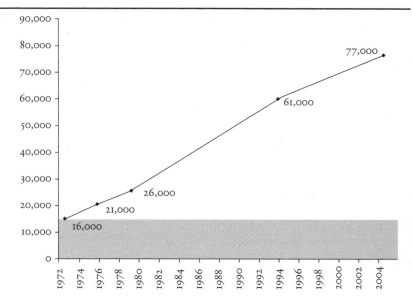

Source: *District of Columbia Bar Association.*

lobbying that year, the U.S. Chamber of Commerce headed the list; the AFL-CIO ranked seventy-fourth. Most public interest groups – advocating such causes as environmental protection, child welfare, or human rights – did not even make the list.[6]

Again, note that the escalation began in the 1970s. In 1950, fewer than one hundred companies maintained Washington offices. After the mid-1970s, the corporate lobbying business exploded. The National Association of Manufacturers moved its headquarters to the nation's capital in 1973, around the same time as the Business Roundtable – an association of chief executives who would travel to Washington to personally lobby – established itself there.[7] By the 1990s, more than 500 American companies maintained permanent offices in Washington, and employed some 61,000 lobbyists, including lawyers who lobbied on their behalf.[8] They were joined by corporate-sponsored foundations, centers, and institutes, staffed with their own policy experts and marketing personnel. To these were added companies specializing in advertising and marketing of public policies favored by one corporation or another.[9]

A similar tide of corporate lobbying has engulfed other global capitals in recent years, as supercapitalism has spread around the world. By 2005, Brussels – which houses the European Commission and other European Union administrative offices – was inhabited by some ten thousand lobbyists, mostly representing large global companies and industry groups.[10] Avenue de Cortenbergh today bears a striking resemblance to Washington's K Street.

2

SOME EXPLAIN this escalating flow of corporate money into politics by positing a deal between big business and the Republican Party that began with the election of Ronald Reagan and has continued through the administration of George W. Bush.[11] According to its supposed terms, big business would give Republicans enough money to guarantee their permanent majority status, in return for which Republicans would promote a resolutely pro-business agenda. Some saw the deal exemplified by the infamous 'K Street Project' during Bush's administration, in which House majority leader Tom DeLay and other Republican leaders pressured corporations and trade groups to hire only GOP lobbyists.

This explanation is too facile. It doesn't explain why corporate lobbying has increased around the world, for example. It also fails to account for the important fact that the increasing flow of corporate money into American politics has been largely bipartisan. By the time Democrats lost control of Congress in 1994, they had already become dependent on corporate money. 'Business has to deal with us whether they like it or not, because we're the majority,' crowed Democratic representative Tony Coelho, who, as head of the Democratic Congressional Campaign Committee in the 1980s, commenced a shakedown of corporate America. Coelho aggressively sought, and finally achieved, a rough parity with Republicans in contributions from corporate campaign coffers. In 1990, for example, the trucking industry divided $1.51 million in contributions in exactly equal installments to Democrats and Republicans, according to the Center for Responsive Politics. The balance persisted until the Republican takeover of 1994, and was restored after the Democratic victories of 2006.[12] (According to Political Money Line, an organization that tracks political giving, PACs gave 56.6 percent of their contributions to Democrats in the first quarter of 2007.)[13] Of course, Coehlo's assumed dependence of corporations on the Democratic Congress also caused Democrats to become dependent on corporate largesse – as became evident when, months before their 1994 trouncing, many Democrats voted against Bill Clinton's health care plan because their corporate sponsors were against it.

Despite that erstwhile plan, the Clinton administration – of which I am proud to have been a part – was one of the most pro-business administrations in American history. In his first two years in office, when Democrats controlled both houses of Congress, Clinton pushed for enactment of the North American Free Trade Agreement, followed by the establishment of the World Trade Organization – two items of central importance to big business. He also committed himself to reducing the federal budget deficit, as Wall Street's bond traders wished. Business never had it so good. Corporate profits exploded, the stock market surged, CEO compensation went into the stratosphere.

These facts alone do not suggest Clinton or any member of his administration was especially beholden to big business or that business dictated Clinton's agenda. But it is notable how much corporate money poured into Clinton's reelection campaign and into the Democratic National Committee, and how assiduously Clinton courted business in pursuit of it. Clinton's generous hospitality toward CEOs who wished to overnight in the Lincoln Bedroom confirmed the old adage that the White House is the only hotel where it's the guests who leave the mint on the pillow. Money guaranteed access, although not necessarily results. Roger Tamraz, an oil tycoon, gave the Democratic National Committee $300,000 in order to meet with Clinton, which prompted Republican senator Fred Thompson to ask Tamraz, during congressional hearings on campaign finance reform, whether he thought he had 'a constitutional right to have your business deal considered personally by the president of the United States'. Tamraz responded with remarkable candor: 'Senator,

I go to the outer limits. Why not? You set the rules and we're following. This is politics as usual.'[14]

The bipartisanship of corporate money in recent years has shaped the careers of many Democrats who, after serving in Washington, have found lucrative work in the service of large corporations. Once it became apparent that Democrats would triumph in the midterm elections of 2006, the K Street Project effectively died. Anticipating Democratic gains months before the election, one of Washington's major law and lobbying firms, DLA Piper, transferred direction of its government affairs practice from Republican Thomas F. O'Neil III to Democrat James Blanchard, a former governor and congressman from Michigan. 'Being a Democrat didn't hurt me, that's for sure,' Blanchard told the *Washington Post.* 'This is going to be a big Democratic year.'[15] Top Democratic staffers for even middle-ranking members of the House were suddenly in great demand.

Bipartisanship in lobbying has become a practical necessity for large corporations because getting a majority of Congress to support a particular policy typically requires bipartisan persuasion. After Senate Democratic minority leader Tom Daschle was defeated for reelection in 2004, he was recruited to the lobbying firm of Alston & Bird by the former Republican majority leader Bob Dole. 'He's got a lot of friends in the Senate, and I've got a lot of friends in the Senate,' quipped Dole. 'And combined, we might have fifty-one.'[16]

Bipartisan lobbying firms serve rosters of blue-chip corporate clients. To push the Bush administration's Medicare drug benefit bill on Capitol Hill, the pharmaceutical manufacturers hired Democratic lobbyists Vic Fazio, a former Democratic congressman; David Beier, who had been a chief domestic policy adviser to Al Gore; and Joel Johnson, a former top aide to President Clinton and Senator Daschle.[17] To push their side, the generic drug manufacturers hired Chris Jennings, who had helped devise Clinton's unlamented health plan, and former Republican aide Mark Isakowitz, who had helped defeat the Clinton plan. Similarly, in 1998, when tobacco companies wanted to sell Congress the settlement they had reached with state attorneys general over tobacco health claims, they turned for help to both Republican and Democratic lobbyists, including former Gore aide Peter Knight, former Democratic governor Ann Richards, and George Mitchell, former Democratic Senate majority leader.

While nonbusiness interests have better access to power under Democratically controlled government than under Republican, businesses have excellent access under both. Upon leaving office, more than half of the senior officials of the Clinton administration became corporate lobbyists. Clinton's first legislative director left his post after less than a year to become chairman of Hill & Knowlton Worldwide. Clinton's deputy chief of staff departed in less than a year to run the U.S. Telephone Association. According to the Center for Public Integrity, between 1998 and 2004 more than 2,200 former high-ranking federal officials, from both Republican and Democratic administrations, registered as federal lobbyists, as did over 200 former members of Congress.[18] By 2003, more than half the total number of former members of Congress who were registered lobbyists had served as Democrats. Almost all were lobbying for large corporations.

The pertinent comparison is not between Democrats and Republicans, but between people who served in Washington decades ago and those who served more recently. In the 1970s, only about 3 percent of retiring members of Congress went on to become Washington lobbyists. By 2005, more than 30 percent of retiring members turned to Washington lobbying – both Republicans and Democrats. More former officials and aides have turned to lobbying not because they have fewer qualms than their predecessors about making money off contacts and experience gained during their government service but because the financial rewards from lobbying have grown considerably larger. Just like restaurant tabs and real estate prices, lobbying fees have escalated due to the large wave of corporate money flowing into Washington. The amount lobbyists charge for new clients rose from about $20,000 a month in 1995 to $40,000 a month in 2005. By 2006, starting salaries for well-connected congressional or White House staffers eager to move to K Street had ballooned to about $500,000 a year. Former chairmen of congressional committees and subcommittees were fetching up to $2 million a year to influence legislation in their former committees.

Relations have been strained between congressional Republicans and Democrats in recent years, especially over the so-called culture wars – abortion, gay marriage, stem cell research, and the Pledge of Allegiance – and over foreign policy. These items tend to make the headlines because they engage the public's attention, as passionate conflicts among public figures will do. But they do not account for most of the day-to-day work of Congress, to which corporate money buys access regardless of party.

ANOTHER THEORY attributes this increasing flow to the increasing size and scope of the federal government. 'There is $2.6 trillion spent in Washington, with the authority to regulate everything in your life,' said former Republican house speaker Newt Gingrich. 'Guess what? People will spend unheard-of amounts of money to influence that. The underlying problems are big government and big money.'[19]

This view is not borne out by the facts, either. The largest increases in postwar public spending at all levels of government occurred between 1947 and 1973, during the Not Quite Golden Age. As a percentage of the total economy, federal outlays peaked in 1983 at around 24 percent, and then declined steadily to under 20 percent. Meanwhile, more and more federal spending has gone to Social Security, Medicare, and national defense. Lobbyists do swarm over these. But nondefense discretionary outlays – which you'd expect most lobbying to focus on, because appropriations vary year by year on them – peaked in 1980, at 5.2 percent of the national economy, and have declined since then.[20] Due to the overall growth of the economy, federal spending has still increased considerably. But the flow of corporate money into Washington has escalated faster.

This escalation cannot be explained by the growth of regulation. As we've seen, most major economic regulations have been repealed or reduced over the last forty years. As measured by the number of final or proposed rules published in the Federal Register, regulation declined after 1980.

Nor, finally, can the escalation of corporate money into politics be explained by the need of corporations to confront the countervailing

FIGURE 4.5

OUTLAYS BY BUDGET ENFORCEMENT ACT CATEGORY, 1962–2011

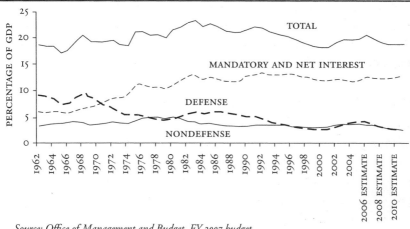

Source: *Office of Management and Budget, FY 2007 budget.*

power of unions. As we have seen, union strength has declined steadily over the last several decades, and its lobbying presence on Capitol Hill is now barely visible relative to the growing presence of corporate lobbyists.

A THIRD THEORY attributes the escalating flow of corporate money into politics to a conspiracy of big business and Wall Street seeking to usurp the machinery of government and co-opt both political parties. Their goal, in this view, is to keep median wages down, avoid costly regulation, reduce taxes on the wealthy, exploit the developing world, and thereby enrich themselves at the expense of everyone else. 'America's bipartisan governing class protects its privileged clients while abandoning the rest of us to an unregulated, and therefore brutal and merciless, global market,' writes Jeff Faux, founder and former president of the Economic Policy Institute. Big business and government are engaged in 'class warfare' against average working people, says Lou Dobbs, a news anchor for CNN.[21]

However attractive this conspiratorial view may be, it also collapses in the face of the facts. Far from conspiring with one another, firms have

FIGURE 4.6

NUMBER OF DOCUMENTS PUBLISHED
IN THE FEDERAL REGISTER, 1976–2004

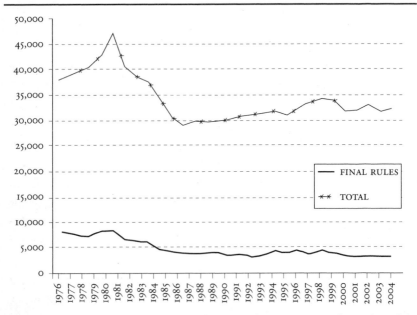

Source: Clyde Wayne Crews, Ten Thousand Commandments: An Annual Snapshot of the Regulatory State, *Competitive Enterprise Institute, June 30, 2005, at http://www.cei.org/pdf/4645.pdf.*

become steadily more competitive with one another. As I'll show in the following pages, this competition has carried over into politics. The fights that actually preoccupy Congress day by day, which consume weeks or months of the time of congressional staffers, and which are often most hotly contested by squadrons of Washington lobbyists and public relations professionals, are typically contests between competing companies or sectors of an industry or, occasionally, competing industries.

The citizen in us has a more difficult time being heard now in Washington and other world capitals not because big business has become more powerfully monolithic but for the opposite reason – because competition among businesses has grown more cutthroat. Companies have entered politics to gain or keep a competitive advantage over their business rivals. The result has been a clamor of competing business interests – a cacophony so loud as to almost drown out any serious deliberation over the public good.

3

THE EXPLANATION for what has happened is the structural shift in the economy, beginning in the 1970s, toward far more intense competition for consumers and investors. Supercapitalism has not stopped at the artificial boundary separating economics from politics. The goal of the modern corporation – goaded by consumers and investors – is to do whatever is necessary to gain competitive advantage. That includes entering any battleground where such gains can be made. Washington – and other capital cities around the world where public policies are devised – have become competitive battlegrounds because public policies often help some companies or industries while putting rivals at a comparative disadvantage.[22]

The flow of corporate money into Washington has accelerated over the last several decades because of supply and demand. The supply of senators, representatives, cabinet members, and senior White House staffers has not substantially increased over this period of time. But the demands of corporations seeking to influence the policy process have grown as competition among them has intensified. It has been like an arms race: The more one competitor pays for access, the more its rivals must pay in order to counter its influence.

Consider one of the most recent additions to the ranks of Washington powerhouses, Google. Until it went public in August 2004, the company took pride in being a maverick outsider in the world of Internet-related software – never venturing inside the Beltway. But once it became a multibillion-dollar public company, it needed to become part of the Washington establishment. In 2005, Google spent more than $500,000 hiring lobbying firms and consultants, and opened its own office complex in Washington's Penn Quarter. Its executives and lobbyists began raising millions of dollars for political campaigns. 'It's been the growth of Google as a company and as a presence in the industry that has prompted our engagement in Washington,' says office director Alan Davidson. 'They are brilliant engineers,' says Lauren Maddox, of the lobbying firm Podesta Mattoon, which Google hired. But, Maddox adds, 'they are not politicians.'23 Podesta Mattoon is a bipartisan influence peddler, exactly what Google needs. Anthony Podesta is a longtime Democrat, and brother of John Podesta, formerly Bill Clinton's chief of staff. His partner, Daniel Mattoon, is a close friend of former Republican speaker Dennis Hastert. Maddox is a former top aide to Newt Gingrich.

Google had no choice. Yahoo, Microsoft, and a gaggle of telecom companies were already well represented in Washington. In 2005 alone, Microsoft spent almost $9 million on lobbying, and its executives donated millions more to politicians on both sides of the aisle. Yahoo spent $1.6 million, according to filings compiled by the Center for Responsive Politics. Microsoft and Google both had economic stakes on a range of policy issues, especially concerning antitrust, intellectual property, and international trade. The outcomes could tip the competitive balance in favor of or against Google, with large financial consequences. Google also began pouring money into Brussels, where Europeans are debating many of these same issues, and where Microsoft and Yahoo were also well entrenched.

One telling example of why Google had to enter the Washington fray: In 2006, Microsoft, with about 80 percent of the Internet browser market, was planning to introduce a new browser – Internet Explorer 7 – featuring a search box that takes users to Microsoft's new search service. Obviously, Google wanted consumers to be able to go directly to the Google search engine when they started up the browser. Just as obviously, Microsoft didn't want them to have this choice. Microsoft argued it would only confuse consumers, but Microsoft's real goal was to draw consumers away from Google's search engine and toward its own.

In April 2006, Google raised its concern with the Justice Department and with the European Commission, deploying its new team of Washington lobbyists and lawyers to show the antitrust authorities it meant business, and simultaneously demonstrating to Microsoft how seriously it took Microsoft's challenge. The underlying strategic question

Google posed to Microsoft by this display was this: How much would Microsoft be willing to pay in legal fees, court costs, and lobbying expenses in order to market an Internet Explorer 7 that excluded Google? Microsoft had been burned before by antitrust. Google was a much more formidable opponent than browser pioneer Netscape had been years before, when Microsoft moved to squeeze it out of the browser market – leading eventually to a federal court ruling that Microsoft repeatedly violated antitrust laws, and a settlement with the Justice Department. Google could put up a far more expensive and presumably even more effective fight.

Microsoft had started pouring money into Washington in 1996, when the Justice Department first issued its antitrust complaint against the company. Microsoft also began investing in Brussels, where the European officials were also charging the company with antitrust violations. Before then, Bill Gates's storied indifference to politics had kept the computer maker out of Washington and Brussels. But soon thereafter, Microsoft executives began making large campaign contributions to Democrats and Republicans – $621,000 in the first half of 1999 alone. Microsoft also hired nine Washington lobbying firms along with ten lobbyists to staff its own Washington office, and a slew of public relations professionals. Within months its lobbyists were urging Congress to deny the Justice Department's antitrust division a requested 16 percent budget hike for 2000, needed to keep up with the litigation. The effort failed – indeed, news of it made Microsoft appear just the sort of behemoth that the antitrust laws were designed to curb – but the lobbyists did succeed on another front. Congress reduced export curbs on encryption software of the sort Microsoft was selling, helping Microsoft's bottom line that year.[24]

After Judge Thomas P. Jackson ruled against Microsoft, denouncing it as a predatory monopolist, the firm unleashed its Washington lobbyists and public relations specialists on anyone who might influence the antitrust division in coming up with a suggested remedy. Two days after the ruling, the media carried photographs of Bill Clinton draping his arm around Bill Gates's shoulders and praising his charitable giving – a public relations coup characterized by *BusinessWeek* as 'an uncomfortable sight for [Justice Department antitrust chief] Joel Klein'.[25]

IBM, Oracle, and Sun Microsystems all supported the Justice

Department's case against Microsoft, as they did the European Commission's. Oracle even went so far as to hire a Washington-based private investigative firm, which found evidence that Microsoft had paid for a New York University study claiming the antitrust case against it damaged state pension funds, and also secretly had paid for full-page ads in major American newspapers defending the company and signed by 240 academics. Oracle's private investigation became public when its detectives bribed some janitors in an effort to try to sift through trash that might contain incriminating evidence. In response, Microsoft issued an angry statement claiming that 'Microsoft's competitors have engaged in an ongoing campaign to promote government intervention'. Oracle's CEO, Larry Ellison, insisted Oracle's investigation was a 'public service'.[26]

Google, Microsoft, Yahoo, IBM, Sun, and Oracle are sending tens of millions of dollars to Washington annually because they understand that, in the words of lobbyist Lauren Maddox, 'the policy process is an extension of the market battlefield'.[27] These companies are motivated in politics by the same intensifying competition that moves them to provide ever-better products and services in the market. If they succeed, their profits increase, their share prices rise, and their top executives make lots of money and earn kudos from Wall Street and the business media. If they fail, their profits drop and their share prices plummet, and their top executives may lose their jobs (although with generous severance). And they are pumping more and more money into Washington because the arms race with their rivals requires it.

Wal-Mart had no full-time representative in Washington before 1999, and only a tiny political action committee, which contributed just $148,250 in 1998. Former Arkansas senator Dale Bumpers claims that during the twenty-four years he served in the U.S. Senate, he had 'no recollection' of Wal-Mart ever lobbying him on a piece of legislation. 'They were simply not tuned into what was going on in Washington,' he says. 'They had a culture there that just didn't include lobbying and directing the way legislation was handled.'[28] According to Blanche Lincoln, an Arkansas Democrat who replaced Bumpers in the Senate, lawmakers would have to call Wal-Mart's Bentonville offices to warn them about legislation that might hurt the company. 'I encouraged them to have some sort of Washington presence,' she says, 'because I thought it was important for them to be able to tell their story to more than just me and the rest of the Arkansas delegation.'

Then came Wal-Mart's equivalent of Microsoft's antitrust shock. Wal-Mart had long wanted to get into the banking business, figuring its millions of consumers would welcome the convenience of banking at Wal-Mart, and the company could make lots of money from banking fees. Wal-Mart hoped to use a loophole in a federal law that generally barred commercial companies from owning banks but exempted stand-alone savings and loans. In 1999, Wal-Mart found a savings and loan in Broken Arrow, Oklahoma, that seemed the perfect vehicle. But the banking industry had been following Wal-Mart's moves carefully. When Wal-Mart sought to buy the bank, the industry unleashed a team of lobbyists on Congress, and Congress abruptly pulled the loophole closed.

It was a lesson Wal-Mart would not forget. Almost immediately, Wal-Mart's PAC increased contributions to House members, senators, and presidential candidates, becoming one of the largest PACs in America. It contributed $2.2 million in the presidential election year of 2004. Although Wal-Mart has donated most heavily to Republicans, it gave Democrats nearly 30 percent of its PAC dollars in the 2006 election cycle. 'We decided ... to do a better job building relationships and political support on both sides of the aisle, but in particular with Democrats,' said Lee Culpepper, head of Wal-Mart's Washington lobbying efforts. Wal-Mart also invested several million dollars to set up its own lobbying shop in Washington and hired a platoon of public relations specialists. 'They have become very sophisticated,' said Ron Ence, vice president of the Independent Community Bankers of America, speaking of Wal-Mart's newly developed Washington clout. '[T]hey are seen at every PAC event and they are walking the halls.'[29]

In July 2005, Wal-Mart requested from the Federal Deposit Insurance Corporation and Utah banking regulators permission to purchase a so-called industrial loan company, which under federal and Utah laws could be controlled by a commercial company. An industrial loan company wasn't a loophole directly into banking, but it was a start. Wal-Mart assured regulators it would be used only to process the credit card purchases of Wal-Mart customers. Yet Wal-Mart's banking rivals feared it could be a Trojan horse for Wal-Mart to enter small-town and suburban banking. Lobbyists representing banks, convenience stores, grocers, and real estate agents descended on the House and Senate banking committees, and flooded the FDIC with more than a thousand complaints requesting that the agency deny Wal-Mart's application. In November 2005, the American Bankers Association, which represents both large and small banks, warned its four thousand members that a law was needed to bar nonfinancial firms, including Wal-Mart, from owning a bank. Wal-Mart's 'reach and influence would be significant,' wrote the association's president. 'Now is the time to act.'[30]

Both sides couched their arguments in terms of the public interest – opponents warning that Wal-Mart's bank would exploit the poor, Wal-Mart arguing its move would lower fees in an industry needing more competition – but the public interest was not the reason for the battle. It was a battle for competitive advantage. In July 2006, the FDIC issued an unprecedented moratorium on all applications for industrial loan banks, thereby freezing Wal-Mart's effort. Ultimately, Wal-Mart withdrew. The bankers won.

4

LIKE THE FIGHT over Wal-Mart's interest in banking, so many of the battles that on the surface seem to concern public policy are, on closer inspection, matters of mundane competitive advantage in pursuit of corporate profit. Almost any seemingly neutral law or regulation creates corporate winners and losers because small differences in the costs of complying can tip the balance. Hence, increasingly in Washington and in other major capitals, the 'stakeholders' who demand to be consulted before legislation is enacted or regulations promulgated are the companies or industries whose competitive positions will be affected by a pending policy, rather than nonbusiness stakeholders such as labor unions, environmentalists, and community groups.

Let's examine closely several matters that preoccupied the 109th Congress, whose sessions extended from 2004 through 2006, and you will see the pattern. Republicans controlled Congress in this interval, but Democrats were deeply involved in most of the following controversies. In truth, party affiliation didn't much matter. Typically, Republicans and Democrats could be found on either side of these battles.

One of the more contentious issues was whether to relax Congress's long-standing ban on oil drilling offshore, especially off the California coast and in the wide swath of the eastern Gulf of Mexico. Not surprisingly, the coalition in favor of doing so included major oil companies, the American Gas Association, and manufacturing groups hard hit by rising fuel costs. But the most powerful opposition did not come from environmental groups, as you might have expected. Environmental groups did oppose the proposal, but their views did not carry much weight; environmentalists had neither the lobbying heft nor the money to play a major role, and their troops were spread so thin over so many issues that they were almost absent from this battlefield. The opposition was led by the tourist industry. Major hotel and restaurant chains feared that an oil spill might damage Florida's pristine beaches and California's dramatic coastline, thereby costing them billions of dollars. Two Republican governors, Jeb Bush of Florida and Arnold Schwarzenegger of California, actively lobbied against the measure. Many representatives from districts on the Gulf were against it. The resulting legislation limited drilling in such a way as to minimize the possible negative effects on tourism.

Even battles that seem to be over the social or 'cultural' agenda can be misleading. In October 2006, Congress passed legislation barring credit card payments for Internet betting – which as a practical matter placed a ban on all online gambling. The ostensible purpose of the legislation was to reduce the public's vulnerability to what is considered an immoral or addictive activity. But the initiative was actually spearheaded by gambling casinos – of which there are more than nine hundred in the United States – which saw the huge growth in online gambling as a potential threat to their profits but wanted their own operations to remain unrestricted. The easier it is to gamble online, obviously, the less incentive to drive several hundred miles to the nearest casino. The legislation was a great victory for the American Gaming Association, which represents the biggest casino operators. As the bill moved through the House, lobbyists for the $1.5 billion racetrack betting industry also did well, carving out an exemption (they had contributed more than $3 million to lawmakers since 2000).[31] Lobbyists for Major League Baseball made sure the bill did not restrict fantasy sports games, which baseball credits in part for its resurgent popularity. And lobbyists for convenience store chains and for the states carefully steered the bill away from lottery tickets.

The big losers were online gambling companies, most of which are based abroad. Several are public companies, listed on the London Stock Exchange, whose investors have included Goldman Sachs and mutual funds affiliated with Fidelity Investments, so some American investors lost, too. It seems doubtful that the legislation will have any effect on the amount of gambling Americans engage in. That was a subterfuge. Its real purpose was to increase the profits on certain kinds of gambling, thereby reducing profits associated with other kinds.

Another hotly contested issue during the session was whether the price of natural gas was being manipulated and what to do about it. Late in 2005, the House passed a bill authorizing the Commodity Futures Trading Commission (CFTC) to investigate gas prices, and requiring gas producers and sellers to keep price records and imposing stiff penalties for violations. It sounded like a battle pitting little old New Englanders and Minnesotans who relied on natural gas to heat their homes against greedy energy companies. But the bill was actually the handiwork of lobbyists representing the Industrial Energy Consumers of America – a coalition of corporations that consume gas – mostly large manufacturers and fertilizer producers. They were upset that shortages of natural gas in 2005 opened the market to speculators.

You might think the bill's opponents would be oil and gas companies, but in fact the loudest opposition came from financial speculators who were making bundles of money in that unstable gas market. They were backed by the financial services lobby. 'We'll do whatever we have to do to make sure [this provision] won't pass,' said Robert Pickel, executive director of the International Swaps and Derivatives Association, which was joined by the Bond Market Association, the Securities Industry Association, and the Futures Industries Association. All argued that giving the CFTC this authority would just cause trading businesses to move to less-regulated foreign markets.[32] In the end, the bill went nowhere.

There was also a congressional debate over whether foreigners should be able to gain control of American airline carriers. Sounds like an issue of broad public interest, doesn't it? What are the national security implications? What would happen to American jobs in the airline industry? In fact, the battle was mainly between two sets of airline lobbyists. United Airlines was in favor of the measure, most likely because it was in bankruptcy reorganization at the time and needed overseas capital to help emerge from it. Opposing the measure was Continental Airlines, whose financial picture was so good it didn't need foreign capital, and stood to gain customers and profits if United went out of business.[33] Airline unions joined with Continental in opposition. In the end, Continental won.

Continental's lobbyists, however, did lose a big one. This was the battle over whether companies should set aside enough money to fully fund their pension plans. Here again, it sounded like an issue of broad public interest, but it really boiled down to a competitive contest between companies that would be affected differently by whatever rule emerged. Airline lobbyists got a special provision giving carriers ten years to get their pension plans in order, while most industries got only seven. This was because United and US Airways had given up on their pension plans when they were in bankruptcy – dumping them on the government's Pension Benefit Guarantee Corporation – and other airlines threatened to do the same thing unless they got the extra years. But lobbyists for Delta and Northwest managed to squeeze in another provision that gave a *seventeen*-year pass to any carrier that froze its pension benefits and closed its plan to new employees. Delta and Northwest had already done this while in bankruptcy, so they'd get the seventeen-year break automatically. But because Continental was flush with cash, its unions would never agree to a freeze; Continental will have to pony up the cash much sooner than its rivals.[34]

Even in congressional fights where you might expect organized labor to be the dominant adversary and the issues of jobs and wages to be front and center – as in the 2005 contest over whether Congress should ratify the Central American Free Trade Agreement (CAFTA) – the actual battle lines run between different segments of industry. In this case, among the loudest voices in opposition was the American Manufacturing Trade Action Coalition and the National Council of Textile Organizations – two groups of domestic manufacturers who still retain a competitive edge in making textiles in the United States but worry that their slim advantage will be whittled away by trade agreements. The Coalition was co-chaired by Roger Milliken, chairman of Milliken & Company, a large privately held textile and chemical manufacturer headquartered in Spartanburg, South Carolina. Milliken and his allies poured money and lobbying strength into battling CAFTA, which, despite Republican control over the House and Senate and a Republican president, ended in one of the closest trade votes in recent history: It passed by just two votes in the House and ten in the Senate.

More recently, the two groups fought off a bill that would have allowed Haiti to use more foreign-made fabric in its clothing exports, such as cheap cloth from China, while still qualifying for duty-free access to the American market. Sixteen southern Republican members of Congress rallied to the cause. And the industry got White House agreement to closely monitor imports from Vietnam, and impose anti-dumping duties on any imports that cause injury to the domestic industry. On the losing side of the battle was the U.S. Association of Importers of Textiles and Apparel, representing J. C. Penney Company and other large retailers wanting access to cheaper imported goods.[35]

COMPANIES OR COALITIONS typically portray themselves as representing the broad public interest when all they really represent is a competitive position relative to their rivals. One big brawl of 2006 concerned implementation of the 2003 Medicare drug benefit. To the public, the issue was whether and how seniors would get better deals on drugs. But to the army of corporate lobbyists brought into the fray, it was a contest over which drug companies' products would be covered, and whether brand-name drug companies or their generic drug rivals would predominate. And the battle continued after the bill was signed into law, as Medicare officials tried to figure out how to implement it. For example, the bill required Medicare to cover 'substantially all' antidepressants but left to Medicare officials which antidepressants should be included. When the officials decided not to cover Lexapro, a drug widely prescribed for depression among the elderly, Forest Laboratories, its manufacturer, hired a team of lobbyists to push them to reverse their decision. Forest Labs garnered letters of support from members of Congress and mobilized mental health advocates. Makers of antidepressants already covered lobbied Medicare officials against reversing course. In the end, Forest Labs won.

Generic drug companies urged Medicare officials to back an electronic prescription system that would automatically remind doctors when generics could be used. Brand-name drug manufacturers lobbied against the system. Medicare sided with the generics. Moody's Investors Service – carefully monitoring this fight – advised its clients the result would mean lower profits for the brand-name makers. 'We expect the implications will become negative,' Moody's analyst wrote, dryly, 'as greater leverage of payers may require drug companies to offer larger discounts and rebates or face steerage away from their products toward lower cost drugs on the formulary.'[36]

In many battles, the hostilities can involve one government body after another as lobbyists and lawyers for competing sides jockey for advantage. If they lose in one house of Congress, they might be able to win in the other and then prevail in conference committee. If they lose in conference, they might be able to regain ground in the White House, which could threaten a veto unless Congress reconsiders. If they still lose, they might recoup in the department or agency charged with implementing the law. If they can't make headway there, they can go back to their allies in Congress in order to pressure the department or agency, or seek an advantageous amendment on the agency's next appropriation bill. Such battles can rage on for years.

The debate over the meaning of the word 'organic' on a food label offers a case in point. Although by 2006 organic food was still a relatively small

$12 billion niche in the $500 billion food industry, its sales were growing 20 percent annually, prompting even Wal-Mart's Lee Scott, Jr., to crow to shareholders, 'We are particularly excited about organic food, the fastest-growing category in all food'. The battle wasn't between small, crunchy Vermont farmers and giant greedy agribusiness; it was between two big sectors of agribusiness. Many organics were produced by large businesses like Cascadian Farm in Washington state, which, in 1999, became a subsidiary of General Mills.[37] On the other side were more traditional food processors, like Kraft, and conventional growers of corn, soybeans, and other fruits and vegetables.

The battle dated back to 1990 when farmers who began using non-synthetic dyes and pesticides in response to consumer demand for more natural foods petitioned the Department of Agriculture to certify their produce as 'organic'. The more traditional segment of agribusiness then lobbied for a looser standard so they could use the increasingly popular 'organic' label, too. When Agriculture caved in to the lower standard, the first group, by now organized into a coalition called the Organic Consumers Association, filed a lawsuit to force Agriculture to go back to its original one. As in most political-economic wars, there were many battles. After a federal judge agreed with the Organic Consumers Association and ordered Agriculture to reinstate its first standard, the second group – who by now were calling themselves, somewhat misleadingly, the Organic Trade Association – slipped an amendment into the department's fiscal 2006 budget, giving it authority to allow conventionally grown corn, soybean oil, tomatoes, and other ingredients into 'organic' food when purer versions were not 'commercially available'.

It became a legislative brawl because the economic stakes were high, although the public had little idea the fight was going on. Lobbyists from both sides descended on key members of Congress and their aides. Charles Sweat, CEO of Earthbound Farm, America's largest grower of the higher-standard organic produce, claimed the amendment would allow any company that couldn't make the grade because it didn't want to pay the higher cost of nonsynthetic ingredients to 'go to the Secretary and claim they need an exemption'.[38] Nonetheless, the amendment passed. It didn't hurt that one of the lobbyists for Kraft, pushing for the amendment, was Abigail Blunt, wife of Representative Roy Blunt, Republican of Missouri, who became the interim House majority leader after Tom DeLay resigned.

The organic wars spread to milk. By the mid-2000s, 'organic' milk was in such demand it sold for up to twice the price of regular milk. According to Agriculture Department regulations, in order to be called 'organic milk', dairy cows that produce it must have 'access to pasture'. But the department didn't define precisely what it meant by this, opening the way for a battle between dairies with lots of pasture for the cows and more industrial-type dairies with very little. (Wal-Mart bought much of its 'organic' milk from giant four-thousand-cow dairies with limited pasture.) Lobbyists for pasture-abundant dairies filed a petition with the department, charging that the industrial dairies cram too many cows into confined areas where most don't graze on pasture but consume high-grain diets. The industrial dairies countered that despite the relative lack of pasture, their cows were 'very healthy and happy'. Lobbyists for both sides pressured members of Congress, in turn, to push Agriculture Department officials.[39] At this writing, the dispute remains unresolved.

As a result of all this lobbying, many of the nation's major behind-the-scenes clashes over regulations – contests that sometimes take years to resolve, often involving the federal courts – result in even more detailed regulations that set out the definitions of certain terms, such as 'access to pasture' or 'substantially all' antidepressants. Conservative ideologues fulminate over the number of regulations (which, as has been pointed out, have actually declined since 1980) without acknowledging that a large portion of them are put on the books because corporate lobbyists and lawyers have gone into battle for them.

In the Not Quite Golden Age, when competition was more limited, there was no reason for these sorts of brawls. AT&T, for example, had a virtual monopoly. Under supercapitalism, though, telecommunications is a wide-open space in which AT&T and other companies compete with cable companies, satellite companies, and Internet companies – all of which are entering or being invaded by other 'content' companies providing entertainment, retail services, search services, and information services.

These rivalries continuously spill over into politics. In 2006, phone and cable companies wanted to charge higher Internet access fees to large providers of Internet content like eBay, Google, and Yahoo, and the providers fought back. In the ensuing battle, both sides sought to portray themselves as representing the public interest – phone and cable companies argued they needed higher fees in order to enlarge the capacity of their systems to handle all the Internet traffic and didn't want to impose the fees on ordinary users; eBay, Google, and Yahoo argued the Internet should be available on an equal basis to anyone who wanted to post content. The latter sought legislation – on the principle cunningly termed 'net neutrality' – that would bar phone and cable companies from imposing higher fees. The phone and cable companies sought to block the legislation, on the principle that government should keep its hands off the Internet. In 2006 alone, the two sides spent $50 million on lobbying and advertising. The war got particularly nasty and unusually public when phone companies ran advertisements attacking Google. This battle, like so many others, would continue for many years, in one form or another.

Although on the same side over 'net neutrality', phone and cable companies squared off on whether phone companies could offer television programming in direct competition with cable operators. The cable operators thought they could block the phone companies by relying on the grassroots legislative power of more than thirty thousand local authorities who depended on cable revenues (typically around 5 percent of cable sales). But in June 2006, phone lobbyists succeeded in having a bill introduced in the House that would put the decision in the hands of the Federal Communications Commission, where the phone companies were confident they could prevail. They were right: Six months later, in December 2006, the FCC ruled that telephone companies could offer TV programming. The cable operators vowed to contest that ruling in federal court. Meanwhile, the phone companies were busily lobbying state legislators for such permission, in order to circumvent the local authorities. These hostilities engaged virtually every major lobbying firm in Washington, representing not only phone and cable but also software and high-tech companies – all of whom were multimillion-dollar contributors to congressional campaigns. This war, too, promises to consume huge amounts of time and energy in the coming years.

It is not unusual for corporate coalitions assembled for one legislative or regulatory brawl to come apart over another, as did phone and cable. The Bush administration had cobbled together a six-thousand-member corporate coalition to back the permanent extension of its 2001 and 2003 tax cuts, but the coalition began falling apart almost immediately, as different groups of companies pushed different priorities. High-tech companies wanted the research and development tax credit extended; others, less dependent on R&D, wanted the emphasis on capital gains tax cuts. When lobbyists for high-tech companies began breaking off from the coalition and freelancing on their own, the White House criticized them publicly for not being team players.[40] But even among high-tech companies there were different views about what the R&D tax credit should cover, depending on the intensity and type of research companies specialized in doing. One of the biggest challenges faced by any trade association is to keep its members in line over legislation that's likely to affect them differently.

Of course, such large armies of corporate lobbyists can coalesce to kill initiatives that would impose large costs on an entire industry or sector of the economy. This happened in the 109th Congress, for example, when environmentalists wanted utilities to use expensive scrubbers when retrofitting their facilities; when public health and human rights advocates wanted pharmaceutical companies to give up patent protections on vital drugs sold in poor nations; and when food safety advocates succeeded in raising standards in a few states, prompting the food industry to seek milder congressional legislation that would preempt the states. But the main reason these armies exist is not because of any imminent threat of public interest legislation welling up from citizens; it is because every major company or sector seeks to gain competitive advantage over another, or to avoid being put at a competitive disadvantage. A potential new cost on one industry or sector of the economy (utilities, pharmaceuticals, food) puts it at a competitive disadvantage relative to other industries or sectors.

As a result, citizens' voices are drowned out. Consumers and investors, as a group, don't come out ahead, either. Unlike competition in the marketplace, political competition doesn't lead to better or cheaper products or services, or to higher returns. It leads to new laws and regulations that typically favor whichever side is more politically potent. Some consumers or investors win, others lose.

5

THE CORPORATE takeover of politics also affects how the public understands the issues of the day. Part of the task of lobbying is to provide evidence of the greater wisdom of your point of view, which often requires the work of economists, policy analysts, and other data gatherers and numbers crunchers, as well as wordsmiths able to make almost any decision sound reasonable. Legislators need to be able to justify their decisions – if not to the broad public directly, at least to a skeptical media sensitive to outright payoffs. Regulators must convince judges they have not acted arbitrarily. Because every side in these contests needs to make the best possible case, large amounts of money are made available to engage experts to provide arguments they may know to be only half-truths or, on occasion, outright deceptions. The result is a broader form of corruption – the corruption of knowledge.

I saw some of this when I ran the policy staff at the Federal Trade Commission in the late 1970s. Corporations would pay 'expert' witnesses to testify to facts that they shaded just enough to make the case for their clients without selling out their own professional integrity. By the time I was at the Department of Labor in the 1990s, more 'experts' had become shameless. Time and again I saw well-respected professors and 'senior fellows' at Washington think tanks make arguments in congressional hearings, regulatory proceedings, and even in the media that they must have known were specious. They rarely revealed they were being paid by corporations or trade associations with direct financial stakes in their conclusions.

Between the 1970s and the 1990s more experts abandoned their integrity because in the intervening years competition had intensified, the economic stakes had become higher, and corporations and their lobbyists were willing to pay experts lots more. Scruples, like other marketable commodities, can be purchased if the price is right.[41]

During these years, expert witnesses became an established part of corporate litigation in federal district courts. The lawsuits were less often between corporations and government prosecutors than between corporations seeking competitive advantage over one another – suing one another for infringing patents or copyrights, engaging in predatory practices in violation of antitrust laws, abrogating contracts or trying to void contracts, or imposing or avoiding liability. Dueling experts often offered contradictory data and analyses that judges and their clerks then spent endless hours trying to sort through. Starting in the 1970s, lawsuits between corporations became the fastest growing category of litigation in the federal courts.[42]

Major legislative battles elicit armies of well-paid experts. In 2003, in anticipation of a contentious debate over the proposed Medicare drug benefit, the Pharmaceutical Research and Manufacturers of America budgeted $1 million for what it described as an 'intellectual echo chamber of economists – a standing network of economists and thought leaders to speak against federal price control regulations through articles and testimony, and to serve as a rapid response team', according to internal budget documents published by the *New York Times*. In the months before Congress formally considered the drug benefit, the trade group spent $2 million to $2.5 million in payments to research and policy organizations 'to build intellectual capital and generate a higher volume of messages from credible sources' sympathetic to the drug industry.[43]

It is often enough merely to cast doubt on an established fact, thereby opening the way for a company or industry to claim that 'experts disagree' or there's a 'lively debate' on an issue, and that any public action (or initiative by opponents masquerading as a public action) should therefore wait 'until all the evidence is in'. The food industry has financed a squad of experts to debunk research showing that childhood obesity leads to health problems in adulthood and that sugar and fatty foods have a direct relationship to weight gain. It is not necessary that the research they sponsor prove otherwise; only that it raise enough questions that a legislator or regulator who wishes to side with the food industry can credibly claim to be unconvinced by the preponderance of research on the other side.

In 1998, Exxon embarked on a campaign to give 'logistical and moral support' to any dissenter from scientific findings documenting global climate change, 'thereby raising questions about and undercutting the "prevailing scientific wisdom" ', according to internal company documents.[44] In 2005, ExxonMobil distributed $2.9 million to thirty-nine groups that would raise doubts about climate change. This prompted even the British Royal Society, one of the world's most prestigious scientific groups, to accuse the firm of creating a 'false sense ... that there is a two-sided debate going on in the scientific community' about the issue.[45]

Enough money, apparently, can even purchase the imprimatur of a great university. In 2002, Stanford University signed a ten-year deal with Exxon and other energy companies in return for $225 million for a 'Global Climate and Energy Project'. Shortly after the deal was signed, Exxon ran ads on the op-ed page of the *New York Times* announcing its new alliance with the 'best minds' at Stanford. One such advertisement read: 'Although climate has varied throughout Earth's history from natural causes, today there is a lively debate about ... the climate's response to the presence of more greenhouse gases in the atmosphere.' The ad was signed by Lynn Orr, the Stanford professor who was to head up the project. The ad also carried the official Stanford University seal.[46]

Even when government pays for neutral expertise, it doesn't necessarily get it. A major academic study released in 2006, finding antidepressants to be safe and effective for pregnant women, was financed by the Food and Drug Administration. But according to the *Wall Street Journal,* most of its thirteen authors, among them prominent professors, were serving at the same time as paid consultants to corporations that manufactured antidepressants.[47] This is not to suggest that these professors – or, for that matter, any experts – understand themselves to be taking bribes that compromise their professional integrity. But human beings are remarkably adept at rationalizing comfortable arrangements. Money induces a generous frame of mind, willing to overlook evidence that might trouble an expert whose judgment is not clouded by a consulting contract.

. . .

THE PREDOMINANCE of corporate-financed 'experts' in policy making, in effect, leads the public to assume the only issues of any importance are those that bear on the welfare of consumers and investors, rather than on the well-being of society or the planet as a whole. Even if conclusions about costs and benefits were not biased in favor of companies willing and able to hire the most – or most prestigious – hired guns, they would still be focused narrowly. Whether in congressional hearings, regulatory proceedings, courts of appeals, op-eds, full-page ads in major newspapers, or in general media coverage – and from whatever competitive side of a given issue they represent – the message from corporate experts is fundamentally the same: Public policies are to be judged by a utilitarian calculus of whether they improve the efficiency of the economy. They are presumed to be wise if consumer-investor benefits exceed consumer-investor costs; unwise, if the opposite holds true.

Absent from any such calculus is consideration of whether the resulting distribution of benefits further widens inequality among citizens or reduces it, provides more or fewer opportunities to the nation's or world's less fortunate, offers more or less economic security to people now lacking it, respects or undermines civil or human rights, promotes or undermines public health and domestic tranquillity, fosters or detracts from community, generates a cleaner or dirtier environment, advances or sets back the cause of tolerance and global peace, or, more generally, strengthens or weakens democracy.

These attributes are clearly difficult to measure or to quantify, but that doesn't make them less worthy of consideration than consumer and investor welfare. Indeed, given widening inequality, heightened economic insecurity, loss of community, and mounting risks to the environment over recent years, it would seem more incumbent than ever to discuss them.

Consider again the battle between phone and cable over whether phone companies may carry television into people's homes. Phone companies argued that consumers would save between $30 and $40 a month; cables disputed this figure and contended video reception would be unreliable.

Almost entirely overlooked were basic issues of accountability and fairness, and concerns about community. If phone companies rather than cable companies provide the video, the fees that cable companies now turn over to towns and cities will evaporate. That means property taxes or other fees would have to be raised for all homeowners to replace them. Moreover, many poor residents won't reap the lower costs of video by phone line because phone companies are not required under federal law – as are cables, under most municipal franchises – to extend their services to poor neighborhoods.[48] Viewed this way, the issue wasn't as simple as regulation or deregulation; it was what sort of regulation would assure both efficiency and fairness.

Similarly excluded from the debate over 'net neutrality' was the larger question of who should bear the costs of additional broadband capacity, including the cost of extending it to rural and inner-city areas still lacking. In 2006, the Government Accountability Office found that 42 percent of households had either no computer or one with no Internet connection, and most of the nation's poor had no access to broadband.[49] Perhaps all these Americans can live without YouTube. But it's far from clear their children can learn all they're capable of learning without access to Google's search engine.

Or look at the ongoing battles between brand-name and generic drugs over Medicare coverage and whether pharmacists or doctors should be able to substitute generics for brands. Generics argue they save consumers money; brands say investors won't finance development of new drugs unless they get a healthy return, and brand-name drugs provide that. Left out of this debate are the fundamental questions of whether drug companies ought to be advertising and marketing prescription drugs to the general public when it is doctors who should be making decisions about medications; how much of the costs of drugs go to advertising and marketing them; and whether there's enough difference between nearly identical drugs to justify the expense of bringing them to market in the first place.

The 'organic' wars could be seen as contests between different groups of consumers and investors, some preferring higher standards and some preferring lower ones. But excluded from this debate are concerns shared by many about the effects of pesticides and synthetics on the environment and on public health. Many citizens would prefer a debate over the ways society should develop and protect the food chain, rather than a battle over the narrow terms of 'organic' consumer labeling.

Microsoft's brushes with antitrust law have also been debated by lawyers and economists mainly in terms of consumer welfare and investor return. This is typical. Under supercapitalism, competition is generally so intense that, as I have said, consumers and investors do very well. As a result, in recent decades antitrust authorities have limited their inquiries to whether consumers could get lower prices if large companies faced fiercer competition on some exclusive feature, such as Microsoft's browser, as against the possibility that those companies will have less incentive to bring new inventions to market if they are not able to make money off of such exclusivity. But entirely overlooked in modern antitrust debates are concerns about the political power that often accompanies large corporate size, and its consequences for small businesses and individuals lacking such power. These were the concerns that first animated antitrust discussions. Senator John Sherman, author of the 1890 antitrust act that bears his name, was not particularly worried about consumers or investors. He was concerned mostly about the 'inequality of condition, of wealth, and [of] opportunity' that was fostered by industrial concentration. For Woodrow Wilson, too, antitrust was mainly a matter of fairness, intended to keep the economy open to 'the beginner', and 'the man with only a little capital'.[50]

6

TO SUMMARIZE: Our voices as citizens – as opposed to our voices as consumers and investors – are being drowned out. We may even be losing confidence that what we have to say as citizens is important. This is not because big corporations have conspired to drown out or marginalize our citizen voices but chiefly because corporations are engaged in escalating competition for political outcomes that advantage them over their rivals. The constantly ascending, hugely elevated decibel level of lobbying is so high in Washington and other capitals that citizens, even when they speak up, can barely be heard by politicians over the cacophony. Supercapitalism has spilled over into politics, and engulfed democracy.

The political competition takes many forms. Elected officials are beholden to corporate lobbyists who put together ever-larger bundles of campaign contributions from their clients; and elected officials, fearing that electoral rivals might get the money instead, extort ever more contributions from lobbyists and their clients. Congressional hearings and regulatory proceedings are increasingly clogged with testimony and filings from corporate experts who represent different companies or industry segments potentially affected by proposed policies. Courts are increasingly jammed with litigation initiated by corporate lawyers appealing regulatory findings or procedures that favor one company or industry segment over another, or appealing trial court decisions in favor of one company and against another, or trial court decisions in favor of a government prosecutor against a company. And with increasing frequency, newspapers and broadcasters run stories spun by corporate public relations spinmeisters in favor of their clients, or defending their clients against stories spun by the public relations specialists of their rivals.

As this competition has escalated, the cost of entering the political fray has continued to rise. Individuals and groups not motivated by the bottom line rarely have the resources to break through. Washington-based 'public interest' groups operate on a tiny fraction of the budgets of corporate lobbyists, and few have any political connections outside the Washington Beltway. The Internet has proven an efficient means of raising campaign money, and the so-called blogosphere a boisterous outlet for airing views and venting frustrations, but there's no direct or systematic link between these forums and decision makers.

Meanwhile, the institutions that once gave voice to citizen concerns have all but disappeared. Unions still have a presence in Washington and their campaign contributions continue to be important, especially to Democrats, but they are no longer large enough to have an effect on any but the most conspicuous issues affecting labor. Regulatory agencies charged with weighing the 'public interest' have been pared back. Localized interest groups, even if organized into national federations, claim less attention from legislators who spend more time seeking large sums of money for their campaign chests from corporate PACs, executives, and corporate lobbyists. Pork continues to flow back home, but that is no longer where the action is. Federated groups like the American Legion, which had been uniquely responsible for gaining passage of the GI Bill in 1947, are no longer as influential. A revealing contrast to the GI Bill occurred in 1994, when Bill Clinton pushed legislation to provide universal health coverage. Despite it being introduced in a Democratic Congress, Clinton's legislation went nowhere. That was partly because the proposal was too complicated and bureaucratic. But it also died because it had no broad-based organization behind it. While corporations vigorously lobbied against it, Clinton had no vehicle to mobilize public support.[51]

Citizen concerns do flare up in politics, especially when the media carry mesmerizing stories about, say, a group of American manufacturing jobs migrating to Asia or the leak of an oil pipeline in the Alaskan wilderness. But the power of these stories to effect political change is limited. Voters have short attention spans. To keep attracting readers and viewers, editors and producers quickly move on to the next 'scandal of the week'. Advocates typically lack resources to mobilize even those who are temporarily outraged and translate the outrage into ongoing political pressure. The major parties are too dependent on corporate funding to risk offending any significant number of companies or Wall Street. In any event, even if populist outrage lingers, it rarely results in sound legislation. It is easily deflected into diffuse resentments directed against business or 'liberal' elites. Such resentments may generate exciting copy for stump speeches, but they do not sustain political movements.

One consequence has been a steady decline in political attention paid to issues of social equity or fairness – even as inequality has widened. Tufts University professor Jeffrey Berry and his colleagues took a close look at Congress in 1963, 1979, and 1991 (all years in which Democrats held a controlling majority). The researchers focused on over two hundred policy issues that were the subject of committee hearings and at least minimal media coverage. Their findings confirm the trend we have been examining. Congress placed steadily decreasing emphasis on economic legislation aimed at reducing inequality – by, for example, raising wages or improving the job skills of the poor. In 1963, Congress passed six of ten bills designed to reduce economic inequality. In 1979, it passed four out of seven of such bills; in 1991, two out of seven.[52]

In politics as in the marketplace, the consumer and investor in us are well represented. But the citizen in us has almost vanished from politics. I own the tiniest sliver of Microsoft stock. I have no doubt that Microsoft is doing everything in its power to maximize the value of that ownership stake, just as it is doing everything possible to attract and retain customers. As an investor in Microsoft, I implicitly supported its political effort to reduce funding of the antitrust division of the Justice Department when the Justice Department was attacking the company, because Microsoft's strategy was calculated to maximize the value of my shares. But as a citizen, I was appalled. It struck me as an abuse of power.

As an investor, I know exactly how to express my displeasure with Microsoft or any other company. I simply sell off shares of its stock. It's exactly what I do as a consumer to express displeasure in a company – just stop dealing with it and go to a competitor that offers a better deal. Wall Street and Wal-Mart have enhanced my power in both regards by giving me easy means of aggregating my preferences with those of others. Internet search engines also give me power; I can find better deals in an instant, and consummate them with a click. In short, supercapitalism allows me to express myself louder than ever as a consumer and investor. But as a citizen, my options for expressing myself have become severely limited – and supercapitalism is largely the cause. How could I express disdain for Microsoft's political strategy? I can no longer count on large mediating institutions to voice my concerns – labor unions, pluralist federations, even political parties. My voice is being drowned out by Microsoft itself, and by other large companies in pursuit of competitive advantage through public policy. I can still register my approval or disapproval of particular candidates when I go to the voting booth, e-mail my representative or senator, send a letter to the White House, fire off letters to newspapers, make a political contribution, or get involved in a political campaign. But chances are, I will not be heard above the corporate din.

The foregoing, it must be stressed, is explanation rather than justification or condemnation. It describes the way our democracy has evolved over the last several decades, as capitalism has been replaced by super-capitalism. The same trend is becoming evident in many other democracies, as supercapitalism is spreading around the world. But it is not the way capitalism and democracy must continue to evolve. We need not be slaves to present trends any more than we were to previous ones. We can, if we choose, fashion a democratic capitalism more suited to our nobler aspirations for the twenty-first century. Yet to do that, it is necessary to separate capitalism from democracy and guard the border between them.

CHAPTER FIVE

POLITICS DIVERTED

IN RECENT YEARS, 'corporate social responsibility' has become the supposed answer to the paradox of democratic capitalism. It is now a hot topic in business schools; as of 2006, more than half of all master of business administration curricula required students to take at least one course on it. Over 80 percent of corporate recruiters say business school graduates should display an awareness and knowledge of the subject.[1] Hundreds of corporate conferences are held on it annually. Tens of thousands of corporate executives listen attentively to consultants who specialize in it explain its importance. The world's top CEOs and officials, gathering annually at the World Economic Forum in Davos, Switzerland, solemnly discuss it and proclaim their commitment to it. Numerous 'social auditors' now measure how well corporations have achieved it, and hundreds of companies produce glossy company reports touting their dedication to it. NGOs – nongovernmental organizations, with full-time staffs, Web sites, newsletters, and funding appeals – develop codes of corporate conduct on aspects of it, and rate corporations on their adherence to it. At least eight hundred mutual funds worldwide say they are devoted to it. The United Nations Global Compact, launched at Davos in 1999, enumerates goals for it, and by 2006 more than three thousand firms had signed on. Great Britain even has a minister for it.

Most of this is in earnest. Much is sincere. Some of it has had a positive impact. But almost all has occurred outside of the democratic process. Almost none has changed the rules of the game. To view it as a new form of democratic capitalism is to fail to understand the logic of supercapitalism. It is also to divert attention from the more difficult but more important job of establishing new rules that protect and advance the common good, and keep supercapitalism from overwhelming politics.

1

THE UPSURGE of interest in 'corporate social responsibility' is related to the decreasing confidence in democracy. These days, reformers often say they find it easier to lobby corporate executives than to lobby politicians; they contend they can be more effective pushing certain large corporations to change their ways than trying to alter public policy. 'Government is failing to provide leadership on environmental concerns, and industry has grown more willing to address them,' says Jonathan Lash, president of World Resources Institute.[2]

Cynicism about politics is perfectly understandable, but this is a curious proposition. A major reason why government is failing to provide leadership is because, as we have seen, big corporations have become so effective in recent years at preventing government from doing much about the environment or any other issue that may require corporations to change in ways they'd prefer not to. Why would industry have grown more willing to address the very concerns it has worked to block government from addressing? Of course, the specific people in a corporation most committed to making it more socially responsible are not likely to be the same people who are lobbying effectively against laws and regulations requiring the firm to be so, but this doesn't change the overriding reality: In supercapitalism, the corporation as a whole must, for competitive reasons, resist doing anything that hurts – and will place a very low priority on anything that doesn't help – the bottom line.

Cynicism about democracy can also become a self-fulfilling prophecy, diverting attention from reforming it. While the citizen of a relatively small nation has little leverage through that nation's own democratic politics to affect the behavior of large global corporations, that is demonstrably not the case for citizens of the United States, or even the European Union. Any corporation that wants to do business in such large and prosperous places must adhere to the laws of these nations. Even the state of California can set its own environmental laws that have bite because most global companies want access to that huge market. Moreover, global firms headquartered in the United States or Europe have significant global activities – Starbucks purchases a large share of global coffee production, McDonald's controls a major portion of the world's beef and chicken markets, Wal-Mart is the world's largest retailer, Home Depot is the largest single purchaser of wood and wood products in the world. American or European laws therefore can control a large percentage of global corporate behavior. Citizens of such big and powerful nations who assume they have more impact pushing corporations to be virtuous than working through the democratic process to require them to be so are simply wrong.

It is easy to understand why big business has embraced corporate social responsibility with such verve. It makes for good press and reassures the public. A declaration of corporate commitment to social virtue may also forestall government legislation or regulation in an area of public concern where one or more companies have behaved badly, such as transporting oil carelessly and causing a major spill or flagrantly failing to respect human rights abroad. The soothing promise of responsibility can deflect public attention from the need for stricter laws and regulations or convince the public that there's no real problem to begin with. Corporations that have signed codes of conduct promising good behavior appear to have taken important steps toward social responsibility, but the pressures operating on them to lure and keep consumers and investors haven't eased one bit. In supercapitalism, they *cannot* be socially responsible, at least not to any significant extent.

Politicians are simultaneously let off the hook. They can applaud some seeming act of corporate virtue – they may even take credit for pushing corporations to sign pledges or promise change – while not having to take any action that might cause negative reaction in boardrooms or among corporate fund-raisers. They don't have to take sides, or take a stand, while appearing to be in favor of virtuous corporate behavior.

Commitments to corporate social responsibility are also conveniently reassuring to talented or privileged young people who want both the sky-high financial rewards of fast-track executive careers and the psychological rewards of doing some good in the world. Rather than labor in the impe-cunious vineyards of social work or teaching school in a poor community, or public service in general, they can get their MBA and thereafter attach themselves to a big corporation that issues an annual report on all the good things it does for society. They can thereby do well and do good at the same time, or so they tell themselves.

But viewed this way, 'corporate social responsibility' is as meaningful as cotton candy. The more you try to bite into it the faster it dissolves. One popular argument is that 'socially responsible' companies are more profitable. Dow Chemical reduces its carbon emissions so it can lower its energy costs. McDonald's employs more humane slaughtering techniques, which prevent costly worker injuries and yield more meat. Wal-Mart has adopted 'green' packaging for its fresh produce – transparent plastics made from corn sugars – because it's cheaper than petroleum-based packaging. Starbucks gives its part-time employees health insurance because that reduces employee turnover and helps its bottom line. Alcoa estimates annual savings of about $100 million from reduced energy use and related environmental improvements.[3]

All these steps may be worthwhile but they are not undertaken because they are socially responsible. They're done to reduce costs. To credit these corporations with being 'socially responsible' is to stretch the term to mean anything a company might do to increase profits if, in doing so, it also happens to have some beneficent impact on the rest of society. Taken to the logical extreme is the textbook economics argument that whenever a company increases its profits it has a positive effect on society because it thereby utilizes assets more efficiently, releasing those that are no longer needed to be used more efficiently elsewhere. In this sense, all profitable companies are socially responsible.

For many years I have preached that social responsibility and profitability converge over the long term. That's because a firm that respects and values employees, the community, and the environment eventually earns the respect and gratitude of employees, the community, and the larger society – which eventually helps the bottom line. But I've never been able to prove this proposition nor find a study that confirms it. More important from the standpoint of the modern firm, the long term may be irrelevant. Under supercapitalism, the 'long term' is the present value of future earnings. There is no better measure of this than share price.

The same confusion is found in so-called socially responsible investing in products likely to become hot in the future due to some emerging public concern. In 2004, CalPERS – the California Public Employees' Retirement System – announced with fanfare it would invest $200 million in what it termed the 'burgeoning environmental technology sector'. This made financial sense, assuming that environmental technologies that burn more cleanly than fossil fuels will reap big rewards in the future. But to describe the move as 'socially responsible' is to confuse what may be a wise investment strategy with an initiative intended to improve society. California's public employees did not agree to sacrifice their retirement incomes for the well-being of the planet. If CalPERS's bet is correct, its public employees will earn higher returns than otherwise. But if it's wrong, California's public employees will be justifiably upset.

Logically, when the extra benefits of some product accrue to consumers individually, they may be willing to pay more for it. This doesn't make the product 'socially responsible', either. Energy-efficient appliances that save consumers money, organic foods that make them feel heathier, gourmet ice cream that's tastier because it's made with cream from cows with access to lots of pasture, salmon that's more delectable because it was caught in the wild rather than brought up in pens, and free-range eggs that make consumers feel more secure against salmonella may all be worth the higher price consumers pay for them. But consumers don't pay extra because of any presumed social good; they pay because it's worth it to them personally. Wendy's restaurants have stopped frying their food in trans fats, which have also been banished from Oreo cookies and Frito-Lay snacks. General Mills now makes its Cheerios and Wheaties out of whole grain. These changes were not made because these firms became more socially virtuous but because consumers have become more conscious about their own health.[4]

Similarly, companies that pay good wages and offer good benefits in order to attract and retain high-caliber employees are not being 'socially responsible'; they are merely practicing good management. 'High ideals don't have to conflict with the bottom line,' says Starbucks in one of its many advertisements touting its special commitment to society. 'When we started providing health coverage to our part-time employees, we noticed a lot less turnover.'[5] That's precisely the confusion. If Starbucks's bottom line is improved because it provides health coverage to part-timers, Starbucks is not acting out of high ideals – regardless of the worthy motives of its founder. Starbucks is acting for the benefit of Starbucks's consumers and investors. The extra costs are more than justified by the savings. It's called smart business.

In general, corporate initiatives that improve the quality of products without increasing their price, or increase efficiency and productivity so that prices can be lowered, or otherwise generate higher profits and higher returns for investors, are not socially virtuous. They're just good management practices that should – and, given the competitive pressures of supercapitalism, will – be undertaken regardless of how much or how little they benefit society.

Economist Milton Friedman argued several decades ago that the business of business is to make a profit, not to engage in socially beneficial acts.[6] Friedman made his argument at a time when many companies still had sufficient discretion to be socially responsible. As noted, big companies tended to be oligopolies with significant power over their prices and markets. His point was companies *should not* seek to accomplish social ends because companies are not the appropriate vehicles for social benevolence. Whether or not you agree with Friedman, companies under supercapitalism no longer have the discretion to be virtuous. Competition is so intense that most corporations *cannot* accomplish social ends without imposing a cost on their consumers or investors – who would then seek and find better deals elsewhere. Even if individual consumers or investors believed in the virtuousness of a particular sacrifice, absent laws requiring all companies and therefore all other consumers and investors to forbear as well, the individual's action would have no effect.

2

AS THE ECONOMY has moved toward supercapitalism, companies that in Friedman's day were known to be the most socially virtuous have been punished by investors. Cummins Engine, one of the pioneers of the corporate social responsibility movement, had to abandon its paternalistic employment policies and its generous contributions to its communities when its investors demanded higher returns. Dayton Hudson, another notably socially responsible company, came close to being swallowed up in a hostile takeover during the 1980s, and has since then paid exclusive attention to its customers and investors. Levi Strauss, also once on everyone's list of America's most socially responsible companies in part because of its commitment to source its clothing from domestic manufacturers, faced plummeting sales in the 1990s and had to eliminate its remaining domestic production. Polaroid, another pioneer, filed for bankruptcy in 2001. The shares of Britain's retailer Marks & Spencer, which had ranked near the top in a survey of worldwide labor standards, performed so poorly the firm attracted a hostile takeover bid in 2004.[7] Both Body Shop International and Ben & Jerry's had been touted as among the nation's most socially responsible companies until investor pressure pushed Body Shop founder Anita Roddick into an advisory role and Ben & Jerry's was taken over by Unilever.

Under supercapitalism, a commitment to social virtue is no substitute for obsessive dedication to shareholder value. George Merck's celebrated motto from the 1950s – 'Medicine is for the people. It is not for the profits. The profits follow' – represented a classic statement of the socially responsible ideal.[8] The company adhered to it in the 1980s when it developed and distributed without charge a drug to cure river blindness that inflicted poor tropical nations, and in more recent years when it decided to make AIDS drugs available in Botswana. But the profits did not necessarily follow, and in recent years Merck's stock price has wallowed. Perhaps this is why the company acted too quickly in putting its painkiller Vioxx on the market, an initiative notably lacking in social virtue. Enron, before its fall, was ranked as one of America's hundred best employers, the recipient of several environmental awards, among the first major companies to issue a 'triple-bottom-line' report enumerating its progress on social and environmental goals, and known for its generous philanthropic contributions. In retrospect, it seems doubtful Enron's commitment to social responsibility was any more sincere than its dedication to its investors.[9]

By the same token, investors don't punish profitable companies or industries notably lacking in social virtue. In the early and mid-2000s,

ExxonMobil had the highest return on equity of any oil company. Shareholders flocked to it despite its being named an 'outlaw' by environmental groups for its highly visible campaigns against non-fossil-based fuels and the reality of global warming.[10] Wall Street analysts and investment bankers concern themselves only with the bottom line, as do most of those whose retirement savings they manage. 'I don't see investors refusing to buy because they think the chief executive is overpaid, and I don't see union members boycotting nonunion stores that sell attractively priced foreign goods,' says Anthony M. Maramarco, a managing director at Babson Capital Management.[11]

Social offensiveness is not necessarily financially offputting. Few industries have been more vilified than tobacco but tobacco companies have had no difficulty obtaining funding from investors eager to make a good return. Firms producing alcohol or firearms, companies relying on revenues from gambling, and firms producing lurid magazines and videos have all done reasonably well on Wall Street – most even outperforming the S&P 500 Index. Defense stocks, considered morally objectionable by some, have likewise outperformed the S&P 500 Index since the late 1980s.[12] It is of course possible that noxious firms must outperform the norm in order to attract capital. Perhaps there is a sleaze premium analogous to a risk premium. But it seems more likely that investors don't know or care. They have instructed the managers of their pension or mutual funds to maximize the value of their savings, regardless. Insulation from the social effects of our market decisions is, again, an essential aspect of supercapitalism.

Investors deeply concerned about corporate morality can park their savings in what are called 'socially responsible investment' funds, which screen out certain offensive industries. But few investors do. In 2004, total shares under the management of such funds comprised less than 2 percent of mutual fund shares outstanding in the U.S. stock market.[13] In Europe, socially responsible mutual funds account for an even lower portion – about a third of 1 percent. If such funds outperformed regular mutual funds more investors would be drawn to them, but their record is decidedly mixed. Besides, most 'socially responsible' fund portfolios include just about every large company featured in a typical mutual fund portfolio. In 2004, thirty-three socially responsible funds held the stock of Wal-Mart, twenty-three held Halliburton's, forty held ExxonMobil's, and almost all held Microsoft's, its antitrust peccadilloes notwithstanding. At the start of the 2000s, many held Enron, WorldCom, and Adelphia stock, and none of these companies went on to distinguish themselves for public service.[14]

Yes, investors are interested in better corporate governance. But better governance makes a firm more responsive to its investors – not to its employees, communities, or society as a whole.

The chances any board of directors will ever again condone the $6,000 floral-patterned shower curtain Tyco's shareholders unwittingly bought for the company's former boss, Dennis Kozlowski; the $100 million Adelphia Communications's shareholders unintentionally gave its former CEO, John Rigas; and the near royal reign of former WorldCom CEO Bernard Ebbers – among other outrages and excesses that came to light in the early 2000s – will hopefully be diminished by moves to improve corporate governance. When shareholders have more say in electing company directors, when top executives have to sign off personally on company audits, and when executive compensation is more fully disclosed, executives presumably will have more incentive to do what they have a fiduciary responsibility to do in the first place.

These initiatives will not make CEOs more responsible to society, however. To the contrary, the more beholden CEOs and other top executives are to investors, the more likely they are to slash payrolls in pursuit of higher profits, uproot themselves from their traditional communities and rely on global supply chains instead, pander to whatever vulgar desires their customers may harbor, subject workers in developing nations to unsafe or unhealthy conditions, and pillage the environment – if these and other such antisocial techniques increase profits and share prices.

Some believe corporate boards should represent all 'stakeholders' – including employees, communities, and society in general – and view this notion of corporate governance as the answer for how to reconcile the interests of investors with those of the rest of society. The idea of 'stakeholder capitalism' was, you recall, put forward by Walter Lippmann,

Adolf Berle, and Gardiner Means in the early twentieth century, and it found expression in the 'corporate statesmen' of the Not Quite Golden Age. There is some appeal in the idea of stakeholder boards. It has worked at other times and in other places. For many years, German companies have had two boards – a traditional one, representing those whose capital is at risk, and a second tier representing other stakeholders. A few American companies, like United Airlines, have experimented with limited board representation of unionized employees in return for their agreement to delay or reduce scheduled increases in wages and benefits. I was an early and loud enthusiast for United's attempt.

Yet it seems doubtful that 'stakeholder' boards can work under supercapitalism. Any company that sacrifices shareholder returns in order to reward some other group of 'stakeholders' will lose its investors, who can easily move their money to where returns are better. Besides, it's proven hard enough on traditional boards to ensure that board members will represent the best interests of shareholders.

The expected profitability of a company is best measured by its share price. But there's no similar way to measure how well a company responds to the interests of its other 'stakeholders'. Some worthy efforts have been made seeking ways to calculate the 'triple-bottom-line' performance of a company in delivering value for its shareholders, employees, and the broader society. None of these attempts at measurement, however, has been able to overcome the most basic problem of all: Under supercapitalism, competitive pressures respond only to how well a company is doing by its consumers and shareholders. If every board became a forum in which different groups of 'stakeholders' devised their own minimum wages, minimum levels of worker safety, minimal protection of the environment, and so on, companies would be competing with one another for consumers and investors from radically different positions. Presumably, those with the lowest standards, and therefore the lowest costs and highest profits, would find it easiest to lure customers and satisfy shareholders. Without laws specifying what is expected of all companies, 'stakeholder' boards would find themselves in a race to the bottom. In supercapitalism, therefore, the elusive promise of corporate democracy is illusory.

. . .

EVIDENCE SUGGESTS consumers, like investors, do not care enough about social responsibility to make financial sacrifices for it. After an exhaustive review of the data, my colleague Professor David Vogel, of the Haas School of Business at the University of California at Berkeley, concluded that 'the social and environmental practices of the vast majority of companies have not had any demonstrated effects on their sales'.[15]

Consumers do like to be associated with likable companies – especially upscale consumers who have extra money to spend on likability. Hence, Starbucks's full-page ads touting such things as the company's grants for children's reading programs. ('On the surface, it might not seem like reading has much to do with coffee, but it has everything to do with being a company that wants to act on its values and engage positively with the world.')[16] It's also true that brand image means more and more. In the Not Quite Golden Age, most companies' book value consisted of physical assets, such as factories and equipment, plus money in the bank. By the early twenty-first century, such hard assets account for only about a third of the typical company's stock market value; the rest is in intangibles – patents, know-how, and the goodwill of a company's brand. This is one reason so-called image advertising has grown so important, and why companies are spending a fortune on public relations, $3.7 billion in 2005.[17] In a world of Internet chat rooms and bloggers, no corporate image is entirely safe.

But, as has been noted, there's a difference between the private wants of a consumer and the public ideals of a citizen. Most consumers want good deals, period. Almost 50 percent of the consumers surveyed in a 2002 poll said they wanted the environment protected but that it was business's responsibility to do so, not theirs. According to another study, consumers buy environmentally friendly products only when they cost no more than regular products, have at least the same level of quality and performance, come from a brand they know and trust, can be purchased at stores where they already shop, and don't require a significant change in habits to use.[18]

After voluntarily adopting a standard for harvesting tuna that protected dolphins, Starkist ran advertisements touting the firm's leadership.

The result was a measurable rise in customer approval and an increase in Starkist's market share. But the company was unable to raise prices to cover the higher costs of protecting the dolphins. Explained J. W. Connolly, president of Starkist's parent company, 'Consumers wanted a dolphin-safe product, but they were not willing to pay more for it. If there was a dolphin-safe can of tuna next to a regular can, people chose the cheaper product. Even if the difference was a penny.'[19]

Consumers say they care about social responsibility, but in practice few care enough to pay more for it. In a European survey of 2004, three-quarters of consumers polled said they would change their buying decisions because of the social or environmental records of companies, but only 3 percent said they had actually done so.[20] Even when they're asked to define 'social responsibility', consumers describe it in terms of personal consumer satisfaction rather than public good. In a survey co-sponsored by the *Wall Street Journal,* people were asked to rank forty-three activities that influence their opinions of corporations as 'good citizens'. The two most often cited as very important were 'standing behind products/services and honoring warranties' and 'producing high-quality products and services'.[21]

Consumers say they want companies they deal with to respect human rights abroad. In 1993, after the events at Tiananmen Square, Levi Strauss decided to phase out its production in China because of that nation's poor human rights record – a decision widely praised.[22] But Levi's customers were unwilling to pay higher prices for jeans produced at higher cost in nations that respected human rights. So in 1998, the company reversed its policy. Either rely on Chinese manufacturers 'or risk losing out in the competitive game of the global apparel business', explained Peter Jacobi, Levi Strauss's president.[23]

On the other hand, a coordinated attack launched on Wal-Mart in 2004 by several unions, environmentalists, and student groups may have had some effect. Wal-Mart's profits have continued to grow as it has added stores, but growth slowed in 2005, as did the growth in profits per store. This may have been because the household budgets of Wal-Mart's customers were squeezed by rising fuel prices and declining wages. But a report prepared by McKinsey & Company for Wal-Mart, made public by an anti-Wal-Mart group, found that 2 to 8 percent of Wal-Mart's former customers said they stopped shopping at the chain because of the 'negative press they have heard'.[24] More on this to come.

3

SOCIAL REFORMERS have long exposed abusive corporate practices as a means of mobilizing political support for new legislation or regulation aimed at curbing them. Progressive-era muckraker Ida Tarbell's *The History of the Standard Oil Company*, published in 1904, inspired the antitrust case that broke up the company. Upton Sinclair's 1906 classic, *The Jungle*, exposed the meatpacking industry and generated the nation's first health and safety regulations. Ralph Nader's 1966 book *Unsafe at Any Speed* revealed the automobile industry's indifference to safety, leading to the creation of the National Highway Safety Administration. The purpose of these and other exposés was not to pressure individual companies to change their ways but to incite political action so all companies would have to. These efforts were not substitutes for political action but preconditions for it.

Starting in the late 1960s, reformers pressured companies doing business in South Africa to adhere to voluntary anti-discrimination guidelines called the Sullivan Principles, named after Leon Sullivan, a minister and member of the board of General Motors. The pressure included consumer and investor boycotts of companies that had not signed on. But the goal was political – to force the government of South Africa to give up apartheid. Agitation in the United States eventually caused Congress to impose economic sanctions on South Africa; other nations did so as well. Many companies closed down their operations there. Finally, apartheid collapsed.

On a smaller scale, Greenpeace's 1995 media campaign against Shell Oil's plan to sink an old oil storage platform in the British North Sea had a specific political objective. Although it involved a consumer boycott of Shell, its purpose was not to shame the company but to mobilize political action so no oil company in the future could dispose of its abandoned rigs by merely jettisoning them in the ocean. The campaign was successful. The Oslo-Paris Commission decreed in 1998 that all such old platforms had to be disassembled and disposed of on land.[25]

These campaigns were designed to change the rules of the game. Consumers or investors as a whole may have ended up paying slightly more for, say, gold, since it was no longer available from South African mines when Congress imposed economic sanctions, or North Sea oil from rigs that had to be disposed of more expensively. But these small price increases were presumably worth the overall social gains, as determined in the democratic process.* Labor organizers also pressure large companies to permit votes on whether workers should form a union – but here, too, the goal is specific and political in the sense of altering the balance of power between owners and employees.

Without a specific political goal, 'corporate social responsibility' is simply a function of a group's organizing heft relative to a particular company or industry – and therefore can mean anything. Should a socially responsible investment fund screen out companies engaged in nuclear energy, as some anti-nuclear advocates urge? Environmentalists who think nuclear energy is the best alternative to fossil-based fuels would disagree. Should consumers prefer eggs produced by agribusinesses with free-range hens, as some animal rights advocates urge? Some food safety advocates prefer that hens be caged in order to avoid contact with migratory birds that may carry avian flu. Should socially responsible investors and consumers eschew companies that produce any alcohol product, including beer or wine, or just hard liquor? Should they avoid media companies that produce any sexual or violent content, or just those that fall below some threshold of decency?

---

* Some consumer boycotts, notably in Europe, have resulted in broadly accepted practices almost the equivalent of laws – such as a 'Rugmark' label certifying that rugs and carpets have been made without child labor, or an agreement to produce batteries that do not contain mercury. One suspects, though, that if competitors could offer nonconforming items at much lower prices many consumers would be tempted to overlook their negative social consequences. If there is broad agreement on the desirability of such norms, it would seem advisable to put them into law.

Absent any political process for deciding questions like these, the answers are completely arbitrary. Electoral democracy is messy and difficult at best. As has been noted, it's now so dominated by large companies that citizen values can barely be heard. Yet there is no means for determining the social obligations of the private sector other than through the democratic process. Making companies more 'socially responsible' is a worthy goal, but it would be better served by making democracy work better.

Pressuring companies to be more virtuous is an unaccountable mechanism for deciding complex social issues better left to legislators. Consider America's gut-wrenching controversies over gay rights, abortion, and guns. Congress and state legislatures have struggled over them for years; some battles have been waged in state and federal courts over them. But even if no consensus is possible, the democratic process and courts at least provide means for weighing and balancing claims. Not so in the private sector.

In 2006, the American Family Association, a nonprofit advocacy group based in Tupelo, Mississippi, attacked Wal-Mart for joining the National Gay and Lesbian Chamber of Commerce, and urged a boycott of the company.[26] Wal-Mart apparently held fast and resisted the boycott. But when other religious groups urged Wal-Mart's pharmacies not to sell the emergency contraceptive commonly referred to as the 'morning-after pill', Wal-Mart caved. When several women's groups then demanded the company offer the pill, Wal-Mart partly reversed itself – stocking the pill but excusing any pharmacist who for personal reasons objected to dispensing it. Women's groups continued to push Wal-Mart to require its pharmacists to fill prescriptions for the pill.[27] What is the socially responsible position for Wal-Mart to take? It has no means for weighing and balancing claims, except by assessing which hurt Wal-Mart's bottom line least.

The American Family Association also organized a boycott of Ford Motor Company for advertising in publications that catered to gays. In response, Ford stopped doing so. Not surprisingly, Ford's decision upset gay rights advocates. 'Where does this leave us if our friends say, "Okay, gay people, we're going to cut you loose because we have the religious right at our heels"?' asked Kevin Cathcart, executive director of the Lambda Legal

Defense fund. 'You don't make deals with bullies, and you don't cut your friends loose.'[28] After meeting with leaders of several gay rights groups, Ford reversed itself,[29] provoking the American Family Association and forty-three other religious groups to reinstate the boycott. 'We cannot, and will not, sit by as Ford supports a social agenda aimed at the destruction of the family,' the groups proclaimed in a letter to Ford CEO William Clay Ford, Jr.[30]

In 2004, Focus on the Family, another conservative religious group, urged consumers to boycott Procter & Gamble's two leading brands, Tide detergent and Crest toothpaste. The firm had provoked the boycott by taking a public position in favor of a Cincinnati ordinance forbidding discrimination against homosexuals. Meanwhile, the pro-life Action League of Chicago called for a boycott of American Girl dolls, owned by Mattel, because the firm donated $50,000 to an organization named Girls, Inc., which had offered after-school programs to disadvantaged girls on subjects ranging from pregnancy prevention to substance abuse and, in one of its publications, supported the Supreme Court decision in *Roe v. Wade*. More recently, the National Rifle Association threatened to run hundreds of billboards casting oil giant ConocoPhillips as an enemy of gun owners. ConocoPhillips had inspired the NRA's wrath by joining a federal lawsuit to block an Oklahoma law allowing employees to bring guns to their work sites. A spokesman for ConocoPhillips explained the firm was concerned about the safety of its employees.[31]

In these and many similar instances, companies get caught in the cross-fire. Because these battles take place outside normal political channels and are aimed at specific firms, they cast corporate executives in the unenviable roles of politicians seeking to broker compromises among competing visions of the common good. Yet executives have no special expertise for doing this. They were hired to give consumers and investors better deals.

That's why, no matter how intense or irritating the advocates for one side or the other may be, in the end the corporation must do whatever is necessary to minimize its costs. If a company were to cave in to a demand that imposed an extra cost on the firm, a rival that isn't party to the agreement could profitably step into the breach. Even if Wal-Mart eventually feels compelled to raise wages and provide broader health insurance coverage – causing it to raise its prices in order to cover the added costs – another big-box retailer could fill the gap by paying lower wages, offering fewer health benefits, and thereby underpricing Wal-Mart.

In the late 1990s, Nike was in the crosshairs of many groups outraged about its treatment of foreign workers in poor countries who stitched together its shoes and clothes. Garry Trudeau's *Doonesbury* comic strip even devoted a full week to attacking the company. Nike eventually set up a system to monitor its foreign subcontractors – firing abusive managers, replacing carcinogenic glues with water-soluble ones, and allowing some plants to unionize. But by the mid-2000s Nike was competing with other companies, such as New Balance, that didn't have such systems in place. Advocates then turned their guns on New Balance, charging in January 2006 that workers at its Chinese factories were forced to labor overtime at meager wages in unsafe conditions.[32] New Balance may eventually mend its ways. But then what's to stop Adidas, Airwalk, and hundreds of other companies from stepping into the breach? With no change in the rules of supercapitalism, competitive advantage simply moves to companies not yet 'socially responsible'. There is no logical stopping place.

Finally, not only are corporations unfit to decide what is socially virtuous, but under supercapitalism they are often unable to deliver services that are inherently public. Pushing them to do so begs the question of whether the responsibilities would be better undertaken by the public sector. The campaign against Wal-Mart charged in full-page advertisements that 'Wal-Mart's low pay and meager employee benefits force tens of thousands of employees to resort to Medicaid, food stamps, and housing assistance. Call it the "Wal-Mart Tax". And it costs you $1.5 billion in federal tax dollars every year'.[33] The problem with this logic is that America had already decided to provide Medicaid, food stamps, and housing assistance to the poor – even if the poor are also working. It seemed more efficient for these benefits to flow from government, and for employers to alert their low-income employees of the availability of them, than for the private sector to provide them as conditions of employment. If we wish to change the rules and require private employers to pay wages and provide health benefits sufficiently high that no employee has to rely on government largesse, we should seek to do that through the democratic process. But it makes little sense to chastise one employer – even one as large as Wal-Mart – for playing by the rules.

Should the rules be altered, as Wal-Mart's critics advocate? That would be a worthy political debate, but we're not having it. I, for one, think the minimum wage should be raised to be about half of the average worker's hourly pay. That was the ratio in the Not Quite Golden Age, and it still seems to me a reasonable compromise. But Wal-Mart's critics also want Wal-Mart to provide employees with good health insurance coverage, which, in my opinion, is no longer a responsibility employers should take on.

Bear with me for a moment, because this is just the sort of issue the nation ought to be debating but that the focus on Wal-Mart obscures. The reason employers got into the business of providing their workers health insurance in the first place, remember, was because it is a form of payment that avoids being taxed. This made it attractive to both employers and employees in the Not Quite Golden Age, before medical costs skyrocketed and competition intensified. Even though employer-provided health care has diminished since then, in 2006 it still constituted the biggest tax break in the whole federal tax system. According to recent estimates, if health care benefits were considered taxable income, employees would be paying $126 billion a year more in income taxes than they do now.[34] In other words, employer-provided health care is a backdoor $126-billion-a-year government health insurance system that's already up and running.

But it's a crazy system. You're not eligible for it when you and your family are likely to need it most – when you lose your job and your income plummets. And these days, as we've seen, no job is safe. Why add to family anxieties by ending eligibility for this backdoor government health insurance just when an employee is shown the front door? The system also distorts the labor market. It prevents lots of people from changing jobs for fear they'll lose their health insurance, or won't get the benefits they do now. And it invites employers to game the system by seeking young, healthy employees who pose low risks of ill health, while rejecting older ones who are likely to have more costly health needs. The system also encourages employers to try to push married employees onto their spouse's health insurance plan so that the spouse's employer bears the cost.

It's also an upside-down system. The lower your pay, the less coverage you're likely to have. Even if Wal-Mart is pressured into providing more health insurance for its lowest-income workers, this wouldn't change the overall pattern across America. Workers in the lowest-paying jobs don't generally get any health insurance from their employers. The higher your pay, the more health coverage you get, with top executives and their families getting gold-plated plans guaranteeing top-notch medical attention for just about every health risk imaginable. As a result, our current $126 billion backdoor government health insurance system mainly benefits upper-income people.

For all these reasons, I've concluded health insurance should be decoupled from employment. Instead of condemning companies like Wal-Mart for providing scant health insurance, we ought to be instructing all companies to stop providing health benefits altogether, and eliminate the whole backdoor $126-billion-a-year government health care system. Better to use the money instead as a down payment on a universal and affordable system that's available to everyone regardless of how much they earn, where they work, or even whether they have a job.

But we can't even begin this conversation as long as the focus is on pushing Wal-Mart to give its employees better health insurance coverage, and as long as this effort occurs outside of and apart from the democratic process. By making it into a moral mission against Wal-Mart, advocates divert attention from what should be a national debate about public policy into a battle over the brand image of a single big company.

4

ALTHOUGH public relations wars over a particular company's virtue may utilize all the paraphernalia of political campaigns, their outcomes are not at all political. No one is elected or deposed, no programs or platforms are put into place, no laws or regulations are changed. The issue in such wars is not what is the best policy overall, but whether a particular company is morally good. It is an ersatz politics – a massive diversion from the real thing.

Participants in the campaign against Wal-Mart have described the battle in lofty terms. 'This is an assault on a business model,' said Carl Pope, a long-standing leader of the environmental movement who signed on in 2005. 'We're not trying to shut Wal-Mart down.'[35] Andrew Grossman, executive director of Wal-Mart Watch, an anti-Wal-Mart coalition, explained, 'We're focusing on Wal-Mart because of the huge impact it has on each of the different parts of American life it touches.' Grossman conceded Wal-Mart does provide many goods at the lowest price, but pointed out that this 'sometimes comes at a high cost to society'. The goal of the campaign was for Wal-Mart to 'make more money, but responsibly'.[36] What precisely did this mean? What exactly were the organizers seeking?

The campaign has used print and broadcast advertisements, videos, books, Web sites, organizing, even a film. Members of America's largest teachers union staged a boycott of Wal-Mart, urging parents and students not to patronize the company for back-to-school supplies. An automated phone system has called tens of thousands of people in Wal-Mart's home state of Arkansas, seeking potential whistle-blowers who will share bad news about the retailer. An online tool kit has been made available to any community group that might want to stop the retailer from entering its town.

The campaign has been run by people with direct experience in real politics. Paul Blank, one of its organizers, had been the political director of Howard Dean's presidential campaign. Chris Kofinis, another organizer, helped create the campaign to draft General Wesley Clark into the 2004 presidential election. Jim Jordan was formerly director of John Kerry's 2004 presidential campaign. Tracy Sefl had been a Democratic National Committee aide responsible for distributing negative press reports about George W. Bush in 2004.

In response, Wal-Mart has spent millions of dollars on a counter-campaign designed to depict the firm as worker-friendly, environmentally conscious, and socially responsible. It hired its own blue-ribbon team of former politicos – headed by Michael Deaver, once Ronald Reagan's image maker, and Leslie Dach, one of Bill Clinton's media consultants who also prepped Al Gore for the 2000 presidential debates, and including Jonathan Adashek, who had directed national delegate strategy for John Kerry, and David White, who helped manage the 1998 reelection of

Connecticut Republican Nancy Johnson. The group was advised by Terry Nelson, who had been national political director of George Bush's 2004 campaign.

It has rolled out commercials showing black, Hispanic, and female employees touting their benefits and career opportunities. It ran Asian-language advertisements targeted to Asian shoppers, others to Hispanics, full-page advertisements in more than a hundred mainstream newspapers, and large ads in select elite media, accusing its critics of distorting its image. 'When critics pervert the facts to serve their financial and potential interests, it's our duty to speak up', H. Lee Scott, Jr., is quoted as saying in an advertisement running across two pages of the *New York Review of Books*. Wal-Mart also ran ads bearing a striking resemblance to Bill Clinton's 'A Place Called Hope' message during the 1992 presidential campaign, starting with a homey image of Sam Walton's first five-and-dime store. 'It all began with a big dream in a small town,' says a sonorous narrator. 'Sam Walton's dream.'

As described by the *New York Times,* Wal-Mart's 'war room' assembles at seven a.m., scans news articles and television transcripts that mention the company, and when it finds any criticism immediately phones the reporters, and issues Web postings and press releases countering the criticism. It even devised a short film to rebut the anti-Wal-Mart film. It feeds releases to bloggers and suggests topics for postings. It has organized and funded a group called Working Families for Wal-Mart, and has recruited Wal-Mart suppliers to join.

Wal-Mart's team even characterizes its counter-campaign in terms usually applied to political battles. They have dubbed it 'Candidate Wal-Mart'. Robert McAdam, a former political strategist at the Tobacco Institute who was brought in to run corporate communications, says Wal-Mart is targeting 'swing voters' – consumers who had not soured on Wal-Mart. He describes the people who watched the anti-Wal-Mart film as 'true believers of their point of view' whose minds were probably already made up. 'They've got their base. We've got ours. But there is a group in the middle that really we all need to be talking to.'[37]

Has Wal-Mart, as a result of all this, been born again as a socially responsible company? Immediately after the devastation caused by

Hurricane Katrina, Wal-Mart pledged $15 million in cash to the Bush-Clinton Katrina Fund, and also gave a million dollars each to the Salvation Army and the American Red Cross. Within a few days, the company was offering any Wal-Mart workers displaced by the floods as much as $1,000 in emergency assistance – about three weeks' wages, tax-free – and guaranteeing them replacement jobs at any Wal-Mart in the country. The company shipped more than a hundred truckloads of merchandise to evacuation centers; offered residents of affected areas free emergency supplies of prescription drugs; and donated at least a dozen Wal-Mart buildings for use as shelters, food banks, and police command centers.[38]

The company has also set out to be – or appear to be – a better employer and citizen in the communities where it does business. It has set up an office of diversity, and expanded health insurance to children of part-time workers. It has announced a plan to help local businesses near its proposed urban stores. And it has become – or appeared to become – a dedicated environmentalist. It has launched a program to recycle shrink wrap, shopping bags, and other plastic items that its consumers normally send to landfills; it has begun testing the use of trees and grasses in parking lots to absorb carbon dioxide emissions and tainted water; it has committed itself to wind and solar energy to generate electricity, to energy-efficient lightbulbs, and to recycled materials to make its outdoor pavements. CEO Scott declared in 2006 that the firm would rely on 100 percent renewable energy sources 'that sustain our resources and environment'.[39]

All these efforts are commendable, but even when added together, their costs still constitute a tiny fraction of Wal-Mart's yearly revenues. Some, like the firm's newfound commitment to renewable energy, have come without a timetable; even Scott admits he is 'not sure how to achieve' them.[40] And it remains unclear to what extent the firm will continue to strive for 'social responsibility' if and when the heat is off and the anti-Wal-Mart campaign has ended – as, presumably, it will end, someday. You don't have to be a cynic to suppose Wal-Mart is doing the least it must do – spending the minimum required – to counter the anti-Wal-Mart camp's negative effects. That's what we'd expect under supercapitalism. There's no way to know whether a subsequent McKinsey study has informed Wal-Mart that its customers are now back in the fold and it has done just about enough, or that 2 or 3 percent are still put off and its reputation still needs some burnishing. But it's a safe bet Wal-Mart is keeping a watchful eye on the polls, and gauging its response accordingly.

Remember, too, Wal-Mart is unusual. It's a huge, ubiquitous, highly visible institution – the largest employer in America, and one of the largest in the world – making it uniquely susceptible to the essentially political tactics of its critics. To the extent the firm has been pushed to be more virtuous, it seems doubtful the tactics for achieving this result are transferable to most other firms.

The fact that a modern corporation can spend its way out of most public relations problems suggests that campaigns to make companies appear more 'socially responsible' are unlikely to establish new norms of corporate conduct. This is true even if the standard they are seeking is precisely drawn, and even if rivals don't jump into whatever lower-cost breach opens up. Political techniques may be employed by both sides, and some candidates for public office may even criticize a company for its irresponsible ways. But in such contests real politics – the stuff of democratic conflict and deliberation – is nowhere to be seen.

5

THE EAGERNESS with which corporations themselves have embraced social responsibility can dull the public's sense that there exist troublesome issues deserving of public attention. Vivid displays of corporate goodness can mask problems a democracy should grapple with – *would* grapple with – if the public understood their true dimensions. And because public attention spans are short, such temporary displays can preempt permanent solutions.

In light of rumblings from the Federal Communications Commission and from conservative legislators concerned about the sex and violence cable companies were pumping out to their subscribers, cable operators in early 2006 announced plans to offer packages of family-friendly channels so parents could shield their children. 'There's no need for legislation now,' said Senator Ted Stevens (R-Alaska), chairman of the Senate Commerce Committee, after being reassured of the cable companies' plans. 'We have to give it a chance to work.'[41] But cable companies had made similar promises before that had never been fulfilled. Presumably, cable companies will continue to pump out sex and violence until Congress or the FCC stops them, because sex and violence make money.

Not long ago, Kraft Foods announced it would stop advertising certain products to children under the age of twelve. The news was hailed as a glowing example of corporate social responsibility. It was no such thing. A government study released before Kraft made its move concluded that advertising directed toward children contributes to child obesity; two bills in Congress proposed that such advertising be regulated. Kraft's initiative was designed to preempt these bills and preserve some degree of discretion to decide how and what to advertise to children. Said Michael Mudd, the chief architect of Kraft's obesity strategy, 'If the tobacco industry could go back twenty or thirty years, reform their marketing, disarm their critics, and sacrifice a couple of hundred million in profits, knowing what they know today, don't you think they'd take that deal in a heartbeat? We have that deal in front of us today'.[42] As public pressure mounted for laws barring advertising of junk food directed at children, Kraft's announcement was followed by commitments from General Mills, McDonald's, and Coca-Cola to dedicate at least half of their child-oriented advertising to messages that encouraged 'healthy lifestyles'.[43] But the firms were conspicuously vague about how they defined healthy lifestyles, or how such ads might compare to the presumably unhealthy lifestyles they would promote with the other half of their advertising budgets.

Similarly, the News Corporation recently launched a multimillion-dollar advertising campaign to promote online safety tips cautioning teenage girls about men they may meet online. A case of social responsibility? Don't believe it. Several state attorneys general had threatened action against News Corp'.s MySpace to force it to make the site safer by providing parents with free software to block access to MySpace from home computers. But these measures would hurt business. The News Corporation launched its 'responsible' campaign to forestall the effort.[44]

Displays of corporate virtue may lull the public into thinking that a company can be trusted to do what's good for society even if costly to customers or shareholders. In 2002, British Petroleum shortened its name to BP and began promoting itself as the environmentally friendly oil company with a vision that went 'Beyond Petroleum' to embrace solar cells and wind power. In a $200 million advertising campaign organized by the advertising firm Ogilvy & Mather, the company transformed its corporate brand insignia from a shield to the more wholesomely natural green, yellow, and white sunburst. BP's chief executive, Lord John Browne, issued warnings about global warming and said the company had a social responsibility to take action.[45]

Notwithstanding its new image, BP continues to be one of the largest producers of crude oil on the planet. Although it committed itself to devoting $8 billion to alternative fuels over ten years, or roughly $800 million a year, that amount is tiny compared to BP's annual profits from oil of over $20 billion and its annual capital expenditures in recent years of over $14 billion.[46] By 2006, with oil hovering above $70 a barrel and BP making record profits, a company dedicated to moving 'beyond petroleum' presumably would invest more in nonfossil energy sources. But BP investors were not interested in being socially responsible. They wanted to maximize their returns – and the returns from nonfossil fuels were, at best, many years away while the returns from oil production were large and immediate. In the summer of 2006, Congress passed an energy bill conspicuously short on money for new non-fossil-based energy sources although generous to oil companies for continued oil exploration and development. It seems plausible that BP's advertising and marketing effort reinforced the public's perception that the private sector was already doing its part.

Meanwhile, BP was not exactly managing itself with the public in mind. In March 2005, corrosion of its pipes and equipment on the North Slope in Alaska led to a spill of 270,000 gallons of oil, the largest spill ever recorded in that fragile territory. Critics said BP wasn't spending enough money to prevent such spills. Only in 2006, after it was forced by the U.S. government to inspect all its pipelines with an automated device that crawled through the pipes, did the company find so much additional corrosion and leakage that it had to shut down a sixteen-mile feeder line to the Trans-Alaska Pipeline. And despite the best efforts of BP's Washington lobbyists and lawyers, BP came under investigation following an explosion at its Texas City plant, which killed fifteen workers and triggered a $21.3 million fine from safety regulators. A federal safety panel attributed it to BP's cutting costs on maintenance and safety.[47] Regulators at the Commodity Futures Trading Commission charged BP with manipulating the price of propane by cornering the market through its dominant position – thereby pushing up heating costs for millions of households at the peak of winter demand.[48] The firm was being investigated by the Environmental Protection Agency for violations of air pollution rules, by the Department of Labor for unsafe work practices, and by the Chemical Safety and Hazard Investigation Board for its unsafe work practices. Perhaps all of these instances of malfeasance or nonfeasance would have come to light in any event, but BP's advertising and marketing success at depicting it as socially responsible arguably dulled the public's outrage and tempered any demand for more comprehensive reform.

Displays of corporate virtue can also obscure conditions that would otherwise generate political heat for reform. Recall the flurry of media attention directed at sweatshop abuses during the mid-1990s. Apparel manufacturers and big retailers avoided any new laws or regulations by promising they would voluntarily clean up their acts. They developed voluntary codes of conduct and began monitoring their overseas factories, especially in China where most were located. But according to an investigation of internal industry documents by *BusinessWeek* in late 2006, the codes are being widely violated. Many Chinese factories keep double sets of books to fool auditors and distribute scripts for employees to recite if they are questioned. Factory managers in China complained in interviews that pressure from American firms to cut prices creates a powerful incentive to cheat. Yet American companies continue to tout the codes as evidence of their social responsibility. And, according to *BusinessWeek,* the codes 'have been important to maintaining political support in the U.S. for growing trade ties with China'.[49]

The preemption of politics often works because the public's memory – and the attention span of the media – are conspicuously short, as I said earlier. The public forgives because it so easily forgets. It can even be persuaded by a clever media campaign that a company once disdained for disregarding the common good is heroically achieving it. Recently, GE has been hailed as an environmental leader for its self-imposed restrictions on greenhouse gases. But the public – and the media – seem to have forgotten GE's role in polluting the Hudson River and its related tributaries with PCBs, the company's tenacious fight with federal regulators against cleaning up the mess, and its insistent lobbying against regulation that would force it to foot more of the bill.[50]

The U.S. government has not increased automobile fuel economy standards in several decades, or made any major move to increase gas taxes to better reflect the true social cost of oil. Part of the reason is that every time the public shows any broad interest in more fuel-efficient cars, major automakers declare themselves born-again environmentalists and commit themselves to fuel efficiency – until the public's interest flags. In 2000, Ford was the largest producer of SUVs and light trucks in North America, and these vehicles were among the nation's most notorious gas guzzlers. (When the Sierra Club sponsored a contest to give a name and advertising slogan to Ford's newest SUV, which used one gallon of gas for every twelve miles it traveled, the winner was 'The Ford Valdez – Have You Driven a Tanker Lately?')[51] But that year Ford effectively preempted political pressure to force it and other automakers to do more by promising to voluntarily increase the fuel economy of its SUVs by 25 percent. Two years later, when Ford's profits began to drop and consumers still wanted big gas guzzlers that were highly profitable to the company, Ford revoked its pledge. It even went so far as to initiate an intense lobbying and advertising effort that successfully defeated a Senate proposal to raise fuel economy standards.[52] In 2005, when oil prices shot upward and consumer interest in gas-guzzling SUVs and pickups began to wane, Ford with great fanfare announced its newfound interest in fuel efficiency. It pledged to voluntarily increase production of hybrid vehicles tenfold by 2010.

Starbucks and Ben & Jerry's are known for their dedication to social responsibility, as I have mentioned, but even these paragons of corporate virtue may have reassured the public more than was merited. Ever since Starbucks's chairman Howard Schultz first sought to transform the coffee bean company into a warmhearted corporate citizen, it has missed no opportunity to advertise its 'guiding principles' – such as 'providing a great working environment'. Yet Starbucks's employment record is not without some large blemishes. In late 2005, the National Labor Relations Board – dominated, it should be noted, by Republican appointees – issued a complaint alleging that Starbucks tried to prevent workers in several of its stores from participating in union activities, and fired at least one who 'supported and assisted' a union.[53] The endlessly soothing cadences about Starbucks's warmheartedness masks a company that is hardheaded when it comes to controlling costs – as it must be under supercapitalism. But the reassuring public relations campaign may also deflect what could be important public discussions about whether workers should be freer to unionize, especially workers in sectors of the economy sheltered from international competition.

Ben & Jerry's puts a great deal of emphasis on the ice cream firm's efforts to save tropical rain forests. The campaign seems to help sell the ice cream because it reinforces the image of Ben & Jerry's as a likable company. Yet conspicuously absent from Ben & Jerry's marketing is any effort to warn the public of the dangers of eating super-premium extra-creamy ice cream, precisely of the sort offered by Ben & Jerry's. Protecting the Amazon is surely a worthwhile goal but protecting people from obesity and diabetes is, too. Ben & Jerry's is not morally or legally responsible for supplying a healthier product, of course. Pursuant to supercapitalism, the company will do whatever is necessary to lure customers and satisfy investors. The problem is that people may be subtly lulled by the happy marketing about keeping the planet healthy into believing they can trust the company to keep them healthy, too. Like Kraft Foods's strategy, this one also diverts the public from pushing the Food and Drug Administration to do such things as bar advertising of fatty and sugary foods directed at children.

6

IN RECENT YEARS, politicians have gotten into something of a habit of publicly shaming companies that have acted badly in some way. Offending executives are typically hauled before congressional committees, where members of Congress berate them. But little legislation emerges to force the companies to behave any differently in the future.

The notion that such public scoldings and the temporarily unflattering publicity that accompanies them will alter corporate practices is another diversion from the work of creating rules that balance the interests of consumers and investors with the broader interests of the public. It also, conveniently, allows politicians to maintain good relations with the same companies and industries – collecting campaign donations, enjoying rounds of golf with their executives, tapping their corporate lobbyists for miscellaneous favors – while showing the public they're being 'tough' on the wrongdoers. Here again, the public is led to believe that democracy is working when all that's really working is public relations.

When oil prices soared in 2005 and early 2006, oil companies reaped extraordinary profits while millions of Americans had to pay more to fuel their cars and heat their homes. This prompted calls for Congress to enact a 'windfall profits tax' on the oil companies, but not even a debate took place. Instead, Congress simply scolded oil company executives and publicly berated the companies. As oil prices and profits approached record levels, Senator Chuck Grassley, an Iowa Republican and chairman of the Senate Finance Committee, issued a public letter reprimanding the oil and gas industry and instructing its companies to make charitable donations – 10 percent of that quarter's profits – to help poor people pay their heating bills that winter. 'You have a responsibility to help less fortunate Americans cope with the high cost of heating fuels,' Grassley said.[54]

Grassley's admonition made the headlines but obviously had no effect. Why would the oil companies voluntarily give away their profits? The only practical effects of the public scolding were to make Grassley and his colleagues seem compassionate, and to reassure some portion of the public that Congress was 'doing something' about record oil prices and profits. But because any real debate about a tax on their windfall profits was deflected by Grassley's moves, the public never had an opportunity to decide whether using the resulting revenues to help low-income oil consumers was worth the risk that oil companies, forced to disgorge some of their profits, might do less exploration and development – leading to higher prices in the future.

When BP's carelessness on the North Slope led to the temporary shut-down of the nation's largest oilfield, in August 2006, Congress demanded

BP executives appear in person to be held accountable. At the ensuing hearing, members from both sides of the aisle accused the executives of crass negligence. Representative Joe Barton, a Texas Republican and chairman of the committee, excoriated them: 'If one of the world's most successful oil companies can't do simple basic maintenance needed to keep the Prudhoe Bay field operating safely without interruption, maybe it shouldn't operate the pipeline,' he fumed. 'I am even more concerned about BP's corporate culture of seeming indifference to safety and environmental issues. And this comes from a company that prides itself in their ads on protecting the environment. Shame, shame, shame.'[55] Committee members then grilled the BP executives about why the company had failed for as long as fourteen years to do the sort of internal inspection and maintenance on its pipelines that was performed every two weeks on the Trans-Alaska Pipeline, into which the BP pipelines feed. The BP executives solemnly promised to be more careful in the future.

But neither the members of Congress nor the BP executives focused on the most pertinent fact: Frequent inspections of the Trans-Alaska Pipeline were required by law, but no similar inspections were required on feeder pipelines such as those owned by BP. If the panel was serious about getting BP to change its ways it would have introduced legislation to close this loophole. Recall that BP did the internal inspection that led to the shutdown only when the government forced it to, after the 2005 oil spill. Why should BP be expected voluntarily to do more thorough inspections in the future? The panel did not introduce such legislation because the hearings were for show. Barton and his colleagues had sponsored many bills favorable to the oil industry, and weren't about to impose any burdens on it. The scolding of BP's executives for being socially irresponsible did nothing to serve the public.

CORPORATE EXECUTIVES are not authorized by anyone – least of all by their consumers or investors – to balance profits against the public good. Nor do they have any expertise in making such moral calculations. That's why we live in a democracy, in which government is supposed to represent the public in drawing such lines.

Consider Yahoo's decision in 2005 when it surrendered to Chinese authorities the names of Chinese dissidents who had used Yahoo e-mail, thinking their e-mail addresses would shield their anonymity. One, a journalist, was sentenced to ten years in prison for sharing with foreigners a message his newspaper had received from Chinese authorities, urging it not to overplay the fifteenth anniversary of the Tiananmen Square disturbances. Another whom Yahoo helped Chinese authorities track down was sentenced to eight years, and a third, to four years. It remains unclear how many more dissidents are in Chinese prisons because of Yahoo's cooperation with Chinese authorities.

Yahoo's decision ignited a temporary firestorm in the United States. Its executives explained that the firm had no choice but to comply with Chinese law if it wanted access to China's huge and growing market – and Yahoo said it needed to be in China to move China toward democracy. 'I've always taken the attitude that you're better off playing by the government's rules and getting there,' Yahoo's chairman told attendees at a Web conference in San Francisco. 'Part of our role in any form of media is to get whatever we can into those countries and to show and enable people, slowly, to see the Western way and what our culture is like, and to learn.'[56] Yahoo's *role*? The firm was never anointed the vessel of Western culture, nor the arbiter of how best to present it to China. That's not the business of any global company. Indeed, most global companies do everything in their power to *avoid* the appearance of representing any particular culture, nationality, or ideology – unless such representation helps them sell their products.

The most damning indictment of Yahoo's decision came from Liu Xiaobo, a Chinese dissident in Beijing who had served time in a Chinese prison, in an open letter to Yahoo's founder, Jerry Yang. 'I must tell you that my indignation at and contempt for you and your company are not a bit less than my indignation at and contempt for the communist regime,' he wrote, according to a translated version appearing on the Web site of the China Information Center, based in Virginia. 'Profit makes you dull in morality. Did it ever occur to you that it is a shame for you to be considered a traitor to your customer?' Liu was unimpressed by Yahoo's argument. 'What you have said to defend yourself indicated that your success and wealth cannot hide your poverty in terms of the integrity of your personality.' His letter concluded with a bitter salvo. '[Y]our glorious social status is a poor cover for your barren morality, and your swelling wallet is an indicator of your diminished status as a man.'[57]

Both sides of this moralistic debate – Yahoo's and Liu's – reflect a fundamental misunderstanding of the role of the modern corporation in a democracy. Yahoo is not a moral entity, and no one authorized it to undertake any ethical balancing between sending dissidents to prison and exposing the Chinese to American culture and democracy. Yahoo's executives have only one responsibility under supercapitalism – to make money for their shareholders and, along the way, satisfy their consumers. In this instance, one of Yahoo's key 'consumers' was the Chinese government, because it was the gateway to all other Chinese consumers. Unless barred by legislation in the United States, Yahoo will continue to do whatever the Chinese government demands of it because the competitive stakes are too high and the potential profits too great to do otherwise. China is the second-largest Internet market in the world after the United States. As of 2006, more than 100 million Chinese had already logged on. At the rate Internet usage is growing there, within a few years there will be more Chinese on the Internet than Americans.

Google also found itself on the hot seat when it created for the Chinese authorities a censored version of its search engine, removing such incendiary words as 'human rights' and 'democracy'. 'I think it's arrogant for us to walk into a country where we are just beginning operations and tell that country how to run itself,' Eric Schmidt, Google's chief executive, told reporters from foreign news organizations.[58] But Google's decision to cooperate with China had nothing to do with arrogance or modesty. Like Yahoo's, it was all about profits, as it *had* to be. A few days before revelations about the firm's complicity with Chinese authorities, Google displayed heroic arrogance toward the United States government, which had demanded from Google information about child pornography searches conducted on Google's Web site, plus a random sample of a million Web searches. The U.S. government was trying to build a case for reinstating the Child Online Protection Act, which the Supreme Court had ruled to be overly broad in violation of the First Amendment. Google refused to cooperate.[59]

Why did Google decide to cooperate with Chinese authorities and not with American? If it were really trying to act morally, it would have resisted the demands of a totalitarian regime and deferred to a democracy. But morality had nothing to do with it. Access to China's huge market depended on the acquiescence of the Chinese government, and Google – like Yahoo – figured the only way to get that acquiescence was to do whatever the Chinese authorities wanted of it. Google didn't want to risk being banned while Microsoft would be free to market its own search engine in China. Access to American consumers, by contrast, does not depend on the acquiescence of the U.S. government. Google can sell its search engine to Americans regardless of whether it complies with a government request, which, in this instance, Google was prepared to fight in court. Indeed, Google's refusal to comply with the U.S. government made good business sense because it protected the privacy of Google's American consumers – who would have been incensed had Google turned over information about them. The difference, of course, is America is a democracy and China is not. Google's executives did not really concern themselves with the moral question of when to defy a government. They have no authority to make such a decision. They are in business to make money for their shareholders.

Any decision about Yahoo's or Google's 'social responsibility' was and is best left to the democratic process in the United States, where the firms are headquartered and whose citizens have a presumed stake in human rights around the world. Hence, one appropriate forum for sorting out these firms' duties is Congress, before whom their executives were summoned to appear. The question that body needed to address was whether American high-tech companies should be barred from cooperating with dictatorial governments to abridge human rights, even if this means losing business. That didn't happen, however.

The House Subcommittee on Human Rights held hearings in February 2006. In addition to Yahoo and Google, the panel summoned the executives of Microsoft and Cisco. Microsoft had removed blogs the Chinese government didn't like; Cisco had peddled its equipment to the Chinese police – creating for them a wireless Internet system to track individual users, a video surveillance system, automated surveillance of telephone conversations, and means of scanning the e-mails of every Chinese citizen.

New Jersey Republican Christopher Smith, chairman of the subcommittee, told the *New York Times* he was incensed. 'This is about accommodating a dictatorship. It's outrageous to be complicit in cracking down on dissenters.'[60] During the hearing, Smith accused Yahoo of entering into a 'sickening collaboration'. He ridiculed the firm's avowed justification for revealing the names of dissenters, saying if Anne Frank had put her diaries on e-mail and Nazi authorities wanted to track her down, Yahoo might have complied if Yahoo's e-mail system had exposed Nazi Germany to American culture. Tom Lantos, a leading Democrat on the committee and the only Holocaust survivor in Congress, asked the assembled executives, 'Are you ashamed? Yes or no?' He called their behavior a 'disgrace' and asked how they could sleep at night. James Leach, a Republican from Iowa, accused Google of serving as 'a functionary of the Chinese government', adding that 'if we want to learn how to censor, we'll go to you'.[61]

Smith subsequently introduced a bill to prevent American companies from, among other things, cooperating with censorship, but no one expected it to pass, and neither Smith nor any other member of Congress pushed for it. Soon thereafter, the State Department announced it was forming a task force about American Internet companies collaborating with China in repressing free speech. A 'task force' is another way to appear to do something in Washington while actually sending the issue back to the circular file.

If the U.S. government wanted to make Chinese human rights a priority, it could pass a law tomorrow barring American companies from helping the Chinese government hobble the free speech of its citizens – just as it once barred trade with South Africa and still bans commerce with countries like Cuba and Burma, and has managed to force most of the world's major banks to eschew business with North Korea.[62] Don't hold your breath. Despite all the self-righteous indignation emanating from Congress, and despite all the talk by the Bush administration about spreading democracy around the world, international human rights don't rank very high in Congress or the White House. First and foremost,

American business wants access to China's huge market without interference. During the hearing, Representative Robert Wexler, a Florida Democrat and another member of the Subcommittee on Human Rights, followed up on Lantos's questioning of the executives and asked if Congress ought to be ashamed of itself for having granted China special trade status as a most favored nation. In a rare moment of candor, another panel member, Dana Rohrabacher, a California Republican, denied Congress's culpability in granting China such trading privileges. 'Who lobbied for that?' he asked, rhetorically shifting responsibility to those who had pushed Congress to grant the trade concessions. 'Come on. The corporations did.'[63]

Lobbyists for Yahoo, Google, Microsoft, and Cisco understood the public's concern about what these companies have been up to in China. Presumably, they also knew the public wanted to be reassured that Congress was 'taking action'. In all likelihood they cooperated with Congress in putting together the conspicuous display of public scolding – for the cameras. They almost certainly knew Congress would do nothing to follow it up.

All the while, as expected, consumers and shareholders of these firms remained unconcerned. A consumer boycott was threatened (booyahoo. blogspot.com urged 'freedom-loving citizens of the Internet to discontinue their use of Yahoo services as a result of their oppressive policies'), but nothing came of it. Reporters Without Borders, a Paris-based organization, got more than two dozen 'socially responsible' asset management firms representing about $21 billion in assets to sign a resolution calling on Internet businesses to ensure their products were not used to commit human rights violations, and to introduce and support shareholder resolutions supporting freedom of expression – but nothing came from the resolution. A UBS analyst warned his clients that 'negative PR will damage Google's brand',[64] but he was proven wrong. A formal shareholder proposal to be voted on at Cisco's annual shareholder meeting requested the firm develop and implement a company human rights policy, but it went nowhere. Did anyone really expect investors to dump Cisco, Microsoft, and Google stock over this imbroglio? To the contrary, access to China's huge market was almost sure to increase profits and share prices in the future. Did anyone suppose American consumers would turn their backs on these companies' products? Not a chance.

None of these companies broke American law when they helped Chinese authorities suppress human rights in China. All obeyed the prevailing rules of the game. In supercapitalism, that's all we can and should expect companies to do. Framing the issue in moral terms – citing the shameless behavior of these companies and their executives – diverted attention from the harder but more important question of whether the rules of the game should be altered.

When Joe Biden, a putative presidential candidate in 2008, attacked Wal-Mart for treating its employees badly, he was credited with being concerned about working people – without having to introduce or push specific legislation to change the rules so Wal-Mart and all its competitors would have to behave differently. When John Kerry, as Democratic candidate for president in 2004, attacked the heads of companies that outsource jobs abroad for being 'Benedict Arnold CEOs', he was similarly credited with having compassion for the millions of American workers whose jobs have been lost and whose wages have been going nowhere for years. His moral outrage, however, only served to divert attention from the sobering fact that Kerry had no real plan then for curbing the practice, and has not followed up with one since.

7

POLITICS IS also diverted when politicians ask corporations to take some action *voluntarily* in the public interest, as Senator Grassley asked the oil companies to do. Early in the Bush administration, the White House embarked on an initiative dubbed 'Climate Leaders', in which the president, with great fanfare, asked the nation's major industrial polluters to commit to reducing their greenhouse gas emissions by at least 10 percent within the decade. The event suggested the administration was taking action on global warming, but it was doing no such thing. By January 2004, only fifty of the thousands of American firms with major greenhouse gas emissions had agreed to become Climate Leaders and reduce their emissions, and of these only fourteen announced specific goals. Although energy utilities are the nation's major polluters, only six of these fifty were utilities. Within a few years the Climate Leaders initiative had died a quiet death. A 2004 report by the World Economic Forum at Davos applauded the efforts of some forward-looking multinational companies to reduce greenhouse gas emissions but concluded that voluntary actions were inadequate to counter effects of climate change.[65]

Of course they're inadequate. Supercapitalism does not permit acts of corporate virtue that erode the bottom line. No company can 'voluntarily' take on an extra cost that its competitors don't also take on – which is why, under supercapitalism, regulations are the only means of getting companies to do things that hurt their bottom lines. As Professor David Vogel concluded after surveying so-called voluntary corporate environmental initiatives in the United States and Europe, few companies undertake them in the absence of regulations or the impending threat of them.[66] To suggest that a vast, untapped reservoir of corporate benevolence is available for the asking is to seriously mislead the public – and once again divert attention from the important job of deciding what such regulations should be. In fact, the outpouring of 'voluntary' corporate initiatives on global climate change is deflecting public attention from the necessary work of enacting tough laws and regulations to deal with it.

It is much the same with what passes for corporate charity. Companies donate money to the extent – and only to the extent – it has public relations value, and thereby helps the bottom line. Shareholders do not entrust their money to corporate executives for them to give it away, unless the return is greater. When the 2005 tsunami devastated Indonesia and other parts of coastal Southeast Asia, President Bush asked American corporations to come to the aid of victims. After several companies contributed millions of dollars, Bush extolled CEOs for their generosity. 'One of the less reported aspects of the U.S. business community is the tremendous amount of good they do, giving back to the communities in which they operate,' he said. '[T]he tsunami has presented the private sector here in America with a genuine watershed moment. I believe it's ushered in a new era of corporate social responsibility.'[67] His words were greeted with loud applause, but they made no sense. The assembled CEOs had not been generous – they had not contributed their own money. They had donated their shareholders' money. Presumably they had done so in the belief that their shareholders would benefit from the public relations value such contributions added to the firms' bottom lines. Otherwise, these CEOs would have violated their fiduciary duties and risked having their shareholders switch to other companies that didn't give away their money. Shareholders do not invest in firms expecting their money will be used for charitable purposes. They invest to earn high returns. Shareholders who wish to be charitable will, presumably, make donations to charities of their own choosing in amounts they decide for themselves.

The larger danger is that these conspicuous displays of corporate beneficence hoodwink the public into believing corporations have charitable impulses that can be relied on in a pinch. An earthquake that hit Pakistan in October 2005 killed more than 87,000 people and displaced three times as many as those affected by the Indian Ocean tsunami. Yet the Bush administration initially pledged only $500,000 in aid – a sum so small as to be derided by many Pakistanis.[68] Bush then pledged more, and also asked five prominent CEOs to mount a major fund-raising effort from American corporations. General Electric contributed more than $5 million in cash and health care and energy equipment; Pfizer, $1 million to relief agencies and $5 million in medicines and health care products; Xerox, $1 million in cash; Citigroup, $3 million. In total, the CEOs raised about $100 million, moving the president to another effusive outpouring of gratitude. 'If the international community had not stepped in,' he told the assembled executives, 'the door might have been opened for more radical Islamic influences.'[69]

Actually, the 'international community' failed to step in as much as it should have. Pakistan needed billions of dollars, not hundreds of millions – and needed it quickly. While more than $3 billion in aid had been distributed to areas hit by the tsunami within two weeks of that disaster, a total of only $17 million had been distributed to Pakistan as late as six weeks after the quake. And according to the United Nations, total pledges to Pakistan still amounted to only a quarter of what was needed to cope with the devastation. The void was partly filled by radical Islamist groups.

The Pakistani interior minister acknowledged that the radicals were 'the lifeline of our rescue and relief work'.[70]

In the wake of Hurricane Katrina in the summer of 2006, the president again asked large corporations to come to the aid of victims – which they did. Steve Odland, CEO of Office Depot, offered some $17 million of the company's office supplies, water, batteries, and school supplies. As noted, Wal-Mart donated millions of dollars. 'We are such a part of the fabric of these communities that you have a responsibility to respond,' Wal-Mart's Lee Scott explained. But responsibility had nothing to do with it. As we've seen, the conspicuous show of corporate kindness was essential to Wal-Mart's strategy of countering the bad press it was getting from the anti-Wal-Mart campaign.[71]

Corporations are not set up to be public charities. The world's biggest philanthropists, Bill and Melinda Gates, do not draw on Microsoft's profits; they draw on their own vast fortune. The only legitimate reason for a corporation to be generous with its shareholders' money is to burnish its brand image, and such a rationale will go only so far. In Katrina's aftermath, Wal-Mart's Scott was candid about the limits of his firm's generosity. 'We can't send three trailer loads of merchandise to every group that asks for it,' he said, turning down a request for two thousand blankets. 'We have to, at the end of this, have a viable business.'[72] Charitable giving by corporations is infinitely small compared to what the public sector dispenses.

Corporate 'thank-you' rituals have become a staple of American public life, but it remains unclear who exactly deserves thanks. 'Ajay, please come up here!' Bill Clinton summoned a Citigroup executive, Ajay Banga, onto the stage at his annual corporate give-a-thon. Before a full house of CEOs and millionaire investors, Clinton praised Citigroup for committing $5.5 million to support financial education for the poor.[73] But who exactly was Clinton praising? The $5.5 million wasn't Banga's money. Presumably, it came out of Citigroup's profits. If Citigroup's shareholders benefited indirectly from the positive publicity because it improved Citigroup's bottom line, the shareholders didn't deserve thanks; they had sacrificed nothing. If they did not benefit, Banga and the other Citigroup executives deserved to be criticized rather than thanked because they had no business giving away their shareholders' money. After Hurricanes Katrina and Rita, and the Indonesian tsunami, the Red Cross ran a two-page spread in the *New York Times,* publicly thanking more than 225 'donors' of a million dollars or more. The list included a few families and foundations, but mostly publicly held corporations. Some of these corporations were recognized for donations made by their employees or customers but most were recognized for making the gifts themselves. 'Thank you for your support during the most demanding time in our 125 years of serving America',[74] read the ad. Here again, it was unclear whom the Red Cross was thanking.

Corporations do some good deeds but corporate thank-you rituals mislead the public into believing companies do these things out of selflessness – indeed, that there is a 'self' there deserving commendation in the first place. But there is no corporate selflessness, and there is no corporate self. In supercapitalism, companies exist only to serve consumers and thereby make money for investors. *This* is how they serve the public.

8

DEMOCRACY and capitalism have been turned upside down. As we have seen, capitalism has invaded democracy. Legislation is enacted with public rationales that bear little or no relation to the real motives of the corporations and their lobbyists who pushed for them and legislators who voted for them. Regulations, subsidies, taxes, and tax breaks are justified as being in the 'public interest' but are most often the products of fierce lobbying by businesses or industries seeking competitive advantage over one another. The broader public is not involved. Citizen voices are drowned out. The public rationales mask what's really going on – which companies and industries gain and which lose.

At the same time, a kind of faux democracy has invaded capitalism. Politicians and advocates praise companies for acting 'responsibly' or condemn them for not doing so. Yet the praise and blame are disconnected from any laws and rules defining responsible behavior. The message that companies are moral beings with social responsibilities diverts public attention from the task of establishing such laws and rules in the first place. It also suggests companies are the moral equivalent to citizens who possess rights, including the right to be represented in a democracy. The praise or blame is soon forgotten, and barely affects the behavior of consumers or investors. Meanwhile, the real democratic process is left to companies and industries seeking competitive advantage.

The first step in turning democracy and capitalism right side up is to understand what is real and what is make-believe.

CHAPTER SIX

A CITIZEN'S GUIDE
TO SUPERCAPITALISM

To reprise: Supercapitalism has triumphed as power has shifted to consumers and investors. They now have more choice than ever before, and can switch ever more easily to better deals. And competition among companies to lure and keep them continues to intensify. This means better and cheaper products, and higher returns. Yet as supercapitalism has triumphed, its negative social consequences have also loomed larger. These include widening inequality as most gains from economic growth go to the very top, reduced job security, instability of or loss of community, environmental degradation, violations of human rights abroad, and a plethora of products and services pandering to our basest desires. These consequences are larger in the United States than in other advanced economies because America has moved deeper into supercapitalism. Other economies, following closely behind, have begun to experience many of the same things.

Democracy is the appropriate vehicle for responding to such social consequences. That's where citizen values are supposed to be expressed, where choices are supposed to be made between what we want for ourselves as consumers and investors, and what we want to achieve together. But the same competition that has fueled supercapitalism has spilled over into the political process. Large companies have hired platoons of lobbyists, lawyers, experts, and public relations specialists, and devoted more and more money to electoral campaigns. The result has been to drown out voices and values of citizens. As all of this has transpired, the old institutions through which citizen values had been expressed in the Not Quite

Golden Age – industry-wide labor unions, local citizen-based groups, 'corporate statesmen' responding to all stakeholders, and regulatory agencies – have been largely blown away by the gusts of supercapitalism.

Instead of guarding democracy against the disturbing side effects of supercapitalism, many reformers have set their sights on changing the behavior of particular companies – extolling them for being socially virtuous or attacking them for being socially irresponsible. The result has been some marginal changes in corporate behavior. But the larger consequence has been to divert the public's attention from fixing democracy.

1

THERE IS no shortage of policy ideas for coping with the social downsides of supercapitalism. I included some of mine at the end of Chapter 3. You may disagree, but we're not even debating them seriously because public policy has become less and less relevant to politics. New ideas are trotted out for public viewing in every election season but they have little bearing on what happens after the election is over. Everyday politics within legislatures, committees, and departments and agencies of government has come to be dominated by corporations seeking competitive advantage. Most new legislation and regulation is at the behest of certain companies or segments of industries; most conflicts and compromises are among competing companies or industries. Should some policy be proposed that might impose costs on many companies or industries, they join together to defeat it.

Without a democracy that will implement them, policy ideas about 'what should be done' are beside the point. A more fundamental question, therefore, is how to make democracy work better.

Many ideas have been proposed here, too: There have been calls to publicly finance election campaigns for all major offices, require broadcasters who use the public airwaves to contribute free campaign advertising to candidates in a general election, prohibit lobbyists from soliciting and bundling big-check donations from their business clients, ban gifts to lawmakers by corporations or executives, prohibit privately financed junkets for legislators and aides, ban parties staged to 'honor' politicians with corporate contributions, prohibit former legislators and public officials from lobbying for at least five years after they leave office, require lobbyists to disclose all lobbying expenditures, and mandate that all expert witnesses in legislative and regulatory hearings disclose financial relationships with economically interested parties. Any such reforms would have to be monitored and enforced by an independent inspector general with power to investigate abuses and impose stiff penalties on violators.[1]

All such steps would be helpful. But the question of how to enact and implement them only leads to a deeper dilemma. Political reforms cannot be achieved as long as public officials and legislators are dependent on the very corporations whose influence is to be limited. The system cannot repair itself from inside. An occasional revelation of outright political bribery causes enough public outrage to elicit solemn pledges by legislators and officials to reform the system. Such promises are forgotten as soon as public outrage fades and memories dim.

In any event, the fundamental problem does not, for the most part, involve blatant bribes and kickbacks. Rather, it is the intrusion of supercapitalism into every facet of democracy – the dominance of corporate lobbyists, lawyers, and public relations professionals over the entire political process; the corporate money that engulfs the system on a day-to-day basis, making it almost impossible for citizen voices to be heard. Not only do campaign contributions have to be severely limited, but also corporate expenditures on lobbying and public relations intended to influence legislative outcomes.

One possible hope for shielding democracy from supercapitalism is the presumed fact that many corporations would rather not pay these escalating costs if they could be certain their competitors would refrain from paying them as well. Firms, therefore, might be amenable to a truce from the political arms race. A few years ago, before the McCain-Feingold Act put a temporary damper on the flow of 'soft money' (donations to political parties for 'issue advertisements' that often end up as thinly veiled attacks on opponents), several hundred business executives in the Committee for Economic Development – including those from General Motors, Xerox, Merck, and Sara Lee Corporation – endorsed stronger campaign finance reform. The group's president, Charles Kolb, summarized their view:

'These people are saying: We're tired of being hit up and shaken down. Politics ought to be about something besides hitting up companies for more and more money.'[2] Their collective support helped pass McCain-Feingold.

It may be possible to craft further deals among corporations to limit the flow of money into politics – perhaps barring lobbyists from soliciting and bundling big-check donations from their business clients and banning gifts to lawmakers from corporations or executives. In 2002, BP's CEO, Lord Browne, announced the firm was voluntarily ending all contributions to political candidates around the world. 'We must be particularly careful about the political process,' he said, 'not because it is unimportant – quite the reverse – but because the legitimacy of that process is crucial both for society and for us as a company working in that society.'[3] Yet it will be far harder to gain agreement among large companies to refrain from flooding Washington and other capital cities with lobbyists, lawyers, and public relations specialists. Notably, BP did not terminate its contracts with such professionals.

To be effective, any such truce would have to be enacted into law. A voluntary truce could not gain the support of every large company. The potential benefits of remaining free to craft advantageous political deals would be too great to pass up. That fact alone would doom any such voluntary effort; as long as some large companies continued to pour money into Washington and other capitals, others would feel compelled to do so as well.

But the largest impediment to reform is one brazen fact: Many politicians and lobbyists want to continue to extort money from the private sector. That's how politicians keep their hold on power, and lobbyists keep their hold on money.

2

GENUINE REFORM will occur only if and when most citizens demand it. In order for that to happen, the public must understand several truths about the present system that are now obscured. The media must understand them as well, and be prepared to convey them when the occasion arises. The half-truths, mythologies, and distortions that now litter the border between the private sector and the public sector make it impossible for the public to keep straight the distinct roles of corporate executives and public officials. Such muddled thinking confounds efforts to prevent supercapitalism from overrunning democracy.

A citizen's guide to supercapitalism would begin by instructing the public to beware of any politician or advocate who blames corporations and corporate executives for the negative social consequences of super-capitalism, whether it be low or declining wages and benefits, job losses, widening inequality, loss of community, global warming, indecent products, or any other of the commonly voiced complaints. Corporate executives are responsible for obeying the law, and should be held accountable for any illegality. But they cannot and should not be expected to do anything more. Their job is to satisfy their consumers and thereby make money for their investors. If they fail to do this as well if not better than their rivals they will be penalized by consumers and investors who take their money elsewhere.

Corporate executives are not engaged in a diabolical plot. The negative social consequences are the logical consequence of intensifying competition to give consumers and investors better and better deals. Those deals may require moving jobs abroad where they can be done at lower wages, substituting computers and software for people, or resisting unions. Or the deals may come at the expense of small retailers on Main Street who can't sell items at prices nearly as low, or at the expense of entire communities that lose a major employer who has to outsource abroad to remain competitive. The deals may require the talents of celebrity CEOs who are paid like baseball stars. Or they may come at the expense of the earth's atmosphere. Good deals may depend on filling the air with gunk, filling the airwaves with sex and violence, or filling our stomachs with junk food. The deals may involve trampling human rights abroad or putting young children to work in Southeast Asia. As long as the deals are legal, and as long as they satisfy consumers and investors, corporations and their executives will pursue them.

This doesn't make them right, but the only way to make them *wrong* — the only way to stop companies from giving consumers and investors good deals that depend on such moves – is to make them illegal. It is illogical to criticize companies for playing by the current rules of the game; if we want them to play differently, we have to change the rules.

It follows that the public must also beware of any claim by corporate executives that their company is doing something in order to advance the 'public good' or to fulfill the firm's 'social responsibility'. Companies are not interested in the public good. It is not their responsibility to be good. They may do good things to improve their brand image, so as to increase sales and profits. They will do profitable things that may happen to have socially beneficial side effects. But they will not do good things because they are considered to be good.

Likewise, when corporate executives or their lobbyists and lawyers fight for certain political or judicial outcomes, do not believe a word they, their spokesmen, or their 'experts' say about why the outcome they seek is in the public interest. The outcome may indeed be in the public interest, but you cannot take their word for it because they are not motivated to do anything mainly because it is in the public interest. Their only legitimate motive, again, is to satisfy consumers in order to make profits that will satisfy investors. The only reason they have for advocating a particular political or judicial outcome is to advance or protect their competitive position. The sole reason they have for claiming an outcome is in the public's interest is to gain public support for it as a means of increasing their political leverage to achieve it.

I hope I've made it clear that you should also be skeptical of any politician who claims the public can rely on the 'voluntary' cooperation of the private sector to achieve some public purpose or goal. Corporations and their executives have no license to use shareholder money to accomplish public purposes. They may 'voluntarily' agree to donate money to a worthy cause, or to forbear from polluting the atmosphere, or to bring more jobs to a particular area – but only if the action is profitable, or if in so doing they burnish their public image and thus improve their bottom lines, or to forestall some new law or regulation that might impose a greater burden. But in the latter instances, such 'voluntary' good deeds are likely to be limited and temporary, extending only insofar as the conditions that made such 'voluntary' action pay off continue. In all such circumstances, you should ask why, if the public goal is so worthy, the politician is not seeking a law requiring the private sector to achieve it.

Similarly, be skeptical of any politician who blames a corporation for doing something that's legal or failing to do something when no law requires that it do so. Find out if the politician is actively supporting legislation to change the rules of the game so that this company and all others must alter their behavior in the prescribed way. If not, you are safe to assume that the politician's words of condemnation are designed to act as a cover for taking no action on the problem.

Be wary, as well, of concerted efforts by advocates and reformers – in the form of public relations campaigns, boycotts, and citizen movements – to force a particular company to be more socially virtuous. Seek to discover the specific goal of any such effort. If you agree with it, ask yourself whether it might be better served by changing laws or regulations that force all companies to alter their behavior in the same way. Sometimes, as we have seen, reformers target specific companies in order to mobilize the public to take political action; sometimes labor organizers target specific companies in order to force them to accept union representation. These may be useful reform strategies. But broad-scale attacks on specific companies to force them to alter their behavior in ways that will cause their prices to increase or their profits to decline should be suspect. Even if socially beneficial, the desired behavior may not seem worth the resulting higher prices or reduced returns. Besides, once the company's prices are raised or returns lowered, other competitors whose behavior has not been altered and whose prices are lower and returns higher may fill the gap, defeating the whole purpose of the effort.

In general, corporate responsibilities to the public are better addressed in the democratic process than inside corporate boardrooms. Reformers should focus on laws or regulations they seek to change, and mobilize the public around changing them. If the campaign against Wal-Mart, for example, is designed to get Wal-Mart to accept unions, that should be made clear. If it is to mobilize the public to accept changes in labor laws that make it easier for low-wage workers to form unions, that goal should be sought directly. The resulting legislative battle would strengthen democracy rather than divert it.

The most effective thing reformers can do is to reduce the effects of corporate money on politics, and enhance the voices of citizens. No other avenue of reform is as important. Corporate executives who sincerely wish to do good can make no better contribution than keeping their company out of politics. If corporate social responsibility has any meaning at all, it is to refrain from corrupting democracy.

3

A FINAL TRUTH that needs to be emphasized – the most basic of all – is that corporations are not people. They are legal fictions, nothing more than bundles of contractual agreements. Yes, there are 'corporate cultures', dominant styles or norms such as characterize any group. But the corporation itself does not exist in corporeal form. This is especially so under supercapitalism, when companies are quickly morphing into global supply chains. Corporations should have no more legal rights to free speech, due process, or political representation in a democracy than do any other pieces of paper on which contracts are written. Legislators or judges who grant corporations such rights are not being intellectually honest, or they are unaware of the effects of supercapitalism. Only *people* should possess such rights.

When companies are invested with anthropomorphic qualities – when they are described in the media or by political leaders as being noble or scurrilous, patriotic or treasonous, law-abiding or criminal, or other qualities that human beings possess – the public is misled into thinking companies resemble people. Even the grammatical convention in America of attaching verbs directly to a company – as in 'Microsoft is trying to …' or 'Wal-Mart wants …' – subtly reinforces the tendency to think about these entities as having independent volition. (The British, with their typical impeccability, use plural verbs to describe corporate conduct, as in 'Rolls-Royce are considering …')

The result of this anthropomorphic fallacy is to give companies duties and rights that properly belong to people instead. This blurs the boundary between capitalism and democracy, and leads to a host of bad public policies. Consider, for example, the corporate income tax. The public has the false impression that corporations pay it, and therefore they should be entitled to participate in the democratic process under the old adage 'no taxation without representation'. But only people pay taxes. In reality, the corporate income tax is paid – indirectly – by the company's consumers, shareholders, and employees. Studies have attempted to determine exactly how the tax is allocated among these three groups, but the distribution remains unclear. What is clear is the corporate income tax is inefficient and inequitable.

It's inefficient because interest payments made by corporations on their debt are deductible from their corporate income tax while dividend payments are not. This creates an incentive for companies to overrely on debt financing relative to shareholder equity, and to retain earnings rather than distribute them as dividends. The result, in recent years, has been for many corporations to accumulate large amounts of money that the company then uses to purchase other companies or to buy back its shares of stock. Capital markets would be more efficient if these accumulated profits were redistributed to shareholders as dividends. Decisions by millions of shareholders about how and when to reinvest these funds are likely to be, as a whole, wiser than decisions made by a relatively small number of corporate executives. Abolishing the corporate income tax would thus help capital markets work better.

The corporate income tax is inequitable in that retained earnings representing the portion held by lower-income investors are taxed at a corporate rate that's often higher than the rate they pay on their other income, while earnings representing the holdings of higher-income shareholders are taxed at a corporate rate often lower than they pay on the rest of their income. As we have seen, under supercapitalism, investors have far more power than they did decades ago. Their decisions about where to put their money to maximize their returns are similar to any other decisions they make about how to increase their earnings. Logically, there is no reason why their 'corporate' earnings should be taxed differently than their other earnings. Abolishing the corporate income tax and treating all corporate income as the personal income of shareholders would rectify this anomaly.

An idea advanced by Professor Lester Thurow of MIT is to get rid of the corporate income tax and have shareholders pay personal taxes on all income earned by the corporation on their behalf – whether the income is retained by the corporation or is paid out as dividends. This would essentially reveal the corporation to be what it is in fact – a partnership of shareholders. All corporate earnings would be treated as personal income. But shareholders would not feel the pinch. As their 'corporate' earnings accumulated throughout the year, the company would withhold taxes owed based on the shareholder's tax bracket – as did the shareholder's employer on his or her salaried earnings. At the end of the year, shareholders would receive from the company the equivalent of a W-2 form telling them how much income should be added to their other sources of income and how much income tax had been withheld. This way, shareholders would automatically pay taxes on 'their' corporate earnings at rates appropriate to their own incomes.[4]

This would rectify the two problems. Corporations would have no artificial incentive to retain earnings, and taxes would be lower for low-income shareholders and higher for higher-income shareholders.* One important by-product of this reform would be to puncture the widespread but false notion that corporations pay taxes and therefore deserve to be represented in the political process. Again, companies should have no rights or responsibilities in a democracy. Only people should.

A SIMILAR CONFUSION and inequity occurs when companies are held criminally liable for the misdeeds of their executives or other employees. Not only does corporate criminal liability reinforce the anthropomorphic fallacy – after all, criminals have rights under most democratic legal systems – but it ends up hurting lots of innocent people.

There is the case of Arthur Andersen, the former accounting firm convicted of obstruction of justice when certain partners destroyed records of the auditing work they did for Enron as the energy giant was imploding,

---

* This integration of corporate and individual income already occurs in so-called S corporations that have fewer than one hundred shareholders and issue only one class of stock. A large public company with different classes of common and preferred stock, and whose shareholders change during the course of a year, would face a more complicated challenge of attributing income to particular shareholders, but computers and software could render this feasible. See John McNulty, 'Corporate Income Tax Reform in the United States: Proposals for Integration of the Corporate and Individual Taxes', *International Tax and Business Lawyer* 12 (1994), pp. 161–259.

shortly before the SEC began its investigation. When Andersen was convicted in 2002, its clients abandoned the company and hired other accounting firms. Andersen shrank from 28,000 employees to a skeleton crew of 200, who attended to the final details of shutting it down. The vast majority of Andersen employees had nothing to do with Enron but lost their jobs nonetheless. Some senior partners moved to other accounting or consulting firms. Joseph Berardino, Andersen's CEO at the time, got a lucrative job at a private equity firm. Some other senior partners formed a new accounting firm. But many lower-level employees were hit hard. Three years after the conviction, a large number were still out of work, according to an Andersen associate who ran a Web site for Andersen alumni. In addition, retired partners and employees lost a substantial portion of their retirement benefits. The Supreme Court eventually reversed the conviction, but by then it was too late. The company was gone. One former employee wrote on the Web site, 'Does this mean we can bring a class action against the DOJ [Department of Justice] for ruining our lives?'[5]

Companies cannot act with criminal intent because they have no human capacity for intent. Arthur Andersen may have sounded like a person but the accounting firm was a legal fiction. The Supreme Court reversed the decision because the trial judge had failed to instruct the jury it must find proof Andersen knew its actions were wrong. Yet how can any jury, under any circumstances, find that a company 'knew' that 'its' actions were wrong? A company cannot know right from wrong; a company is incapable of knowing anything. Nor does a company itself take action. Only people know right from wrong, and only people act.* That is a basic tenet of democracy.

On the other hand, corporate civil liability – where a company is fined for illegal actions by certain of its executives or employees that profit the firm – is perfectly consistent with the idea of personal responsibility. There is no good reason why shareholders or other employees should reap

---

* Prosecutors point to the difficulty of proving individual intent when transactions involve many people, as is typically the case in a large corporation. This is hardly an argument for inflicting punishment on low-level employees – who are least likely to have been involved in a criminal matter but most likely to be harmed when the corporation as a whole shrinks or dissolves as a result of the criminal action.

the gains from illegal acts, even those of which they had no knowledge. But the fine must be proportional to the illegal gain. Punitive damages that go so far beyond the illegal gains as to jeopardize the company's continued existence are more like criminal penalties, and therefore should not be allowed.

SIMILARLY, it makes no sense to criticize or penalize companies headquartered in the United States for sending jobs abroad or parking their profits in other nations. Nor does it make sense for the U.S. government to favor companies headquartered in the United States over companies headquartered elsewhere, on the assumption that American-based companies are somehow more patriotic than companies headquartered abroad. Companies are not patriotic. To believe they should be – even could be, under the logic of supercapitalism – is to further anthropomorphize the corporation, and confuse the set of legal contracts that comprise a company with rights and responsibilities of citizenship that only people can exercise. Under supercapitalism, all global companies, wherever headquartered, are coming to resemble one another because they are competing against one another for global consumers and investors. All are turning into global supply chains – seeking the best deals from all over the world.

Corporate executives who outsource abroad are not treasonous 'Benedict Arnolds'. They cannot sacrifice good deals for their customers and investors in the belief that their company has a patriotic duty to hire more Americans or otherwise be a good American citizen. If they did so, customers and investors would abandon them in favor of other companies that provided better deals through outsourcing abroad. By 2006, as has been noted, American-based companies accounted for almost half of American imports. The biggest exporter of German-made washing machines was Whirlpool. Whirlpool's American employment has not increased since 1990, while its overseas workforce has tripled. Yet two-thirds of its revenue still comes from American consumers.[6] Even Wal-Mart is becoming a global company, growing faster abroad than in the United States.

For the same reason, it makes little sense to limit certain military contracts to so-called American companies. The ostensible reason for doing so is that American companies will do their research, design engineering, and manufacturing in the United States, and that the nation's security depends on having such crucial activities done within the nation's borders. But in fact, American-based defense contractors increasingly rely on the same worldwide supply chains that other companies do. A significant amount of military software is developed offshore. In 2006, 90 percent of all printed circuit boards were made overseas. If defense contractors had to custom-make everything inside the United States, defense costs would be even more astronomical than they are today.[7]

The logic of limiting certain public responsibilities to American companies is similarly dubious. It fails to distinguish between who owns a company and who actually works for it, and it assumes that the nationality of a global company's executives or other employees alters its performance. In 2006, Congress succumbed to this fallacious logic when it moved to stop Dubai Ports World, owned by the emir of Dubai, from taking over contracts to run six American ports, fearing a security risk. But at the time, about 80 percent of American ports were already run by foreign-based companies, including the six in question. Most of these companies had hired American nationals to undertake day-to-day management of the ports, because they were the most experienced. Dubai Ports World's chief operating officer was an American, as was its former chief executive, as were the American port executives of the British company that was seeking to sell its contracts to Dubai Ports World. In any event, day-to-day operations of the ports would still be done by American longshoremen, clerks, and technicians. And control over port security would remain with the U.S. government, the Coast Guard, Customs, harbor police, and port authorities, who make and enforce the rules.[8]

Subsidizing the research of American-based companies is just as illogical. It does not make America more competitive, because American-based companies are doing their research and development all over the world. Such subsidies merely underwrite research that would have been undertaken here anyway while freeing up more corporate research money to be spent outside the United States. Microsoft recently announced a $1.7 billion investment in India, about half of which will go to its R&D center in Hyderabad, in southern India. In early 2006, IBM announced it was opening a software laboratory in Bangalore, India. Dow Chemical is building a research center in Shanghai that will employ six hundred engineers when completed in 2007, and a large installation in India. In a survey of more than two hundred American and European global corporations conducted by the National Academies, 38 percent planned to shift more of their R&D work to China and India, and to decrease R&D in the United States and Europe.[9]

The goal of government policy should be to make Americans more competitive, not to make American companies more competitive. This is an important distinction that most corporate executives understand. Big companies are global entities; people are not. 'For a company, the reality is that we have a lot of options,' says William Banholzer, Dow's chief technology officer. 'But my *personal* worry is that an innovative science and engineering workforce is vital to the economy. If that slips, it is going to hurt the United States over the long run' (italics added).[10] The federal government should subsidize the basic R&D of any company regardless of its headquarters as long as it does its work in the United States, developing on-the-job skills of American-based engineers and scientists.

IT MAKES no sense to treat companies as 'persons' with legal rights to challenge in court duly enacted laws and regulations. That should be left to real citizens. Investors, consumers, or employees already have the right to go to court – as individuals or as members of a class action – to challenge laws and regulations that allegedly impose economic injuries on them. They do not need the corporation to litigate on their behalf. Moreover, because almost all large companies depend on pools of capital derived from investors all over the world, giving companies standing to sue effectively confers on some non-American investors the right to seek to overturn American laws and regulations. Noncitizens should have no right to do so unless the law or regulations breach some international treaty. Otherwise, decisions arrived at democratically can be overturned by people who are not even American citizens.

Yet this is happening all the time when companies are allowed to sue. In January 2005, nine global automakers sued California to block California's new 'clean cars' law, which requires cars sold in California to reduce greenhouse gas emissions 30 percent by model year 2016, on grounds that the legislation amounted to an unconstitutional restraint on interstate commerce. A majority of the shareholders of at least seven of these automakers were not American citizens yet the court gave them standing to challenge, and potentially overturn, a law enacted by the citizens of California. This is nonsensical. Real citizenship should be the criterion – and by allowing only people rather than companies to sue, it can be. Any American citizen or group of American citizens claiming they are injured by California's law should be able to challenge it – including, for example, American investors in Toyota, but not including non-American investors in General Motors.

FINALLY, and most fundamentally, since only people can be citizens, only people should be allowed to participate in democratic decision making. Consumers, investors, executives, and other employees all have a right to advance their interests within a democracy. But as Yale political scientist Charles Lindblom concluded many years ago, neither ethically nor logically do corporations have a legitimate role in the democratic process.[11]

For many years, anti-union lobbyists have pushed what they call 'paycheck protection' laws, supposedly designed to protect union members from being forced, through their dues, to support union political activities they oppose. Under such laws – already in effect in several states – no union dues can be spent for any political purpose, including lobbying, unless union members specifically agree. It would seem logical to apply the same principle to protect shareholders from being forced through their investments to support political activities they oppose. 'Stockholder protection'[12] would require that shareholders specifically agree to any corporate political activity. If a company dedicates, say, $100,000 to political action in a given year – including lobbying, campaign contributions, and gifts or junkets for elected officials – shareholders who do not wish their money to be used this way would get a special dividend or additional shares representing their pro rata share of that expenditure. Mutual funds and pension plans would have to notify their shareholders of such political activity, and seek their acquiescence. Such political activity would thereby be paid for by shareholders who wished to spend their portion of company profits on it.

Even if it is assumed that political activities of corporations reflect the consumer and investor in us, the citizen in us has nowhere near the same political clout. Another way to redress the imbalance would be to allow taxpayers a tax credit of up to, say, $1,000 a year, which we could send to any organization that used the money to lobby on behalf of our citizen values – groups seeking, for instance, a higher minimum wage, a cleaner environment, or limits on videos and music featuring lurid sex and violence. The group would have to be nonprofit, but the choice of group and goal would be up to each of us. The point would be to give the citizen in us a louder voice in our democracy.[13]

These are illustrations of how we might better ensure that only people have the rights and responsibilities of citizenship. Along with the other measures – abolishing the corporate income tax, ending the practice of prosecuting corporations for criminal conduct, no longer expecting or insisting that companies be patriotic, not granting them standing to challenge duly enacted laws in court – they offer a realistic and logically coherent view of the corporation as a legal fiction, and of people as citizens. I have used the United States as my primary example here, but the same logic would apply in any democracy.

4

THE TRIUMPH of supercapitalism has led, indirectly and unwittingly, to the decline of democracy. But that is not inevitable. We can have a vibrant democracy as well as a vibrant capitalism. To accomplish this, the two spheres must be kept distinct. The purpose of capitalism is to get great deals for consumers and investors. The purpose of democracy is to accomplish ends we cannot achieve as individuals. The border between the two is breached when companies *appear* to take on social responsibilities or when they utilize politics to advance or maintain their competitive standing.

We are all consumers and most of us are investors, and in those roles we try to get the best deals we possibly can. That is how we participate in a market economy and enjoy the benefits of supercapitalism. But those private benefits often come with social costs. We are also citizens who have a right and a responsibility to participate in a democracy. We thus have it in our power to reduce those social costs, thereby making the true price of the goods and services we purchase as low as possible. Yet we can accomplish this larger feat only if we take our responsibilities as citizens seriously, and protect our democracy. The first step, which is often the hardest, is to get our thinking straight.

NOTES

INTRODUCTION: THE PARADOX

1. In his *Capitalism and Freedom,* first published in 1962, Friedman made clear that, in his view of history, 'capitalism is a necessary condition for political freedom ... [but] not a sufficient condition'. He noted that fascist Italy and fascist Spain, Germany at various times in the twentieth century, and Japan before the two world wars were dominated by private enterprise, yet were not politically free. 'It is therefore clearly possible to have economic arrangements that are fundamentally capitalist and political arrangements that are not free.' *Capitalism and Freedom* (Chicago: University of Chicago Press, 1962; 2002 ed.), p. 10.

   Since the eighteenth-century Enlightenment, much Western thought has assumed a connection between market freedom and political freedom. Both Adam Smith at the University of Glasgow and Anne Robert Jacques Turgot at the Sorbonne in Paris came to see economies progressing through predictable stages, with each stage giving rise to progressively more complex political and legal institutions, and social advance. Smith's thoughts were contained in his *Lectures on Jurisprudence,* which exist today only in the form of notes taken by students who heard them delivered between 1762 and 1764. Turgot's musings appear in his *Plan of Two Discourses on Universal History,* originally written in 1750 or 1751, and not published until the nineteenth century. See also Sir John Dalrymple, *Essay Towards a General History of Feudal Property* (London, 1757). See generally Ronald L. Meek, *Smith, Marx and After: Ten Essays in the Development of Economic Thought* (London: Chapman & Hall, 1977), Chapter 1, and Benjamin M. Friedman, *The Moral Consequences of Economic Growth* (New York: Alfred A. Knopf, 2005), Chapter 2.

2. See *The American National Election Studies,* University of Michigan, at http://www.umich.edu/~nes/nesguide/toptable/tab5.

3. See, for example, Hans-Dieter Klingemann and Dieter Fuchs, eds., *Citizens and the State* (New York: Oxford University Press, 1995); Michael Adams and Mary Jane Lennon, 'Canadians, Too, Fault Their Political Institutions and

Leaders', *The Public Perspective* 3 (September–October 1992), p. 19; Susan Pharr, 'Confidence in Government: Japan', prepared for the Visions of Governance for the Twenty-first Century Conference in Bretton Woods, New Hampshire, July 29–August 2, 1996.

4. I first heard the term 'authoritarian capitalism' applied to China from Orville Schell, a China scholar at the University of California at Berkeley.

5. Data on civil liberties are from Freedom House.

6. John Maynard Keynes, *The General Theory of Employment, Interest and Money* (London: Longmans, Green, 1936), Chapter 12, p. 134.

CHAPTER ONE: THE NOT QUITE GOLDEN AGE

1. The most useful polling series on American attitudes toward government is *The American National Election Studies,* undertaken by the University of Michigan. It can be found at http://www.umich.edu/~nes/nesguide/toptable/tab5.

2. Figures from Simon Kuznets, *Economic Growth and Structure* (New York: W. W. Norton, 1965), pp. 305–27.

3. Figures from U.S. Bureau of the Census, *Historical Statistics of the United States: Colonial Times to 1970* (Washington, D.C.: U.S. Government Printing Office, 1975), Vol. 1, pp. 201–2, 224.

4. At the end of the nineteenth century, British citizens were treated to series of lurid accounts of German and American economic onslaught and baleful consequences for Britain. Among them were E. E. Williams, *Made in Germany* (London: William Heinemann, 1896), and Frederick McKenzie, *American Invaders* (London: G. Richards, 1902). In form and substance, this literature bore remarkable resemblance to accounts of Japanese 'invasions' offered American readers a century later.

5. Figures from Jerehmiah Jenks and Jett Lauck, *The Immigration Problem* (New York: Funk & Wagnalls, 1926), p. 148.

6. Cited in W. A. Williams, *The Tragedy of American Diplomacy* (Cleveland: World, 1959), p. 44.

7. J. A. Hobson, *Imperialism* (London: J. Nisbet, 1902), p. 112.

8. Selected from Harris Corporation, 'Founding Dates of the 1994 *Fortune* U.S. Companies', *Business History Review* 70 (Spring 1996), pp. 69–90.

9. Ibid.

10. Quoted in Richard S. Tedlow, *Keeping the Corporate Image: Public Relations and Business, 1900–1950* (Greenwich, Conn.: JAI Press, 1979), p. 5.

11. *The Papers of Woodrow Wilson,* Arthur S. Link, ed. (Princeton: Princeton University Press, 1977).

12. Acceptance address, Philadelphia, June 27, 1936, *Speeches of Franklin D. Roosevelt* (New York: Dutton, 1949).

13. Gustav Stolper, *German Economy* (New York: Reynal & Hitchcock, 1940), p. 83.

14. See, for example, Barrington Moore, Jr., *The Social Origins of Dictatorship and Democracy* (Boston: Beacon, 1966).

15. Richard Hofstadter, 'What Happened to the Antitrust Movement?' in his *The Paranoid Style in American Politics and Other Essays* (Chicago: University of Chicago Press, 1952).

16. Herbert Croly, *The Promise of American Life* (New York: World, 1909), pp. 362, 379.

17. Quoted in Robert M. Collins, *The Business Response to Keynes, 1929–1964* (New York: Columbia University Press, 1984), pp. 29–30.

18. Quoted in Ellis Hawley, *The New Deal and the Problem of Monopoly* (Princeton: Princeton University Press, 1966), p. 19.

19. Ibid., p. 27.

20. Walter Lippmann, *Drift and Mastery* (Englewood Cliffs, N.J.: Prentice Hall; originally published 1914; reprinted 1961), pp. 22, 23.

21. Adolf A. Berle and Gardiner C. Means, *The Modern Corporation and Private Property* (New York: Macmillan, 1932), p. 302.

22. Ibid., p. 312.

23. David Lilienthal, *Big Business: A New Era* (New York: World, 1953), pp. 47, 190.

24. *Fortune,* October 1955, p. 81.

25. *Fortune,* September 1953, p. 94.

26. U.S. Senate, Armed Services Committee, *Confirmation Hearings on Charles E. Wilson as Secretary of Defense,* February 18, 1953.

27. P. Armstrong et al., *Capitalism Since 1945* (Oxford: Blackwell, 1991), table 10.1.

28. M. A. Adelman, 'The Measurement of Industrial Concentration', *Review of Economics and Statistics* 33 (November 1951), pp. 275–77.

29. John Kenneth Galbraith, *The New Industrial State* (London: Hamish Hamilton, 1968), pp. 24, 26.

30. A. Maddison, *Monitoring the World Economy, 1820–1992* (Paris: Organization for Economic Cooperation and Development, 1995), table D.

31. Heller Committee for Research in Social Economics, *Quantity and Cost Budgets for Three Income Levels, Prices for San Francisco* (Berkeley: University of California Press, 1946).

32. Quoted in Joseph C. Goulden, *The Best Years, 1945–1950* (New York: Atheneum, 1976), p. 116.

33. Quoted in Daniel Bell, 'The Language of Labor', *Fortune,* September 1951, p. 86.

34. Jacob Hacker, *The Divided Welfare State* (New York: Cambridge University Press, 2002).

35. *Fortune,* October 1951, p. 114.

36. From U.S. Bureau of the Census, *Historical Statistics of the United States: Colonial Times to 1957* (Washington, D.C.: U.S. Government Printing Office, 1960).

37. Joseph Kahl, *The American Class Structure* (New York: Holt, Rinehart, 1956), pp. 109–10. See also Robert Dahl, *Who Governs?* (New Haven: Yale University Press, 1961).

38. The 1952 survey was included in a book published by *Fortune* called *The Executive Life* (Garden City, N.Y: Doubleday, 1956), p. 30.

39. William H. Whyte, Jr., *The Organization Man* (New York: Simon & Schuster, 1956), pp. 143, 145.

40. Among the most influential statements of the pluralist perspective are David Truman, *The Governmental Process* (New York: Alfred A. Knopf, 1951); Robert A. Dahl, *A Preface to Democratic Theory* (Chicago: University of Chicago Press, 1956); Nelson W. Polsby, *Community Power and Political Theory* (New Haven: Yale University Press, 1963); Arnold M. Rose, *The Power Structure* (New York: Oxford University Press, 1967); Edwin Epstein, *The Corporation in American Politics* (Englewood Cliffs, N.J.: Prentice Hall, 1969).

41. Truman, *The Governmental Process,* p. 535.

42. Dahl, *A Preface to Democratic Theory.*

43. See, generally, Theda Skocpol, *Diminshed Democracy* (Norman: University of Oklahoma Press, 2003).

44. John Kenneth Galbraith, *American Capitalism: The Concept of Countervailing Power* (Boston: Houghton Mifflin, 1952).

45. Ibid., p. 147.

46. Ibid., 151.

47. Harry Truman, inaugural speech, 1949, in *Speeches of President Harry S. Truman* (Washington, D.C.: U.S. Government Printing Office, 1952).

48. Quoted in *Fortune,* October 1951, pp. 98–99.

49. Galbraith, *The New Industrial State,* p. 394.

50. New York Stock Exchange, *Fact Book, 1991* (New York: New York Stock Exchange, 1991).

51. See *The American National Election Studies,* University of Michigan.

52. John F. Kennedy, commencement address at Yale University, June 11, 1962, *Speeches of President John F. Kennedy* (Washington, D.C.: U.S. Government Printing Office, 1964).

CHAPTER TWO: THE ROAD TO SUPERCAPITALISM

The literature on America's and the world's transition to supercapitalism between the 1970s and the end of the twentieth century is sparse, but I have found the following books and articles useful in illuminating particular aspects of that transition. See, for example, Alice Amsden, *Asia's Next Giant: South Korea and Late Industrialization* (New York: Oxford University Press, 1989); Leszek Balcerowicz, *Socialism, Capitalism, Transformation* (London: Central European University Press, 1995); Robert Barro, *Getting It Right: Markets and Choices in a Free Society* (Cambridge: MIT Press, 1996); Richard Baum, *Burying Mao: Chinese Politics in the Age of Deng Xiaoping* (Princeton: Princeton University Press, 1996); Stephen Beckner, *Back from the Brink: The Greenspan Years* (New York: John Wiley & Sons, 1996); Suzanne Berger and Ronald Dore, eds., *National Diversity and Global Capitalism* (Ithaca: Cornell University Press, 1991); Richard Bernstein and Ross Munro, *The Coming Conflict with China* (New York: Alfred A. Knopf, 1997); Jagdish Bhagwati, *India in Transition: Freeing the Economy* (Oxford: Oxford University Press, 1995); Matthew Bishop, John Kay, and Colin Mayer, eds., *The Regulatory Challenge* (Oxford: Oxford University Press, 1995); Stephen Breyer, *Regulation and Its Reform* (Cambridge: Harvard University Press, 1982); Lowell Bryan and Diana Farrell, *Market Unbound: Unleashing Global Capitalism* (New York: John Wiley & Sons, 1996); Shahid Javed Burki and Sebastian Edwards, *Dismantling the Populist State: The Unfinished Revolution in Latin America and the Caribbean* (Washington, D.C.: World Bank, 1996); Richard Cockett, *Thinking the Unthinkable: Think-tanks and the Economic Counter-Revolution, 1931–1983* (London: Fontana, 1995); Christopher Colclough and James Manor, eds., *States or Markets? Neo-Liberalism and the Development Policy Debate* (Oxford: Oxford University Press, 1995); Clive Crook, ed., 'The Future of the State: A Survey of the World Economy', *Economist*, September 20–26, 1997; Christopher DeMuth and William Kristol, eds., *The Neoconservative Imagination* (Washington, D.C.: AEI Press, 1995); Jorge Domínguez, *Technopols: Freeing Politics and Markets in Latin America in the 1990s* (University Park: Pennsylvania State University Press, 1997); Grzegorz Ekiert, *The State Against Society: Political Crises and Their Aftermath in East Central Europe* (Princeton: Princeton University Press, 1996); James Fallows, *Looking at the Sun: The Rise of the New East Asian Economic and Political System* (New York: Pantheon, 1994); Martin Feldstein, ed., *American Economic Policy in the 1980s* (Chicago: University of Chicago Press, 1994); Milton Friedman, *Capitalism and Freedom* (Chicago: University of Chicago Press, 1982); Francis Fukuyama, *The End of History and the Last Man* (New York: Free Press, 1992); William Greider, *One World, Ready or Not: The Manic Logic of Global Capitalism* (New York: Simon & Schuster, 1998); Bennett Harrison and Barry Bluestone, *The Great U-Turn* (New York: Basic Books, 1988); Paul Holden and Sarath Rajapatrirana, *Unshackling the Private Sector: A Latin American Story* (Washington, D.C.: World Bank, 1995); Douglas Irwin, *Against the Tide: An Intellectual History of Free Trade* (Princeton: Princeton University Press, 1996);

Christopher Johnson, *The Economy Under Mrs. Thatcher, 1979–1990* (London: Penguin, 1991); Alfred Kahn, *Economics of Regulation: Principles and Institutions* (New York: John Wiley & Sons, 1970); Ethan Kapstein, *Governing the Global Economy: International Finance and the State* (Cambridge: Harvard University Press, 1996); Paul Krugman, *The Age of Diminished Expectations: U.S. Economic Policy in the 1990s* (Cambridge: MIT Press, 1995); Steven A. Morrison and Clifford Winston, *The Evolution of the Airline Industry* (Washington, D.C.: Brookings Institution, 1995); William Niskanen, *Reaganomics: An Insider's Account of the Policies and the People* (New York: Oxford University Press, 1988); Sylvia Ostry, *The Post-Cold War Trading System: Who's on First?* (Chicago: University of Chicago Press, 1997); Peter Temin and Louis Galambos, *The Fall of the Bell System: A Study in Prices and Politics* (New York: Cambridge University Press, 1987); Raymond Vernon and Debora Spar, *Beyond Globalism: Remaking American Foreign Economic Policy* (New York: Free Press, 1989); John Vicker and George Yarrow, *Privatization: An Economic Analysis* (Cambridge: MIT Press, 1993); Daniel Yergin and Joseph Stanislaw, *Commanding Heights: The Battle Between Government and the Marketplace That Is Remaking the Modern World* (New York: Simon & Schuster, 1998).

1. D. Comin and T. Philippon, 'The Rise in Firm-Level Volatility: Causes and Consequences', NBER Working Paper No. 11388, May 2005; D. Comin, E. Groshern, and B. Rabin, 'Turbulent Firms, Turbulent Wages?', NBER Working Paper No. 12032, February 2006.
2. J. Micklethwait and A. Wooldridge, *The Company: A Short History of a Revolutionary Idea* (New York: Modern Library, 2003), pp. 129–30.
3. 'Pass the Parcel', *Economist,* February 11, 2006, p. 61.
4. On this point, see Chris Anderson, *The Long Tail: Why the Future of Business Is Selling Less of More* (New York: Hyperion, 2006).
5. Kate Hafner, 'For eBay, Departures Underscore a Risky Time', *New York Times,* July 10, 2006, pp. C1, C3.
6. On this point, see William Nordhaus, 'Retrospective on the Postwar Productivity Slowdown', Cowles Foundation Discussion Paper No. 1494 (2004), http://cowles.econ.yale.edu/P/cd/d1494.pdf.
7. Ira Magaziner and Robert Reich, *Minding America's Business* (New York: Harcourt Brace Jovanovich, 1982), pp. 230–31.
8. *Computer Aided Engineering,* January 1981, pp. 25–30.
9. Marc Levinson, *The Big Box: How the Shipping Container Made the World Smaller and the World Economy Bigger* (Princeton: Princeton University Press, 1996).
10. A. Jung, 'The Box That Makes the World Go Round', *Spiegel Online,*

November 25, 2005, at http://www.spiegel.de/international/spiegel/0,1518, 386799,00.html.

11. Figures from Alan Greenspan, 'Goods Shrink and Trade Grows', *Wall Street Journal,* October 24, 1988, p. A1.

12. That year, according to the Department of Commerce, 66 percent of the TVs and radios purchased by Americans, 45 percent of all machine tools, 28 percent of all autos, and 25 percent of all computers were produced outside the United States. For summary, see Monroe W. Karmin, 'Will the U.S. Stay Number One?', *U.S. News & World Report,* February 2, 1987, p. 18. See also Robert Reich, *The Work of Nations* (New York: Alfred A. Knopf, 1991), p. 72.

13. *BusinessWeek,* June 30, 1980, p. 12.

14. M. Dertouzos et al., *Made in America: Regaining the Productive Edge* (Cambridge: MIT Press, 1989), p. 1.

15. Figures from J. Grunwald and K. Flamm, *The Global Factory: Foreign Assembly in International Trade* (Washington, D.C.: Brookings Institution, 1985), pp. 14–20.

16. Louis Uchitelle, 'Made in the U.S.A. (Except for the Parts)', *New York Times,* April 8, 2005, p. C1.

17. For a more detailed analysis of the changed meaning of national competitiveness, see my *The Work of Nations.*

18. P. Panchak, 'Shaping the Future of Manufacturing: A Tour Through Manufacturing's Recent History Reveals Clues of What's to Come', *Industry Week,* January 1, 2005, p. 38.

19. Anderson, *The Long Tail.*

20. Betsy Morris, 'The New Rules', *Fortune,* July 24, 2006, p. 80.

21. On airline and other deregulation, see R. Fox, *Managing Business-Government Relations: Cases and Notes on Business-Government Problems* (Homewood, Ill.: Richard D. Irwin, 1982).

22. See P. Strahan, 'The Real Effects of U.S. Banking Deregulation', *Federal Reserve Bank of St. Louis,* July–August 2003; R. Kroszner and P. Strahan, 'What Drives Deregulation? Economics and Politics of the Relaxation of Bank Branching Restrictions', *Quarterly Journal of Economics* 114 (November 1999), pp. 1437–67.

23. Thomas H. Hammond and Jack Knott, 'The Deregulatory Snowball: Explaining Deregulation in the Financial Industry', *The Journal of Politics* 50 (1988), pp. 3–30.

24. Quoted in 'A Quantum Leap for Communications', *BusinessWeek,* November 28, 1983, p. 92.

25. Quoted in 'Revolution in Financial Services', *BusinessWeek,* November 28, 1983, p. 89.

26. Data from New York Stock Exchange, Securities Industry Association, Economic Policy Institute.

27. Data from the New York Stock Exchange Statistic Archive, at http://www.nyse.com/marketinfo/1022221393023.html.

28. During the 1990s, total equities held by households increased 443 percent, from $1.81 trillion to $8.01 trillion. Total equities held by mutual funds increased three times as fast, growing from $233 billion to $3.36 trillion. In 1980, there were only 228 stock mutual funds with $44.4 billion in net assets. By 1999, the total had reached 3,952 mutual funds with $4.04 trillion in net assets. An additional $2.5 trillion was socked away in private pension funds (up from $595 billion in 1990, a gain of 420 percent). Another sizable chunk was owned by insurance companies ($1.17 trillion of stock in 1999, up from $162 billion in 1990), and bank trusts and estates. Data from the Investment Company Institute, *2000 Mutual Fund Fact Book* (New York: Investment Company Institute, 2000), pp. 69, 71. See also U.S. Census Bureau, *Statistical Abstract of the United States, 2000*, p. 523.

29. Bureau of Economic Analysis, National Income and Product Accounts, table 1.14, at http://www.bea.gov/bea/dn/nipaweb/TableView. See also Andrew Glyn, *Capitalism Unleashed* (New York: Oxford University Press, 2006), p. 52.

30. Quoted in 'Time of His Life', *Economist*, February 9, 2006, p. 64.

31. Floyd Norris, 'Executives' Downfall: The "Managing" of Numbers Turned into Manipulating Them', *New York Times*, May 27, 2006, p. C4.

32. Quoted in Ian Somerville and D. Quinn Mills, 'Leading in a Leaderless World', *Leader to Leader*, Summer 1999, p. 32.

33. Cited in Jason Leow, 'Sell = Fire: Analysts' Views Cloud CEO's Jobs', *Wall Street Journal*, August 5–6, 2006, p. B3.

34. C. Lucier, P. Kocourek, and R. Habbel, *The Crest of the Wave* (New York: Booz Allen Hamilton, 2006).

35. Gretchen Morgenson, 'McKinnell Fumbled Chance to Lead', *New York Times*, August 6, 2006, p. C1.

36. Quoted in Jack Welch, *Jack: Straight from the Gut* (New York: Warner, 2001), p. 161; and also in Robert Slater, *Jack Welch and the GE Way* (New York: McGraw-Hill, 1999), pp. 38–39.

37. Bill Hutchinson, 'Pittsfield Fears PCBs Are Taking Lethal Toll', *Boston Herald*, September 8, 1997, p. 6.

38. John Byrne, *Chainsaw: The Notorious Career of Al Dunlap in the Era of Profit-at-Any-Price* (New York: HarperBusiness, 2003), p. 155.

39. Scott Malone, 'Spillane: Malden's Next Chapter', *Women's Wear Daily*, April 18, 2005, p. 24.

40. S. Friedman et al., eds., *Restoring the Promise of American Labor Law* (Ithaca: ILR Press, 1994).

41. R. Prosten, 'The Rise in NLRB Election Delays: Measuring Business's New Resistance', *Monthly Labor Review* 102, no. 2 (1979), p. 59.

42. Commission on the Future of Worker-Management Relations, 'Fact Finding Report' (Washington, D.C.: U.S. Department of Labor, May 1994).

43. See, for evidence on growth of nonunionized sectors of economy, Henry Farber and Bruce Westera, 'Round Up the Usual Suspects: The Decline of Unions in the Private Sector, 1973–1998', Industrial Relations Section, Princeton University, Working Paper No. 437, April 2000.

44. Cited in Lee Hawkins, Jr., 'Fitch Takes Dim View of GM's Moves', *Wall Street Journal,* November 23, 2005, p. A3.

45. Micheline Maynard, 'Delphi Chief Fights Battle of Detroit', *New York Times,* November 23, 2005, p. C1.

46. Louis Uchitelle, 'Two Tiers, Slipping into One', *New York Times,* February 26, 2006, p. C1.

CHAPTER THREE: OF TWO MINDS

There is little literature on, or even study of, the cognitive dissonance between the relative euphoria of the consumer and investor side of our brains and the growing concerns of the citizen side. In recent years, each side has had its share of champions. Good summaries of the euphoric consumer and investor can be found in Michael Cox and Richard Alm, *Myths of Rich and Poor: Why We're Better Off Than We Think* (New York: Basic Books, 2000); Gregg Easterbrook, *The Progress Paradox: How Life Gets Better While People Feel Worse* (New York: Random House, 2003); Lawrence Kudlow, *American Abundance: The New Economic and Moral Prosperity* (New York: HarperCollins, 1997); Stephen Moore, *It's Getting Better All the Time* (Washington, D.C.: Cato Institute, 2000).

Good summaries of the increasingly concerned citizen can be found in Robert Bork, *Slouching Towards Gomorrah* (New York: HarperCollins, 1997); Lou Dobbs, *War on the Middle Class: How the Government, Big Business, and Special Interest Groups Are Waging War on the American Dream and How to Fight Back* (New York: Viking, 2006); Byron Dorgan, *Take This Job and Ship It: How Corporate Greed and Brain-Dead Politics Are Selling Out America* (New York: Thomas Dunne, 2006); Jeff Faux, *The Global Class War* (New York: John Wiley & Sons, 2006); David Gordon, *Fat and Mean: The Corporate Squeeze of Working Americans and the Myth of Managerial Downsizing* (New York: Free Press, 1996); Al Gore, *An Inconvenient Truth* (New York: Rodale, 2006); Jacob Hacker, *The Great Risk-Shift: The Assault on American Jobs, Families, Health Care, and Retirement* (New York: Oxford University Press, 2006); Robert Kuttner, *Everything for Sale: The Virtues and Limits of Markets* (New York: Alfred A. Knopf, 1997); Louis Uchitelle, *The Disposable American: Layoffs and*

Their Consequences (New York: Alfred A. Knopf, 2006); William Wolman, *The Judas Economy: The Triumph of Capital and the Betrayal of Work* (New York: Perseus, 1997).

1. Adam Nagourney and Michael Barbaro, 'Eye on Election, Democrats Run as Wal-Mart Foe', *New York Times,* August 17, 2006.
2. *Wall Street Journal,* December 3–4, 2005, p. A9.
3. Dan Mitchell, 'Manufacturers Try to Thrive on Wal-Mart Workout', *New York Times,* February 20, 2005, p. C1.
4. There has been an abundance of research on Wal-Mart's effects on consumer prices. See, for example, Emek Basker, 'Selling a Cheaper Mousetrap: Wal-Mart's Effect on Retail Prices', *Journal of Urban Economics* 58, no. 2 (September 2005), pp. 203–29; Jason Furman, 'Wal-Mart: A Progressive Success Story', New York University, November 28, 2005; this paper can be found at http://homepages.nyu.edu/~jf1264/walmart.pdf. See also Jerry Hausman and Ephraim Leibtag, 'Consumer Benefits from Increased Competition in Shopping Outlets: Measuring the Effect of Wal-Mart', MIT and Economic Research Service, U.S. Department of Agriculture, October 2005. Hausman and Leibtag found that Wal-Mart's prices averaged 15 to 25 percent below the prices of identical food items at traditional supermarkets. With typical household products like shampoo, toothpaste, and laundry detergents, the average savings to consumers from shopping at Wal-Mart range from 1.5 to 3 percent in the short run to four times that in the long term. Wal-Mart held down prices of food by 9.1 percent nationwide and of nonfood goods by 4.2 percent between 1985 and 2005.
5. Data from 'Residential Energy Consumption Survey, 2001', U.S. Department of Energy, Energy Information Administration, table HC5–3a; 'Supplemental Measures of Material Well-Being: Basic Needs, Consumer Durables, Energy, and Poverty, 1981 to 2002', U.S. Bureau of the Census, December 2005. See also Cox and Alm, *Myths of Rich and Poor.*
6. Paul Liegey, 'Hedonic Quality Adjustment Methods for Microwave Ovens in the U.S. CPI', at http://www.bls.gov/cpi/cpimwo.htm.
7. Bureau of Labor Statistics, Department of Labor; DePaul University, newspaper archives, the Tax Foundation, at http://www.bbhq.com/prices.htm.
8. Gregg Easterbrook, 'What's Bad for G.M. Is …', *Nation,* June 12, 2005; see also J. McCaracken, 'U.S. Automakers in Price Squeeze', *Detroit Free Press,* June 4, 2004.
9. Data from Air Transport Association, Bureau of Labor Statistics, Energy Information Administration, Federal Communication Commission, Paul Kagan Associates, assembled by *Consumer Reports,* at www.consumerreports.org/cro/consumer-protection/deregulation-702/overview.htm.

10. Hubert B. Herring, 'Lower the Fares and They Will Fly (a Bit More Slowly)', *New York Times,* June 5, 2005, p. C2.

11. Robert W. Crandall and Clifford Winston, 'Unfriendly Skies', *Wall Street Journal,* December 18, 2006, p. A16.

12. Linda Blake, *Trends in the U.S. International Telecommunications Industry,* Federal Communications Commission, September 2005.

13. See, generally, Easterbrook, *The Progress Paradox.*

14. One possible explanation: Universities are competing with one another for students from upper-middle-class families who are willing to spend tens of thousands of dollars a year – indeed, who consider high price to be a sign of high value – not only for classes, laboratories, and professors, but also for amenities like plush student centers, dormitories with every modern convenience, and platoons of counselors. Another: As the economist William Baumol has noted, productivity gains are harder to achieve in labor-intensive industries that depend on human interactions, such as education and the performing arts.

15. See also U.S. Department of Labor, Bureau of Labor Statistics, Displaced Worker Survey, 2002, at http://www.bls.gov/opub/mir/2004/06/art4full.pdf. See also Lori G. Kletzer, *Job Loss from Imports: Measuring the Costs* (Washington, D.C.: Institute for International Economics, 2001).

16. Quoted in Jeff Bailey, 'Northwest and Its Flight Attendants Await a Strike Ruling', *New York Times,* August 25, 2006, p. C3.

17. Furman, 'Wal-Mart: A Progressive Success Story'.

18. Quoted in Ann Zimmerman, 'Costco's Dilemma: Be Kind to Its Workers or Wall Street', *Wall Street Journal,* March 26, 2004, p. B1.

19. S. Greenhouse, 'How Costco Became the Anti-Wal-Mart', *New York Times,* July 17, 2005, p. B1.

20. *National Compensation Survey: Employee Benefits in Private Industry in the United States,* U.S. Department of Labor, Bureau of Labor Statistics, March 2006, at http://www.bls.gov/ncs/ebs/sp/ebsm0004.pdf. Historical data are available on the Internet at http://www.bls.gov/ncs/ebs/home.htm.

21. 'Employer Health Benefits 2005', Kaiser Family Foundation and Educational Trust, 2005, p. 114.

22. Panel Study of Income Dynamics, at http://psidonline.isr.umich.edu. See Jacob Hacker, *The Great Risk Shift* (New York: Oxford University Press, 2006); Mark Rank, *One Nation, Underprivileged: Why American Poverty Affects Us All* (New York: Oxford University Press, 2004), p. 93.

23. See, for example, Pew Social Trends Poll, August 30, 2006. A representative sample of Americans was asked: 'Compared to 20 or 30 years ago, do you think the average working person in this country … has more job security, less job security, or about the same amount?' Results: More job security, 11 percent of

respondents; less job security, 62 percent; about the same, 24 percent; don't know or refused to say, 3 percent.

24. James Banks, Michael Marmot, Zoe Oldfield, and James P. Smith, 'Diseases and Disadvantage in the United States and England', *Journal of the American Medical Association* 295, no. 16 (May 3, 2006), pp. 2037–45.

25. Data from Internal Revenue Service, posted September 22, 2006, at http://www.irs.gov/taxstats/indtaxstats/article/0,,id=129406,00.html.

26. Thomas Piketty and Emmanuel Saez, 'Income Inequality in the United States, 1913–1998', *Quarterly Journal of Economics* 118, no. 1 (February 2003), with updated figures for 2004 from the authors' Web site, http://www.econ.berkeley.edu/~saez/TabFig2004.xls. Capital gains were excluded from this calculation. See also Ian Dew-Becker and Robert J. Gordon, 'Where Did the Productivity Growth Go?', paper presented at the Brookings Panel on Economic Activity, September 8–9, 2005, at http://faculty-web.at. northwestern. edu/economics/gordon/BPEA_Meetingdraft_Complete_051118.pdf.

27. Lucien Bebchuk and Yaniv Grinstein, 'The Growth of Executive Pay', *Oxford Review of Economic Policy* 21, no. 2 (2005), pp. 283–303, at http://www.law.harvard.edu/faculty/bebchuk/pdfs/Bebchuk-Grinstein. Growth-of-Pay.pdf.

28. Carola Frydman and Raven E. Saks, 'Historical Trends in Executive Compensation, 1936–2003', working paper, November 15, 2005, at http://tinyrl.com/f3pzz. See also survey of 200 large companies by Pearl Meyer & Partners, the compensation practice of Clark Consulting: Pearl Meyer & Partners, '2006 Compensation Report', at http://www.pearlmeyer.com. Another study by Mercer Human Resource Consulting showed that in 2005 median pay packages for CEOs of America's 350 largest companies was $6.8 million, including stock options, but excluding pensions, deferred compensation, and other perks.

29. This phenomenon is related to, but not quite the same as, 'winner-take-all' markets characterized by large demand for a few star players. See Robert H. Frank and Philip S. Cook, *The Winner-Take-All Society: Why the Few at the Top Get So Much More Than the Rest of Us* (New York: Free Press, 1995).

30. Xavier Gabaix and Augustin Landler, 'Why Has CEO Pay Increased So Much?', MIT Working Paper No. 06-13, May 8, 2006, at http://papers.ssrn.com/so13/papers.cfm?abstract_id=901826.

31. Calculations from Fadel Gheit, senior energy analyst with Oppenheimer & Co., in Alan Murray, 'Some Executives Get What They Deserve', *Wall Street Journal*, April 19, 2006, p. A2.

32. James Surowiecki, 'Net Worth', *New Yorker*, March 14, 2005, p. 62.

33. The survey was done in February 2006. See Eric Dash, 'Off to the Races Again, Leaving Many Behind', *New York Times*, April 9, 2006, p. C1.

34. Jenny Anderson, 'Big Bonuses Seen Again for Wall Street', *New York Times,* November 7, 2006, p. C1.

35. 'The Very Richest Hedge Fund Managers', *New York Times,* May 26, 2006, p. C1.

36. Ellen E. Schultz and Theo Francis, 'The CEO Health Plan in Era of Givebacks, Some Execs Get Free Coverage After They Retire', *Wall Street Journal,* April 13, 2006, p. B1.

37. 'Creative Destruction', editorial, *Wall Street Journal,* September 7, 2006, p. A20.

38. Economic Policy Institute, *State of Working America, 2006–2007,* Chapter 5, table 5.9; U.S. Bureau of the Census, American Community Survey, 2004.

39. Piketty and Saez, 'Income Inequality in the United States'.

40. Edward N. Wolff, 'Recent Trends in Wealth Ownership', New York University Working Paper, December 12, 1998, table 2.

41. John Heilemann, 'Unstoppable', *New York,* August 15, 2004, p. 23.

42. David Neumark, Junfu Zhang, and Stephen Ciccarella, 'The Effects of Wal-Mart on Local Labor Markets', NBER Working Paper No. 11782, November 2005, at http://papers.nber.org/papers/w11782.pdf?new_windows=1.

43. Patrick McGeehan, 'Top Executives Return Offices to Manhattan', *New York Times,* July 3, 2006, p. A1.

44. Bork, *Slouching Towards Gomorrah,* pp. 125, 139.

45. Ibid., pp. 126–27.

46. See, for example, Jacques Steinberg, 'Censored "SNL" Sketch Jumps Bleepless onto the Internet', *New York Times,* December 21, 2006, p. D1.

47. Data from Marion Nestle, *Food Politics* (Berkeley: University of California Press, 2002), pp. 8–9.

48. Ibid., p. 25.

49. Robert Reich, 'Look Who Demands Profits Above All', *Los Angeles Times,* September 1, 2000.

50. Raymond Bonner and Jane Perlez, 'New York Urges U.S. Inquiry in Mining Company's Indonesia Payment', *New York Times,* January 28, 2006, p. A6.

51. *Play Fair at the Olympics* (Oxford: Oxfam, 2004), p. 36.

52. See A. Atkinson, *Economic Inequality in OECD Countries: Data and Explanations,* CesIFO Discussion Paper, 2003, figure 1-9; T. Smeeding, 'Public Policy and Economic Inequality: The United States in a Comparative Perspective', Luxembourg Income Study Working Paper No. 367 (2004), figure 3, and (2002), figure 4. Benchmark data for many countries are found in Forster and D'Ercole, *Income Distribution and Poverty in OECD Countries in the Second Half of the 1990s,* OECD Social Employment and Migration Working Paper (2005) No. 22. According to the Luxembourg Income Survey, the ratio of post-tax incomes at 10 percent from the top of the income

distribution to incomes 10 percent from the bottom increased in Germany from 3.1 in 1980 to 3.3 in 2000; in Sweden from 2.4 in 1980 to 3 in 2000; in the United Kingdom from 3.5 in 1980 to 4.6 in 2000; and in the United States from 3.7 in 1980 to 5.4 in 2000.

53. 'Europe Auto Relations Get Testy', *Wall Street Journal,* June 15, 2006, p. A8.

54. 'Hard New Realities of the Marketplace for German Labor', *New York Times,* October 26, 2005, pp. C1, C4.

55. By 2005 the median pay for chief executives of the largest American-based companies was still more than 50 percent higher than the median pay for top executives in British companies listed on the Financial Times Stock Exchange 100 Index, but the gap was closing. In 1998, American executives took home more than four times what the CEO of a big British company made. Pay was also rising for CEOs of big French companies listed in the CAC-40 benchmark stock index, rising to $3 million in 2004, from about $780,000 in 1998, accoding to Proxinvest, an adviser to pension funds and mutual funds. In Germany, a recent survey by *Die Welt* showed nearly an 11 percent increase in 2005 in the average salary of management board members from thirty blue-chip DAX Index companies. See, generally, Geraldine Fabrikant, 'U.S.-Style Pay Deals of Chiefs Become All the Rage in Europe', *New York Times,* June 16, 2006, pp. A1, C4.

56. Norimitsu Onishi, 'Revival in Japan Brings Widening of Economic Gap', *New York Times,* April 16, 2006, p. A1.

57. Andrew Batson and Shai Oster, 'As China Booms, the Poorest Lose Ground', *Wall Street Journal,* November 22, 2006, p. A4.

58. Thomas Friedman, 'Bring in the Green Cat', *New York Times,* November 15, 2006, p. A27; Jason Dean, 'How Capitalist Transformation Exposes Holes in China's Government', *Wall Street Journal,* December 18, 2006, p. A2.

59. Joseph Stiglitz and Andrew Chartlton, *Fair Trade for All* (New York: Oxford University Press, 2006).

60. Harvard economist Gregory Mankiw, a former adviser to President George W. Bush, correctly noted on his blog that 'CEOs are paid what they're worth to their companies, and their high pay reflects the extraordinary value of their talent. But the supply of talent is inelastic and the allocation of talent would not be affected if everyone faced high tax rates'. Quoted in David Wessel, 'With CEO Pay, Size Does Matter', *Wall Street Journal,* November 2, 2006, p. A2.

61. Editorial, 'The Only Certainty Is More Uncertainty', *Independent,* April 12, 2006.

CHAPTER FOUR: DEMOCRACY OVERWHELMED

The literature on corporate influence on the U.S. government is large but uneven. Among the most thoughtful books I've read in recent years are William Greider's two volumes, *The Soul of Capitalism* (New York: Simon & Schuster, 2003), and *Who Will Tell the People? The Betrayal of American Democracy* (New York: Touchstone, 1992); and Kevin Phillips's two books, *Arrogant Capital* (Boston: Little, Brown, 1994), and *Wealth and Democracy* (New York: Broadway, 2002). I have also found particularly helpful David Kay Johnson, *Perfectly Legal: The Covert Campaign to Rig Our Tax System to Benefit the Super Rich – and Cheat Everyone Else* (New York: Portfolio/Penguin, 2003).

Before the 2006 midterm elections reversed course, a number of authors studied the rise of Republican influence at the behest of the American business community. I've found especially useful in this regard John Micklethwait and Adrian Wooldridge, *The Right Nation: Why America Is Different* (London: Allen Lane, 2004); E. J. Dionne, Jr., *They Only Look Dead* (New York: Simon & Schuster, 1996); Jacob Hacker and Paul Pierson, *Off Center: The Republican Revolution and the Erosion of American Democracy* (New Haven: Yale University Press, 2005).

There is also a large literature detailing corporate influence on politics. See, for example, Jeffrey Birnbaum, *The Lobbyists: How Influence Peddlers Work Their Way in Washington* (New York: Times Books, 1992); and Lee Drutman and Charlie Cray, *The People's Business: Controlling Corporations and Restoring Democracy* (San Francisco: Barrett-Koehler, 2004).

Some recent reportage is interesting and useful, notwithstanding its somewhat conspiratorial view. See, for example, Joel Bakan, *The Corporation* (New York: Free Press, 2004); Carl Boggs, *The End of Politics: Corporate Power and the Decline of the Public Sphere* (New York: Guilford, 2000); Charles Derber, *Corporation Nation* (New York: St. Martin's, 1998); Jeff Gates, *Democracy at Risk* (Cambridge, Mass.: Perseus, 2000); Mark Green, *Selling Out: How Big Corporate Money Buys Elections, Rams Through Legislation, and Betrays Our Democracy* (New York: HarperCollins, 2002); Noreena Hertz, *The Silent Takeover: Global Capitalism and the Death of Democracy* (New York: HarperBusiness, 2003); David Korten, *The Post-Corporate World* (San Francisco: Barrett-Koehler, 2004); Lawrence Mitchell, *Corporate Irresponsibility* (New Haven: Yale University Press, 2001); Greg Palast, *The Best Democracy Money Can Buy* (New York: Plume, 2003); David Sirota, *Hostile Takeover: How Big Money and Corruption Conquered Our Government – and How We Take It Back* (New York: Crown, 2006).

1. On survey research about America's loss of confidence in government and the democratic process, see sources cited in the Introduction. For data on a similar

decline in confidence in many other democracies, see, for example, Hans-Dieter Klingemann and Dieter Fuchs, eds., *Citizens and the State* (New York: Oxford University Press, 1995); Michael Adams and Mary Jane Lennon, 'Canadians, Too, Fault Their Political Institutions and Leaders', *The Public Perspective* 3 (September–October 1992), p. 19; Susan Pharr, 'Confidence in Government: Japan', prepared for the Visions of Governance for the Twenty-first Century Conference in Bretton Woods, New Hampshire, July 29–August 2, 1996.

2. Although the Tillman Act of 1907 barred direct campaign contributions from corporations, passage of the Federal Election Campaign Act, in 1971, legalized corporate political action committees. Subsequent campaign finance reforms limited what PACs could do but created a loophole for unlimited 'soft money' contributions to state and local affiliates of national parties. The Bipartisan Campaign Reform Act of 2002 (commonly referred to as the McCain-Feingold Act) closed that soft money loophole but allowed unlimited dollars to flow to so-called 527 groups not under the control of a candidate or party. None of these reforms limited the ability of corporate executives to 'bundle' individual contributions from fellow executives in the same corporation, or corporate lobbyists to bundle contributions from executives of an entire industry, or anyone else to bundle contributions from any other group of people.

3. Cited in 'Washington', *Encyclopedia Britannica* online, at http://www.britannica.com/eb/article-24527.

4. See Kevin Phillips, *Arrogant Capital* (New York: Little, Brown, 1994), pp. 26–27, 32.

5. The official estimate of lobbyists in Washington is probably lower than the actual number because many people who engage in lobbying do not formally register as lobbyists. The rules requiring registration are vague and the penalties for failing to register are minimal. A law enacted in 1995 to register and track lobbyists was singularly lacking in teeth; Capitol Hill staffers responsible for implementing it have been perennially shorthanded and without auditing and investigative powers necessary to enforce it. Estimates of the amount of money spent on lobbying each year are based on reports filed with the House of Representatives and the Senate, and suffer limitations similar to those affecting estimates of the number of lobbyists. Several authors and studies have sought to document the trend in the increasing scope and dominance of the lobbying industry in Washington, D.C., over the last decades. See, for example, Todd Purdum, 'Go Ahead, Try to Stop K Street', *New York Times,* January 8, 2006, p. A1; Jeffrey Birnbaum, 'The Road to Riches Is Called K Street', *Washington Post,* June 22, 2005, p. A1; and Jonathan Rauch, 'The Parasite Economy', *National Journal,* April 25, 1992. See also

Phillips, *Imperial Washington,* pp. 22–40. See also studies by the Center for Public Integrity and data from Political Money Line, various years.

6. Center for Public Integrity, www.publicintegrity.org.

7. David Vogel, 'The Power of Business in America: A Re-appraisal', *British Journal of Political Science* 13 (1979), pp. 19–43.

8. See data from Burdett Loomis and Michael Struemph, 'Organized Interests, Lobbying and the Industry of Politics', paper prepared for Midwest Political Science Association meeting, April 4–7, 2003, Chicago, Illinois.

9. S. Prakash Sethi, *Advocacy Advertising and Large Corporations* (Lexington, Mass.: Lexington Books, 1977), updated in S. Prakash Sethi, 'Grass-roots Lobbying and the Corporation', *Business and Society Review* (Spring 1979), pp. 8–14. For a discussion of Mobil's effort, see Randall Poe, 'Masters of the Advertorial', *Across the Board* (September 1980), pp. 15–28. See also David Liff, Mary O'Conner, and Clarke Bruno, *Corporate Advertising: The Business Response to Changing Public Attitudes* (Washington, D.C.: Investor Responsibility Research Center, October 1980).

10. See, for example, EurActiv report, 'EU and US Approaches to Lobbying', *EurActiv,* August 29, 2005.

11. For a fuller account, see J. Micklethwait and A. Woodridge, *The Right Nation: Conservative Power in America* (New York: Penguin, 2004). See also Nolan McCarty, Keith Poole, and Howard Rosenthal, *Polarized America: The Dance of Ideology and Unequal Riches* (Cambridge: MIT Press, 2006).

12. Robert Kuttner, *The Life of the Party: Democratic Prospects in 1988 and Beyond* (New York: Viking, 1987), p. 62.

13. B. Mullins and D. Treftz, 'Companies Shift More Donations to Democrats', *Wall Street Journal,* April 30, 2007, pp. A1, A9.

14. Cited by Bill Moyers in 'Hostel Takeover', *Sojourner,* July–August 1998, p. 18.

15. Quoted in Jeffrey H. Birnbaum, 'Democrats' Stock Rising on K Street', *Washington Post,* August 17, 2006, p. A1.

16. Christopher Lee, 'Daschle Moving to K Street', *Washington Post,* March 4, 2005, p. 17A.

17. Robert Pear, 'Drug Companies Increase Spending on Efforts to Lobby Congress and Governments', *New York Times,* June 1, 2003, p. A20.

18. See research reports from the Center for Public Integrity, at http://www.publicintegrity.org/lobby/report.aspx?aid=774 and http://www.publicintegrity.org/lobby/report.aspx?aid=678.

19. Ibid.

20. Alice Rivlin, *Reviving the American Dream: The Economy, the States and the Federal Government* (Washington, D.C.: Brookings Institution, 1992), p. 50.

21. Jeff Faux, *The Global Class War* (New York: John Wiley & Sons, 2006), p. 3; Lou Dobbs, *War on the Middle Class: How the Government, Big Business, and*

Special Interest Groups Are Waging War on the American Dream and How to Fight Back (New York: Viking, 2006), p. 12.

22. This point has been understood by political scientists but they have tended to limit their inquiries to campaign spending, and have, for the most part, failed to study the vast sea of corporate money financing efforts to influence policy. See, for example, Stephen Ansolabehere et al., 'Why Is There So Little Money in Politics?', *Journal of Economic Perspectives* 17, no. 1 (2003) pp. 105–30.

23. Kate Phillips, 'Once a Maverick, Google Joins the Lobbying Herd', *New York Times,* March 28, 2006, pp. A1, A13.

24. Amy Borrus, 'It's Back to Charm School for Microsoft', *BusinessWeek,* November 8, 1999.

25. Mike France, 'The Unseemly Campaign of Mr. Microsoft', *BusinessWeek,* April 24, 2000, p. 53.

26. 'Dirty Dealings', *Economist,* June 29, 2000.

27. Phillips, 'Once a Maverick, Google Joins the Lobbying Herd'.

28. Quoted in Michael Crittenden and Rebecca Adams, 'Mr. Sam Comes to Washington', *CQ Weekly,* November 7, 2005, p. 1.

29. Quoted in Kim Chipman and Lauren Coleman-Lochner, 'Wal-Mart Girds for Showdown with New Congress on Unions, Trade', Bloomberg.com, December 4, 2006, at http://www.bloomberg.com/apps/news?pid= 20601103&sid=a6JOvd6gbkog&refer=news.

30. Bernard Wysocki, Jr., 'How Broad Coalition Stymied Wal-Mart's Bid to Own a Bank', *Wall Street Journal,* October 23, 2006, p. A1.

31. Kate Phillips, 'Interest Groups Lining Up to Lobby on Web Gambling', *New York Times,* July 4, 2006, p. A11.

32. Michael Schroeder, 'Futures Traders Resist Tighter Oversight Plan', *Wall Street Journal,* February 10, 2006, p. A6.

33. David Rogers, 'House Deals Blow to "Open Skies" as It Passes Latest Spending Bill', *Wall Street Journal,* June 15, 2006, p. A4.

34. Deborah Solomon and Evan Perez, 'Airlines Split over Pension Package', *Wall Street Journal,* July 31, 2006, p. A3.

35. Greg Hitt, 'Textile Makers Tap Political Opportunity', *Wall Street Journal,* October 18, 2006, p. A4.

36. Cited in Christopher Bowe, 'US Pharmaceutical Industry Limbers Up for Medicare's Brave New World', *Financial Times,* January 4, 2006, p. 2.

37. See, generally, Michael Pollan, *The Omnivore's Dilemma* (New York: Penguin, 2006).

38. Melanie Warner, 'A Struggle over Standards in Fast-Growing Food Category', *New York Times,* November 1, 2005, p. C1.

39. Ibid.

40. Brody Mullins and Ethan Wallison, 'Another Coalition of the Willing', *Roll Call,* May 7, 2003.
41. David Vogel, 'The Politics of Risk Regulation in Europe and the United States', *Yearbook of European Environmental Law* (New York: Oxford University Press, 2004), vol. 3, p. 42.
42. Data from Marc Galanter, 'The Life and Times of the Big Six; or, The Federal Courts Since the Good Old Days', *Wisconsin Law Review* (1988), pp. 921–54. See also William Nelson 'Contract Litigation and the Elite Bar in New York City, 1960–1980', *Emory Law Review* 39 (1990), pp. 413–62.
43. Robert Pear, 'Drug Companies Increase Spending on Efforts to Lobby Congress and Governments', *New York Times,* June 1, 2003, p. A20.
44. Paul Krugman, 'Enemy of the Planet', *New York Times,* April 17, 2006, p. A21.
45. Heather Timmons, 'Exxon Accused of Deception on Climate Change, Royal Society in U.K. Complain to Firm', *International Herald Tribune,* September 22, 2006, p. A1.
46. Jennifer Washburn, 'The Best Minds Money Can Buy', *Los Angeles Times,* July 21, 2006, p. 13.
47. David Armstrong, 'Drug Interactions: Financial Ties to Industry Cloud Major Depression Study', *Wall Street Journal,* July 11, 2006, p. A1.
48. Stephen Labaton, 'House Expected to Back Bill Favoring Phone Companies', *New York Times,* June 9, 2006, p. C1.
49. U.S. Government Accountability Office, *Access to Broadband* (Washington, D.C.: U.S. Government Accountability Office, May 2006).
50. Quotes in my 'Let's Bring Back Antitrust', *Inc. Magazine,* October 1982, pp. 12–13.
51. On this point, see Theda Skocpol, *Diminished Democracy* (Norman: University of Oklahoma Press, 2003). Skocpol has carefully documented the decline in locally based but nationally federated citizen organizations.
52. Jeffrey Berry, *The New Liberalism: The Rising Power of Citizen Groups* (Washington, D.C.: Brookings Institution, 1999), p. 56.

CHAPTER FIVE: POLITICS DIVERTED

There is a large and growing literature on corporate social responsibility. Among the best recent books I have found are David Vogel, *The Market for Virtue* (Washington, D.C.: Brookings Institution, 2006); Michelle Micheletti, *Political Virtue and Shopping: Individuals, Consumerism, and Collective Action* (New York: Palgrave Macmillan, 2003); and David Henderson, *Misguided Virtue: False Notions of Corporate Social Responsibility* (London: Institute of Economic Affairs, 2001). Most contemporary writing on the subject emphasizes the connection between corporate social responsibility and corporate profitability. See, for example, Christine Arena, *Cause for Success: Ten Companies That Have Put Profits Second and Come in First* (Novato, Calif.: New World, 2004); Michael Hopkins, *The Planetary Bargain: Corporate Social Responsibility Matters* (London: Earthscan, 2003); Ira Jackson and Jane Nelson, *Profits with Principles: Seven Strategies for Delivering Value with Values* (New York: Currency/Doubleday, 2004); Kevin Jackson, *Building Reputational Capital: Strategies for Integrity and Fair Play That Improve the Bottom Line* (New York: Oxford University Press, 2004); Malcolm McIntosh, Deborah Leipziger, Keith Jones, and Gill Coleman, *Corporate Citizenship: Successful Strategies for Responsible Companies* (London: Financial Times, 1998); Robert Willard, *The Sustainability Advantage: Seven Business Case Benefits of a Triple Bottom Line* (Gabriola Island, B.C.: New Society, 2002).

1. Both surveys are from Ronald Alsop, 'Recruiters Seek MBAs Trained in Responsibility', *Wall Street Journal,* December 13, 2005, p. B6.
2. Quoted in Claudia H. Deutsch, 'Companies and Critics Try Collaboration', *New York Times,* May 17, 2006, p. E1.
3. For information on Dow's efforts to reduce its carbon emissions, see the Dow Web site for energy and climate change, at http://www.dow.com/energy/. On McDonald's shift to more humane slaughtering techniques, see Joby Warrick, 'Big Mac's Big Voice in Meat Plants', *Washington Post,* April 10, 2001, p. A11. On Wal-Mart's adoption of green packaging, see Harold Brubaker, 'Wal-Mart Picks Corn for Its Packaging', *Houston Chronicle,* October 21, 2005, Business Section, p. 4. On Starbucks's employee health insurance, see Lisa Schmeiser, 'Perks Can Aid Bottom Line', *Investor's Business Daily,* October 17, 2005, p. A10. See also Vogel, *The Market for Virtue,* p. 130.
4. On these instances of corporate sensitivity to consumer concerns about fatty foods, see 'Wendy's Cuts Trans Fats in Fries and Chicken', *Consumer Affairs,* June 9, 2006, at http://www.consumeraffairs.com/news04/2006/06/wendys_transfat.html; 'Oreo Takes on a New Twist with New Varieites That Contain Zero Grams of Trans Fat Per Serving', *PR Newswire,* April 6, 2004; 'Frito-Lay Chips Down – to Zero Trans Fat', *Houston Chronicle,* September 28, 2003, Business Section, p. 10; 'Cereals Will Get Healthier', *Houston Chronicle,* October 1, 2004, Business Section, p. 1.
5. Starbucks full-page ad, *New York Times,* July 24, 2005, p. 13.
6. Milton Friedman, 'The Social Responsibility of Business Is to Increase Profits', *New York Times Magazine,* September 13, 1970.
7. For these illustrations of how investors have punished companies that sacrifice

profits to 'social responsibility', see, on Cummins Engine, Michael Oneal, 'Global Economy Strains Loyalty in Company Town', *Chicago Tribune,* April 4, 2004; on Dayton Hudson, Caroline Mayer, 'Dayton Hudson Acts to Fend Off Hafts', *Washington Post,* June 20, 1987, p. C1; on Levi Strauss, 'Levi Strauss Announces Intention to Close Six Plants', Associated Press State & Local Wire, April 8, 2002; on Polaroid, Claudia Deutsch, 'Deep in Debt Since 1988, Polaroid Files for Bankruptcy', *New York Times,* October 13, 2001; on Marks & Spencer, Michael Skapinker, 'Why Corporate Laggards Should Not Win Ethics Awards', *Financial Times,* July 21, 2004, p. 8.

8. Peter Landers and Joann Lublin, 'Merck's Big Bet on Research by Its Scientists Comes Up Short', *Wall Street Journal,* November 28, 1993, p. A1.

9. On this point, see Alison Maitland, 'Scandals Draw Attention to "Superficial" Measures', *Financial Times,* December 10, 2002, Management Section, p. 1.

10. Felicity Barringer, 'ExxonMobil Becomes Focus of a Boycott', *New York Times,* July 12, 2005, p. A19.

11. Claudia H. Deutsch, 'New Surveys Show That Big Business Has a P.R. Problem', *New York Times,* December 9, 2005, p. C1.

12. See Dan Ahrens, *Investing in Vice: The Recession-Proof Portfolio of Booze, Bets, Bombs and Butts* (New York: St. Martin's, 2004). See also Oaul Koku, Aigbe Akhigbe, and Thomas Springer, 'The Financial Impact of Boycotts and Threats of Boycott', *Journal of Business Rresearch* 40, no. 1 (1997), pp. 15–20.

13. Jeffrey Hollender and Stephen Fenichell, *What Matters Most: How a Small Group of Citizen Pioneers Is Teaching Social Responsibility to Big Business and Why Big Business Is Listening* (New York: Basic Books, 2004), p. 47.

14. Paul Hawken and Natural Capital Institute, *Socially Responsible Investing* (Sausalito, Calif.: Natural Capital Institute, October 2004).

15. Vogel, *The Market for Virtue,* p. 73.

16. Starbucks full-page ad, *New York Times,* August 10, 2006, p. A7.

17. 'Do We Have a Story for You!', *Economist,* January 21, 2006, p. 57.

18. Dara O'Rourke, 'Market Movements: Nongovernmental Strategies to Influence Global Production and Consumption', *Journal of Industrial Ecology* 9, nos. 1–2 (2005), citing J. Makower, 'Whatever Happened to Green Consumers?', Organic Consumer Association, July–August 2000.

19. Vogel, *The Market for Virtue,* p. 135.

20. Michel Capron and Françoise Quairel-Lanoizelée, *Mythes et réalités de l'enterprise responsable* (Paris: La Découverte, 2004), p. 57.

21. Vogel, *The Market for Virtue,* p. 54.

22. Ibid., p. 154.

23. Ibid.

24. Michael Barbaro, 'A New Weapon for Wal-Mart: A War Room', *New York Times*, November 1, 2005, p. A1.

25. Vogel, *The Market for Virtue*, pp. 112–13.

26. See the AFA's online petition, at http://www.afa.net/Petitions/ IssueDetail.asp?id=220.

27. Ann Zimmerman, 'Morning-After Pill Comes to Wal-Mart', *Wall Street Journal*, March 18–19, 2006, p. A2.

28. Jeremy Peters, 'Gays Pressure Ford to Reject Boycott Group', *New York Times*, December 13, 2005, p. C4.

29. Jeremy Peters, 'Ford, Reversing Decision, Will Run Ads in Gay Press', *New York Times*, December 15, 2005, p. C3.

30. Donald E. Wildmon, Chairman, American Family Association, Letter to Chairman Bill Ford, January 10, 2006, available at http://afa.net/fordletter.asp.

31. On Focus on the Family's urging consumers to boycott Procter & Gamble, see David Kirkpatrick, 'Conservatives Urge Boycott of Procter & Gamble', *New York Times*, September 17, 2004, p. A18. On the Action League of Chicago's attempt to boycott American Girl dolls, see Laura Berman, 'Don't Drag Girls into Debate', *Chicago Sun-Times*, November 28, 2005, p. 61. On the National Rifle Association's attempt to pressure ConocoPhillips, see Ralph Blumenthal, 'N.R.A. Fights Energy Giant over Stance on a Lawsuit', *New York Times*, August 3, 2005, p. A13.

32. On Nike, see Tom McCawley, 'Inside Track: Racing to Improve Its Reputation', *Financial Times*, December 21, 2000, p. 14; on New Balance, see Chris Reidy, 'Labor Group Hits New Balance', *Boston Globe*, January 7, 2006, p. 4.

33. The text of this advertisement appeared in many newspapers. See, for example, *New York Times*, April 20, 2005, p. A20. It can also be found at the 'Wal-Mart Watch' Web site, http://walmartwatch.com/pdg/ad-nyt-042005.pdf.

34. This estimate can be found in Executive Office of the President of the United States, Office of Management and Budget, *Analytic Perspectives, Budget of the United States Government, Fiscal Year 2006* (Washington, D.C.: U.S. Government Printing Office, 2006), p. 324.

35. Steven Greenhouse, 'Opponents of Wal-Mart to Coordinate Efforts', *New York Times*, April 3, 2005, p. A12.

36. Ibid.

37. Barbaro, 'A New Weapon for Wal-Mart: A War Room', p. A1.

38. On Wal-Mart's response to Katrina, see Michael Barbaro and Justin Gillis, 'Wal-Mart at Forefront of Hurricane Relief', *Washington Post*, September 6, 2005, p. D1.

39. On Wal-Mart's environmental initiatives, see Mark Gunther, 'The Green Machine', *Fortune,* August 7, 2006. Scott is quoted in Matther Wald, 'What's Kind to Nature Can Be Kind to Profits', *New York Times,* May 17, 2006, p. E1.

40. Wald, 'What's Kind to Nature Can Be Kind to Profits', p. E1

41. Jennifer Kerr, 'Comcast to Help Shield Kids from Smut on TV', *Detroit Free Press,* December 13, 2005, p. 4.

42. Sarah Ellison, 'Why Kraft Decided to Ban Some Food Ads to Children', *Wall Street Journal,* October 31, 2005, p. A1.

43. Andrew Martin, 'Leading Makers Agree to Put Limits on Junk Food Advertising Directed at Children', *New York Times,* November 16, 2006, p. C1.

44. Julia Angwin, 'News Corp. Sets Online-Safety Ads', *Wall Street Journal Online,* April 10, 2006, retrieved November 3, 2006, from http://online.wsj.com/purblic/us.

45. Joe Nocera, 'Green Logo, but BP Is Old Oil', *New York Times,* August 12, 2006, p. C1.

46. Ibid. See also Eric Reguly, 'Facts Discolour BP's Green Image', *Globe and Mail,* September 21, 2006, p. B2.

47. Jim Carlton, 'BP Finds New Pipeline Rupture Caused by Corrosion in Alaska', *Wall Street Journal,* April 17, 2006, p. 14. See also Ralph Blumenthal, 'Company Deficiencies Blamed in 2005 Texas Explosion', *New York Times,* March 21, 2007, p. A15.

48. Jad Mouawad, 'BP Named in Inquiry on Pricing', *New York Times,* June 29, 2006, p. C1.

49. Dexter Roberts and Peter Engardio, 'Secrets, Lies, and Sweatshops', *BusinessWeek,* November 27, 2006, p. 50.

50. 'Waiting for GE', *New York Times,* March 26, 2006, Section 14 WC (Westchester Weekly Desk), p. 15.

51. Vogel, *The Market for Virtue,* p. 122.

52. Ibid.

53. Carol Hymowitz, 'Big Companies Become Big Targets Unless They Guard Images Carefully', *Wall Street Journal,* December 12, 2005, p. B1.

54. 'Mr. Grassley Goes Begging', *New York Times,* November 14, 2005, p. 20.

55. Felicty Barringer, 'Panel Questions BP on Managing Alaska Oil', *New York Times,* September 8, 2006, p. A16.

56. Tom Zeller, Jr., 'To Go Global, Do You Ignore Censorship?', *New York Times,* October 24, 2005, p. C3.

57. Ibid.

58. Jim Yardley, 'Google Chief Rejects Putting Pressure on China', *New York Times,* April 13, 2006, p. C7.

59. Jon Swartz, 'Google, Justice Department Face Off on Search/Privacy Issue', *USA Today,* March 14, 2006, p. 3B.

60. Zeller, 'To Go Global, Do You Ignore Censorship?'
61. Joseph Nocera, 'Enough Shame to Go Around on China', *New York Times,* February 18, 2006, pp. B1, B13; Tom Zeller, Jr., 'Web Firms Are Grilled on Dealings in China', *New York Times,* February 16, 2006, p. C1.
62. Nocera, 'Enough Shame to Go Around on China', pp. B1, B13. See also Joel Brinkley, 'U.S. Squeezes North Korea's Money Flow', *New York Times,* March 10, 2006, p. A12.
63. Zeller, 'Web Firms Are Grilled on Dealings in China', p. C1.
64. On the Reporters Without Borders resolution, see Tom Zeller, 'Critics Press Companies on Internet Rights Issues', *New York Times,* November 8, 2005. The UBS analyst is quoted in Lee Drutman, 'Google May Be the Least of Three Evils', *Providence Journal,* February 21, 2006.
65. Vogel, *The Market for Virtue,* pp. 131, 132.
66. Ibid., p. 134.
67. 'Corporate Social Responsibility in Action: Private Sector Summit on Post-Tsunami Rehabilitation and Reconstruction', Asia Society, Washington, D.C., May 12, 2005.
68. Elizabeth Davies, 'Earthquake Tragedy: West's Response Condemned as Slow and Inadequate', *Independent,* October 11, 2005, p. 1.
69. William Holstein, 'The Impact of Image on the Bottom Line', *New York Times,* April 9, 2006, p. C13.
70. Husain Haqqani and Kenneth Ballen, 'Earthquake Relief: If We Don't Help Pakistan, Al-Qaeda's Friends Will', Carnegie Endowment for International Peace, November 17, 2005.
71. Alan Murray, 'The Profit Motive Has a Limit: Tragedy', *Wall Street Journal,* September 7, 2005, p. A2.
72. Ibid.
73. Celia W. Dugger, 'Clinton, Impresario of Philanthropy, Gets a Progress Update', *New York Times,* April 1, 2006, p. A9.
74. A copy of the Red Cross advertisement can be found at www.nestle-watersna. com/PDF/ARC.

CHAPTER SIX: A CITIZEN'S GUIDE TO SUPERCAPITALISM

1. Any such reforms would also have to be consistent with the First Amendment to the Constitution. At this writing, the Supreme Court is narrowly divided on whether campaign finance limits violate the First Amendment. *First National Bank of Boston v. Bellotti,* 435 U.S. 765 (1978) had been brought by a group of major corporations wanting to spend money to publicize their views on a state ballot question. Massachusetts law barred corporations from buying advocacy ads. The Supreme Court found the Massachusetts law to be in violation of

the First Amendment. Yet, twelve years later, the Court upheld the constitutionality of a Michigan law that placed limits on corporate campaign expenditures from general corporate funds. See *Austin v. Michigan State Chamber of Commerce* 494 U.S. 652 (1990).

2. Don Van Natta, Jr., 'Defying Senator, Executives Press Donation Rules Change', *New York Times,* September 1, 1999, p. A1.

3. John Browne, 'Leading Toward a Better World? The Role of Multinational Corporations in Economic and Social Development of Poor Countries', April 3, 2002, speech at Harvard University, at http://www.greenmoneyjournal.com/article.mpl?newsletterid=2&articleid=177.

4. Lester Thurow, *The Zero-Sum Society* (New York: Basic Books, 1980).

5. Jonathan Glater and Alexei Barrionuevo, 'Decision Rekindles Debate over Andersen Indictment', *New York Times,* June 1, 2005, p. C1.

6. Louis Uchitelle, 'Globalization: It's Not Just Wages; for Whirlpool, High-Cost Germany Can Still Have Advantages', *New York Times,* June 17, 2005, p. C1.

7. See, for example, 'Is Offshoring a National Security Threat?' *CIO Magazine,* November 13, 2006, p. 1.

8. Simon Romero and Heather Timmons, 'A Ship Already Sailed: America Ceded Its Seaport Terminals to Foreigners Years Ago', *New York Times,* February 24, 2006, p. C1.

9. William Broad, 'Advisory Panel Warns of an Erosion of the U.S. Competitive Edge in Science', *New York Times,* October 13, 2005, p. A16.

10. Steve Lohr, 'Outsourcing Is Climbing the Skills Ladder', *New York Times,* February 16, 2006, pp. C1, C17.

11. Charles Lindblom, *Politics and Markets* (New York: Basic Books, 1977).

12. This idea was suggested to me by John Wilson.

13. This idea was suggested to me by Stephen Sugarman, a professor of law at the University of California at Berkeley.

ACKNOWLEDGMENTS

This book is the fruit of several years of research, including the insights of many people in business, government, and the academy. To thank all of them adequately would be an impossible task, but several deserve mention. My Berkeley colleagues Brad DeLong, Laura D'Andrea Tyson, Stephen Sugarman, David Vogel, Eugene Smolensky, David Kirp, Michael O'Hare, Lee Friedman, John McNulty, Ramona Naddaff, and Alan Auerbach read early drafts and offered helpful suggestions. My dear friend and sorely missed colleague, the late Nelson Polsby, contributed many useful ideas. I am also grateful to my former colleagues Peter Orzsag, Lawrence Katz, and Dorothy Robyn. Several people subjected earlier drafts to the sort of withering criticism only close friends can be counted on to provide; in this regard I am particularly indebted to Clare Dalton, John D. Donahue, Erik Tarloff, Douglas Dworkin, and John Heilemann. Special thanks are due to Perian Flaherty for her thoughtful insights. I also want to thank several graduate students here at the University of California at Berkeley – Stephen Wald, Karin Martin, Ernie Tedeschi, Joshua Shakin, Rick Wilson, and Lee Drutman. The book could not have been written without the generous support of Steve Silberstein and the unflagging enthusiasm of Michael Nacht, dean of Berkeley's Goldman School of Public Policy. My able assistant, Rebecca Boles, watched over preparation of the manuscript and managed everything else that needed doing, a miracle of efficiency. As on prior occasions, special thanks are due my talented literary agent and friend, Rafe Sagalyn, and my perspicacious editor and friend, Jonathan Segal.

INDEX

Italicized page numbers refer to figures.

abortion issue, 182–3
Abrams, Frank, 45
academics, influence of, 11–12
Ackermann, Josef, 124
Adelphia Communications, 176
Advanced Micro Devices (AMD), 102
advertising, see marketing; public relations
AFL-CIO, 35–6, 86, 133–5
agriculture, 24, 123, 125, 154, 181
    Not Quite Golden Age and, 17–18, 30, 41–2, 47
Agriculture Department, U.S., 24, 154–5
airlines, airline industry, aircraft industry, 11, 127, 151
    deregulation of, 66–70, 83, 87
    Not Quite Golden Age and, 24–5, 34, 39, 43, 47
    and social consequences of supercapitalism, 93, 100, 113, 118
    and transition to supercapitalism, 52, 58–9, 62, 66–70, 83, 87
air traffic controllers, firing of, 80
Alaska, 165, 190, 192, 196–7
Alcatel, 122
Aluminum Company of America (Alcoa), 19, 118–19, 171
American Bankers Association, 148
American Class Structure, The (Kahl), 38
American Family Association, 182–3
antitrust laws, 8, 66
    and corporate influence on government, 144–7, 159, 163, 166
    corporate social responsibility and, 176, 180

Not Quite Golden Age and, 23, 32, 41
apartheid, 180
Arthur Andersen, 218–19
Asia, Asians, 9, 165, 188
    and social consequences of supercapitalism, 122–5, 127, 129–30
assembly lines, 19, 62
AT&T, 94
    Not Quite Golden Age and, 19, 23–4, 30, 155
    and transition to supercapitalism, 52, 66, 68, 76
automobile industry, automobiles, 6, 8, 10
    and citizen's guide to supercapitalism, 222–3
    corporate social responsibility and, 180, 182–3, 194, 196
    Not Quite Golden Age and, 19–21, 25, 28–34, 39, 42–3, 48
    and social consequences of supercapitalism, 93, 99–100, 105, 113, 115, 118, 124
    and transition to supercapitalism, 52, 57, 62–4, 83–5

Bain & Company, 65
Banga, Ajay, 206–7
Barton, Joe, 197
Baumol, William, 237n
Bebchuk, Lucien, 107–8
Belda, Alain, 118–19
Bell System, see AT&T
Ben & Jerry's, 174, 194–5

A NOTE ABOUT THE AUTHOR

Robert Reich is Professor of Public Policy at the Goldman School of Public Policy at the University of California at Berkeley. He has served in three national administrations, most recently as secretary of labor under President Bill Clinton. He has written eleven books, including *The Work of Nations*, which has been translated into twenty-two languages, and the best sellers *The Next American Frontier, The Future of Success,* and *Locked in the Cabinet.* His articles have appeared in *The New Yorker, The Atlantic Monthly,* the *New York Times,* the *Washington Post,* and the *Wall Street Journal.* He is also co-founding editor of *The American Prospect* magazine. His weekly commentaries on public radio's *Marketplace* are heard by nearly five million people. In 2003, Reich was awarded the prestigious Václav Havel Foundation Prize for pioneering work in economic and social thought.

A NOTE ON THE TYPE

This book was set in Adobe Garamond. Designed for the Adobe
Corporation by Robert Slimbach, the fonts are based on types first cut by
Claude Garamond (c. 1480–1561). Garamond was a pupil of Geoffroy Tory
and is believed to have followed the Venetian models, although he introduced a number of important differences, and it is to him that we owe the
letter we now know as 'old style'. He gave to his letters a certain elegance and
feeling of movement that won their creator an immediate reputation and the
patronage of Francis I of France.